After the Peace

AFTER THE PEACE

Loyalist Paramilitaries in Post-Accord Northern Ireland

CAROLYN GALLAHER

Cornell University Press

ITHACA AND LONDON

First published 2007 by Cornell University Press
First printing, Cornell Paperbacks, 2007

Printed in the United States of America

Library of Congress Cataloging-in-Publication Data

Gallaher, Carolyn, 1969–
 After the peace : Loyalist paramilitaries in post-accord Northern Ireland / Carolyn Gallaher.
  p. cm.
 Includes bibliographical references and index.
 ISBN 978-0-8014-4570-5 (cloth : alk. paper) —ISBN 978-0-8014-7426-2 (pbk. : alk. paper)
  1. Ulster Volunteer Force.   2. Ulster Defence Association.   3. Loyalist Volunteer Force.
 4. Paramilitary forces—Northern Ireland.   5. Political violence—Northern Ireland.   6. Protestants—Northern Ireland—Political activity.   7. Northern Ireland—Politics and government—1994–   I. Title.
  DA990.U46G333 2007
  941.60824—dc22

                                                                              2007018951

Cloth printing   10 9 8 7 6 5 4 3 2 1
Paperback printing   10 9 8 7 6 5 4 3 2 1

Contents

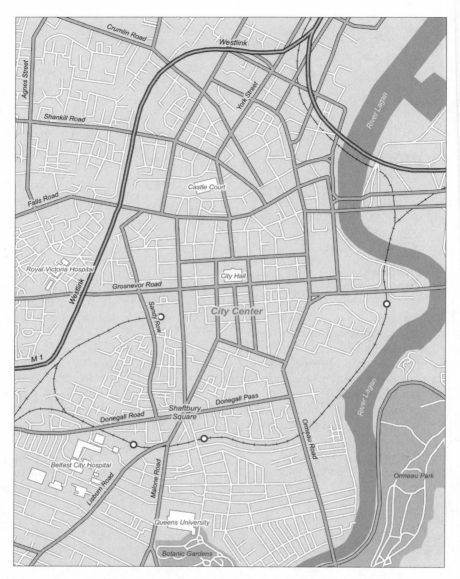

Fig. 1. Central Belfast. By Nuala M. Cowan, Department of Geography, George Washington University.

Preface

This book is about the backwash of a conflict that has largely ended. It has been almost a decade since a peace agreement was signed in Northern Ireland and even longer since a joint 1994 cease-fire was announced. This is a significant duration of time—most conflicts have a high likelihood of reigniting within the first five years of peace. Northern Ireland has witnessed its share of brinkmanship in the intervening years, but its peace has held. Nevertheless, formal peace has failed to rid the province of its paramilitaries. Loyalist paramilitaries, the subject of this book, have killed over fifty people, mostly Protestant, since 1999. They have maimed or otherwise wounded countless others. Indeed, they continued to recruit as if the Troubles were ongoing.

In Northern Ireland, as in any society emerging from conflict, the preferred scenario is for paramilitaries to demilitarize (or be demilitarized) shortly after a peace agreement is signed. With paramilitary members sent home and weapons put beyond use, civil society can emerge and peace can take root. When wars were primarily state-on-state affairs, demilitarization was routine. The victor state seized the enemy state's weapons, imprisoned or killed its military leaders, and decommissioned the rest. Contemporary warfare is different. States still fight wars (no one has yet figured out how to eliminate them), but increasingly guerillas, paramilitaries, and contract fighters join states on the battlefield. When such conflicts end, there is usually no clear victor and no entity capable of forcibly demobilizing all the armed factions.

Unfortunately, paramilitaries have a poor track record of dismantling themselves. And as contradictory as it may seem, most paramilitaries lack the wherewithal to do so. Indeed, while paramilitaries generally have enough largesse to provide members with generous "retirement" payouts, one-time payments, even large ones, tend to be less attractive than the promise of continued kickbacks from racketeering, smuggling, and the like. The horizontal leadership that benefits paramilitaries on the battlefield is also an obstacle at peace time. A flat organizational chart means that brigades are designed to operate autonomously; they purchase and store their own weapons, and they run their own rackets. In short, a battalion can afford to ignore a stand-down order if it so chooses. Even in organizations that have sufficient power to enforce dismantlement, the motivation to shut down can be weak. Protracted fighting often becomes a way of life—a source of income, status, and security. Convincing hardened fighters, or their admirers down the demographic ladder, to forgo the life is easier said than done. Indeed, some fighters grow weary of fighting, but others fear their prospects under peace and resist it. Fighting the "traitors" in the ranks becomes a new casus belli and a reason not to stand down.

After World War II, the nature of warfare changed. Intrastate wars gave way to so-called low-intensity conflicts. Like contemporary conflicts in Colombia and East Timor, as well as more recent wars in Sierra Leone, Chechnya, and the Balkans, the Troubles of Northern Ireland involved a mix of state forces, guerilla groups, and paramilitaries loyal to the government. Many of these societies are currently at peace, but organized violence remains a problem in all of them. In some cases fighters have refused to fully demobilize. In others, fighters have demobilized, but they have simply shifted their efforts into criminal enterprises. In Colombia, for example, the right-wing paramilitary—the United Self-Defense Forces of Colombia (AUC)—has murdered over three thousand people since its cease-fire in 2002 (Vieira 2006). In the spring of 2006 the East Timorese military, made up of former combatants, fragmented into warring factions that mirrored the old conflict divide. Dili, the capital, became a battlefield, with jobless youths and common street gangs joining the fray.

Peace agreements are never perfect. Far more fail than succeed. And many have only partial success. The Belfast Agreement certainly has its problems, and I discuss many of them here, but my primary focus is on the paramilitaries themselves. Their continuing violence and descent into criminality cannot be blamed on the agreement alone. Indeed, the agreement was signed by the same Loyalist paramilitaries that chose to ignore its mandate to decommission and otherwise dismantle in a timely manner.

Loyalist recalcitrance has as much to do with internal divides as external forces. Since the march to peace began in the run-up to the 1994 cease-fire, Loyalist paramilitaries have become trenchantly divided. The split began as a divide about the peace process but has since morphed into a wider struggle. On the one hand are Loyalists, many of them ex-prisoners, who helped negotiate the 1994 cease-fire and the 1998 peace accord. They still support peace, but they find themselves in the unenviable position of supporting peace from *inside* a paramilitary structure that was meant to be dismantled long ago. On the other hand are Loyalists who decry peace as a form of capitulation and spend most of their time running criminal enterprises that have nothing to do with maintaining the province's union with Great Britain. The intricacies of this divide are fascinating in their own right, but they beg larger questions: why did Loyalist paramilitaries stay on the battlefield after peace, and what can convince or force them to leave it for good? This question is the subject of this book. It is clear there is much yet to learn about the topic in Northern Ireland, and beyond, as the problems in Colombia, East Timor, and other places suggest.

Before delving into the issue of paramilitary reintegration, it is worth noting the baggage that comes with any study of Northern Ireland. It is heavy baggage. As John Whyte once famously observed, "in proportion to size, Northern Ireland is the most heavily researched area on earth." The level of scrutiny is particularly noteworthy when one considers that between 1969 and 1998 only 3,480 people were killed. Of course, even one death is too many. And, to be sure, the numbers are more significant when put into demographic and geographic context—the population is just under 1.5 million, and most murders were concentrated in a handful of neighborhoods in West and North Belfast. A new researcher to Northern Ireland, as I am, cannot help but wince at Whyte's observation. It was with not a little trepidation that I embarked on this study.

I am not a specialist in Northern Ireland. I cut my research teeth an ocean and mountain range away, studying the militia movement in central Kentucky. Militia groups have certainly enacted their fair share of violence, but even the Kentucky movement's most ardent opponents would never put them in the same league as the Ulster Volunteer Force or the Ulster Defence Association. Although this project was never intended to be a comparative one, I prefaced most of my interviews for this project with a brief introduction to my previous work. I wanted Loyalists to know that I had some experience with armed groups, that I was not as green as I looked. I also wanted my research subjects to know that I could engage fairly with maligned or otherwise unpopular groups. Indeed, the militias are routinely dismissed as anachronistic—disaffected white men who cannot deal with the changing face of power in the United States. I did not agree with my militia informants' worldview, but I did my best to present the militia as it was and to analyze it without reference to stereotyping. And I tried to consider alternatives to the grievances they identified. I would, I told my informants, be as fair to Loyalists as I had been to the militia.

My brief introduction, however, seemed to give my informants more pause than comfort. Indeed, many of them assumed I was doing a comparative study and warned me off it. One community worker bluntly interrupted my preview to advise me, "You'd be well to steer clear of that comparison." An ex-prisoner suggested my foray into Loyalism would be more complicated. There is, he told me, "no single ideology that explains Loyalism." Even people I was not interviewing thought my experience with militias was irrelevant. When I remarked on my background to a Unionist in a pub one night, he retorted, "But, those people are crazy!" My response, "They're not as crazy as you think," did little to soften the blow I had unwittingly delivered.

John Whyte's solution to writing about a well-covered and controversial topic was to reconsider the literature rather than add to it. "In these circumstances," he explained, "the most useful contribution which a specialist on Northern Ireland can make is, not to add yet another item to the already daunting pile of research, but to provide a guide through it" (Whyte 1990, viii). Although I deeply admire Whyte's work, my study will add to, rather than sort through, the daunting pile. I believe, however, that there are contributions still to be made.

For starters, research on combatant groups in Northern Ireland has been heavily weighted toward the study of the Provisional Irish Republican Army (PIRA, or IRA for short). Academics, journalists, and even IRA men have taken their turn explaining the group. By contrast, relatively few books have been written about Loyalist paramilitaries. Steve Bruce's *The Red Hand* remains the definitive account fifteen years after it was published. Although the method is hardly scientific, a quick search on Amazon.com is telling. A search for books about the IRA returns over 37,000 entries. The combined total of searches for the Ulster Volunteer Force, the Ulster Defense Association, and the Loyalist Volunteer Force is ten entries.

This book is also designed to examine the aftermath of the Troubles rather than the Troubles itself. Comprehending contemporary Loyalism obviously requires an awareness of the past, but peace has presented paramilitaries with a new set of opportunities, and it has prompted new reactions from them. My examination of the post-peace landscape has benefited greatly from the work of scholars such as Pete Shirlow, Brian Graham, Steve Bruce, and James McAuley, who have done much to rescue the Loyalist paramilitary figure from caricature by acknowledging their motivations and fears as well as their internal debates in this new context. I see this book as a continuation of their work, for it could not have been conceived without it.

Finally, this book is designed to provide an analytic counterweight to the recent crop of journalistic accounts of Loyalism. It is an attempt to analyze the factual information presented in these accounts (as well as information gathered in my own research) in a wider frame. I hasten to add, however, that I remain appreciative of the genre even as I depart from it. Veteran reporter Peter Taylor's *Loyalists*, for example, is an important exposition of Loyalist history; the book is all the more significant because it is the first to lay out Loyalist history using first-person accounts. I frequently turned to it as I tried to put the Loyalist present into its historical context. Jim McDowell's *Godfathers* and David Lister and Hugh Jordan's *Mad Dog* are equally compelling. Both accounts juxtapose details of the paramilitary high life with gory facts about betrayal, untimely death, and bereaved families. These accounts are certainly salacious, with voyeuristic asides about paramilitary vanities and conceits, but they lay bare the often arcane personal grudges that lie behind the ideological banners raised to legitimate Loyalist criminality. Although this book contains no gossipy tidbits, I believe Loyalist criminality is an important topic of analysis. Indeed, the changing balance between criminal and ideological motivations underpins the current divide within Loyalist paramilitaries and helps explain why everyday Loyalists, trapped in desolate neighborhoods between feuding paramilitaries, feel peace has passed them by.

This book raises as many questions as it answers. My hope is that by laying out the complexities of paramilitary demobilization in one small place, I can provide insight and prescriptions, however tentative, for peacemakers in Northern Ireland and abroad. Northern Ireland is a small place, but its experiences carry lessons beyond its borders.

I must also say a few words on terminology. Like many conflict zones, terminology varies depending on which side of the fence you are standing. The terms used to describe the peace accord prove a cogent example. Catholics refer to it as the Good Friday Agreement, after the day it was signed, while Protestants call it the Belfast Agreement for the city in which it was signed. Because this book is about Loyalists and relies in part on ethnographic methods, I use the term my informants use: the Belfast Agreement.

There is also debate about what to call the territory that is Northern Ireland. Catholics prefer to call it the North because the term denotes geographic location in the Republic, as in the north of the country. Protestants tend to use the formal appellation, Northern Ireland. Here, I stick to the formal name or to the term "province." Again, I do so because these are the terms my informants use. In using Protestant terminology I mean no disrespect to Catholics or nationalists. At the end of the day, the future of the place is not in my hands. I only hope to chart it, however briefly, for the lessons it might teach us. Finally, I try to avoid the term "conflict resolution." Not only do few people use the term in Northern Ireland, but many actually despise it. Indeed, a number of my informants pointed out that the underlying problem around which the conflict revolved—the constitutional status of the province—has not been resolved. The Loyalist paramilitaries, ex-prisoners, and community workers I spoke to stressed that conflict was not the problem; instead, it was the manner in which the conflict was handled, with violence, that was the real problem. Thus, the most urgent thing peacemakers can do is to shift the conflict away from violence. Only then can a real resolution be found. It is only fitting then that this book is about the transformation of Loyalism rather than its resolution per se.

Finally, as transformations occur, so do passings. During the write-up phase of this book, two of the Loyalists I interviewed—Billy Mitchell and

David Ervine—died. While political Loyalism's future may look grim without them, it is also clear that they were much more than charismatic leaders. They worked hard to build a base from which political Loyalism could grow into the future, and the fruits of their hard work can and will live on.

My first research trip to Belfast was in the summer of 2002. I had no paramilitary contacts then and only a hazy idea about what it was about Loyalist paramilitarism that I wanted to study. I viewed the trip as a sort of fact-finding mission. I wanted to develop my research questions *after* talking to a few men in the Loyalist paramilitary structure so that I could tailor my questions around what Loyalists themselves saw as important.

It was a lucky fluke, therefore, that one of the first articles I stumbled across in my research at the Linen Hall Library in Belfast was written by Martin Snodden, an ex-prisoner with the Ulster Volunteer Force. I am especially grateful that Martin agreed to sit down for a chat with the nosy American who cold-called him a few days later. It is hard for me to overstate how important that interview was for this project. Martin put a human face on Loyalism for me. We began our chat with scones and tea—Northern Ireland's thirty-year civil war has done nothing to diminish the graciousness of its people—and we progressed to cigarettes in short order. For me, sharing food and vice leads to good conversation, and we had one. It was not a happy conversation, nor an easy one for either of us to have. Martin told me about his path into paramilitarism and later into jail. His story was short on bravado and long on humility and regret, but it was told with hope and humor. Martin showed me that ex-prisoners could leave prison and give back, that they could help others pull back from the brink. It was only one interview, but it convinced me that the story I needed to tell was not just about Loyalist paramilitary violence but also about what individuals within these structures could do to stop it. It is not a stretch to say that I do not think this book would have come to pass without Martin.

I am also indebted to Pete Shirlow, Mary Gilmartin, and Gerald Mills. Research is often a lonely endeavor, and all three cut the loneliness for me in ways big and small. Pete took me on my first tour of Belfast and to Belfast haunts I would never have gone to on my own. I learned more about the Troubles and their aftermath from him than from any book I read, before or since. Often times I did not even realize I was learning something until several months later when I would stumble across a fact, figure, or anecdote only to recall a conversation we'd had that would put it all into context. In Dublin, Mary Gilmartin was my savior. She was always ready to collect me at the airport, feed me, and send my jet lag on its way. She diverted my attention when I was tired, acted as a sounding board when I needed it, and kept me laughing all the way to Sligo and Kathleen's potatoes. For his part, Gerald Mills (often in concert with Mary) made sure I was a true geographer, getting me out of my research shell, taking me on tours, hikes, and the pub, and always to good effect. Pete, Mary, and Gerald always made me feel like I was home.

I am also grateful for the institutional support I received for this project. American University's summer research stipend was crucial in helping me pay for my research. When I began this project I chose not to apply for outside grant funding. I certainly wanted the money a grant would provide, but I did not want the baggage that could come with it. I knew paramilitary men would already be wary of an outsider from the States, and I did not want to add suspicion of third-party interests to the mix. I am also grateful to Rob Kitchin at the National Institute for Regional and Spatial Analysis (NIRSA) at the University of Ireland, Maynooth. The fellowship I received for the spring of 2005 allowed me the time and space to begin writing this book and to conduct more interviews as well. The NIRSA folks were an inviting lot, and I enjoyed their institutional and personal support.

Finally, no manuscript ever comes to print without the careful and sage handling of an editor. For me, fortunately, Peter Wissoker was that person. Peter proved invaluable in helping me chart the unknown waters of a university press review process. When I grew dejected, he put things into context. When I was exasperated, he helped me steer my energy into more productive emotions. And he was always willing to give my ideas a chance. Peter also chose excellent external reviewers for this project. Steve Bruce and Brian Graham both gave my initial manuscript a careful, meticulous read. Their advice was detailed and substantive. They pointed out factual errors and analytic gaps and helpfully offered nuance to my interpretation. Most importantly, both helped me avoid pitfalls I did not know existed. Both took more care and time than the average reviewer, and I am grateful for it. Their care helped me take this book to another level. Of course, any errors that remain are my responsibility. Thanks also to the rest of the Cornell team—Susan Specter, Karen Hwa, Kathryn Gohl, and Lou Robinson—for their eagle eyes. They smoothed out punctuation, grammar, and spelling errors I did not even see and got my graphics up to par. This is a far more readable book because of them. And a heartfelt thanks to Priya Dixit for doing such a meticulous index for this book.

As always, thanks to Morris and Carrie Gallaher. You both inspire me!

Abbreviations

Armed Groups

CIRA	Continuity Irish Republican Army
CLMC	Combined Loyalist Military Command
INLA	Irish National Liberation Army
IRA	Irish Republican Army
LVF	Loyalist Volunteer Force
OIRA	Official Irish Republican Army
PIRA	Provisional Irish Republican Army
UDA	Ulster Defence Association
UFF	Ulster Freedom Fighters
UVF	Ulster Volunteer Force

Paramilitary-Affiliated Groups

EPIC	Ex-Prisoners' Interpretive Centre
LINC	Local Initiatives for Needy Communities
MARC	Multi-Agency Resource Centre
UPRG	Ulster Political Research Group

Political Parties

DUP	Democratic Unionist Party
PUP	Progressive Unionist Party
UUP	Ulster Unionist Party
UDP	Ulster Democratic Party

Civil Society and Governmental Entities

EU	European Union
NICEM	Northern Ireland Council for Ethnic Minorities

NICVA Northern Ireland Council for Voluntary Action
NIHE Northern Ireland Housing Executive
NISRA Northern Ireland Statistics and Research Agency
PSNI Police Services of Northern Ireland
RUC Royal Ulster Constabulary

1   *Staying Put*

Paramilitaries respond to formal peace in different ways. Some issue prompt stand-down orders and implement them with efficiency. Others drag their feet, dismantling by fits and starts. Still others stay put, endorsing peace but refusing to stand down.

In Northern Ireland a formal peace accord was signed in April 1998. Nine years later the Ulster Volunteer Force (UVF) finally stood down. Its counterpart, the Ulster Defence Association (UDA) remained on the battlefield. Loyalist paramilitary foot-dragging defies the accord they signed and the aspirations of the citizens who supported it. This book is about the delayed business of Loyalist demilitarization. It explains why Loyalist demilitarization included more fits than starts in the decade since formal peace arrived and how Loyalist paramilitary recalcitrance has affected everyday Loyalists.

Loyalist paramilitaries are a vestige of Northern Ireland's thirty-year civil war, known locally and euphemistically as the Troubles. Although the war began in 1968, enmity between the province's two ethnoreligious blocks— Catholics and Protestants—stretches back to British colonization of the island in the sixteenth century.[1] At the time, the British established control through a razed-earth campaign; locals were driven from their land and threatened with reprisal if they returned. Protestant "planters" from England and Scotland were then brought in to resettle the land. The goal of the plantation period was to stamp the island with a politically British and culturally Protestant imprint while developing a thriving export economy in

---

[1] Most scholars define Northern Ireland's Catholic and Protestant populations as ethnoreligious groups. Centuries of each group's segregation from the other and the secular nature of contemporary Northern Ireland mean that religion is primarily a marker of one's "descent group" (McGarry and O'Leary 1995, 218).

agricultural goods (Mulholland 2002). To secure its objective the British established a rigid social hierarchy in which Irish Catholics were deprived of basic rights and privileges. Protestant settlers often lived marginal lives (the majority were peasants), but they were spared many of the degradations, symbolic and otherwise, of their Catholic counterparts. When Ireland gained its independence in 1921, the British retained control of the northern portion of the island, where Protestants were in the majority. And they continued to support local Protestant dominance in political and economic affairs. The Protestant elite who ruled the province called themselves Unionists and vowed the province would remain British.

The war that began in 1968 was set against this historical backdrop. It pit the Provisional Irish Republican Army (known commonly as the IRA or Provos) against the British government and the Unionist elite in a protracted, often nasty fight. The conflict began benignly enough, when Catholics embarked on a civil rights struggle in the late 1960s. A harsh response by law enforcement upped the ante, however, and the civil rights campaign soon morphed into an armed "liberation struggle." Using guerilla tactics such as targeted bombing and hit-and-run assaults on police and military installations, Republicans hoped to force a British retreat from the province—achieving victory by a war of attrition. Many of their assaults, however, affected everyday Protestants. And not surprisingly, many in their ranks rose up to protect themselves and defend the state. These paramilitaries called themselves Loyalists and vowed to defend the Union to the death.[2] Embracing the tactics of their Republican counterparts, they argued that if the Unionist state would not destroy Republicanism, they would do it themselves.[3] The UVF and the UDA were seen by many Protestants as an important bulwark against IRA violence.[4]

After almost thirty years of fighting, the IRA announced a cease-fire in 1994. The UVF and the UDA responded in kind a few weeks later. These announcements were met with relief and guarded optimism by a war-weary population. Four years later, on Good Friday 1998, the province's armed groups signed a joint peace accord in Belfast. The agreement, known by

[2] Scholars of political violence make a distinction between guerilla and paramilitary groups. Both are nonstate actors, but guerillas fight the state whereas paramilitaries fight on its behalf and often have structural links to it. Steve Bruce (1992) uses the terms "anti-state terrorism," and "pro-state terrorism" to mark this distinction in Northern Ireland. As a matter of convenience, however, most people in Northern Ireland refer to groups on both sides as paramilitaries.

[3] This rhetoric signaled the emergence of a key divide within the Protestant fold. The Unionist label came to be associated with establishment forces and a law-and-order ethos. By contrast, Loyalism implied lower rank on the social hierarchy and a greater tolerance for stepping outside legal bounds to fight the IRA.

[4] The UVF was actually formed in 1966, before the civil rights movement. The group was formed to protest Prime Minister Terrence O'Neill's efforts to bring Catholics into the Unionist fold. It is not likely, however, that the group would have consolidated into a full-scale paramilitary without an organized and armed enemy on the Catholic side of the equation.

Catholics as the Good Friday Agreement and by Protestants as the Belfast Agreement, was designed to bring paramilitaries out of violence by bringing them into the political system of the province. The accord required paramilitaries to decommission their weapons within two years and established a power-sharing Assembly that would include both paramilitary and traditional political parties.[5]

Demilitarization did not, however, proceed as hoped. Indeed, the IRA only formally dismantled in July 2005, a full seven years after the agreement. Loyalist demilitarization remains incomplete. And almost a decade into the peace process, everyday Loyalists have grave doubts about the agreement. Their antipathy to it, often encouraged by paramilitaries, has become a serious impediment to complete peace (Hayes, McAllister, and Dowds 2005; McAdam 2005).

This book proffers three broad findings about the delayed business of Loyalist demilitarization. First, because pro-state paramilitaries are as a rule less politically developed than anti-state groups, they are poorly positioned to follow the paramilitary-cum-political-party trajectory laid out in the agreement.[6] Second, and as a consequence, a formal state-run demilitarization scheme is needed to effectively dismantle paramilitaries and end their individual members' violence.[7] Indeed, even though the UVF has finally issued a stand-down order, it is likely that many of its former members will remain in the violence "business." Most have few marketable skills and limited hopes of finding alternative employment. Residual violence will likely continue, therefore, under new flags of allegiance, whether to a local "boss," a turf-based gang, or the like. Finally, although Loyalist paramilitarism has left an indelibly negative imprint on the province, there are people *within* Loyalist paramilitary structure who support peace and whose efforts deserve support despite their location within the paramilitary fold. Indeed, these men, though few in number, have access and credibility that few outsiders possess. They are therefore better positioned than any other entity in Northern Ireland to push Loyalism toward peace.

Lest readers think Loyalist paramilitaries are inherently atavistic, I begin with a brief explanation of why contemporary demilitarization is such a

[5] Most of the paramilitaries that signed on to the Belfast Agreement had at least nascent political parties. The largest, most developed paramilitary party was the IRA's Sinn Fein Party. The Progressive Unionist Party (PUP) and the Ulster Democratic Party (UDP), affiliated with the UVF and the UDA, respectively, were smaller and less developed.

[6] Because anti-state groups want to seize power from the state, they are compelled to develop a political alternative. Pro-state groups do not have a similar impetus. Their goal, at least initially, is to protect the political establishment (Bruce 1992). Although most paramilitaries go on to form their own political parties, they must compete (for votes, allegiance, "airtime") with the political establishment they claim to protect. And they must explain why they chose illegal means to fight when their side had legal means to fight the enemy.

[7] Demilitarization schemes usually embrace a wide array of programs, including gun buybacks, job training, and counseling. The goal is to dismantle paramilitary structures, decommission their weapons, and reintegrate members into mainstream society.

difficult endeavor. Indeed, although the continued existence of Loyalist paramilitaries after almost a decade of formal peace is an aberration, demilitarization is not as simple or speedy as it used to be.

Demilitarization and Its Complexities

THE DIFFICULTIES IN GENERAL

When wars were primarily fought between states, demilitarization was usually a straightforward process. The winner confiscated enemy weapons, executed or imprisoned military leaders, and discharged soldiers. The victor then sent its own soldiers home, *without* their weapons.

Warfare today is different. States continue to fight wars, but increasingly they are joined on the battlefield by guerillas, paramilitaries, mercenaries, and even criminal gangs. Conflicts with nonstate actors are known by a variety of labels, including low-intensity conflict (Kitson 1991), postmodern war (Gray 1997), criminal warfare (Mueller 2004), and new war (Kaldor 1999, 2001). Although scholars have found much to debate about these conflicts,[8] they generally agree that demobilizing nonstate actors is more difficult than demobilizing conventional forces. A number of reasons explain the increased difficulty.

For starters, states find themselves in a relatively weakened position in contemporary warfare. Guerillas have both inferior numbers and firepower, but they have an important advantage—flexibility. Free from cumbersome command chains, bulky weapons systems, and technological dependence, guerillas elevate hit-and-run tactics to a full-blown strategy (Guevara 1998). Thus, although they can rarely overthrow a state, guerillas can nag it endlessly, zapping its strength in the process. As Mao Tse-tung succinctly explained in his treatise *On Guerilla Warfare*, "when guerillas engage a stronger enemy, they withdraw when he advances; harass him when he stops; strike him when he is weary; pursue him when he withdraws" (2000, 46).

To defeat a guerilla movement (and there is no consensus that guerillas are beatable), states must adopt aggressive counterinsurgency tactics such as internment, "draining the swamp," and collusion.[9] These tactics carry risks, however. They tend to harm as many civilians as guerillas, and over

---

[8] The debate about contemporary wars largely centers on how to categorize them, with secondary debates stemming from these varied positions. Some scholars argue that contemporary warfare represents a radical break in the nature of war (Kaldor 1999; Münkler 2004; van Creveld 1991). Other scholars argue that contemporary warfare represents a return to primitive violence (Ignatieff 1998; Kaplan 1994, 2001). Still others argue that warfare is in serial decline and that contemporary conflicts are the "remnants of war" (Mueller 2004).

[9] Martin van Creveld argues that counterinsurgency operations usually fail. "The British lost India, Palestine, Kenya, Cyprus, and Aden, to mention but the most important places where they tried to make a stand. The French spent six years fighting in Indochina and another

time their use may erode the state's moral authority and legitimacy. Given the high costs, it is not surprising that many states opt to use such tactics sparingly, to contain rather than eliminate guerillas. And, when most low-intensity conflicts end, they do so in a draw (van Creveld 1991). This state of affairs is reflected at the peace table, where guerillas and paramilitaries are usually able to win broad concessions, including amnesty, release of prisoners, and flexible decommissioning. In some conflicts, armed groups are even allowed to decommission on their own or to join state-run demobilization programs voluntarily rather than by force.

Contemporary conflicts are also difficult to demilitarize because they contain more armed factions than conventional wars do. Although low-intensity conflicts usually begin with two warring parties—a guerilla group and the state—they grow to include many more. When a state becomes mired in a guerilla conflict, its advocates often form private armies to help, reasoning that paramilitaries can operate free of the constraints that limit the state. Moreover, because paramilitaries tend to be organized locally, they spring up at different times and places, substantially adding to the mix of groups already on the battlefield. Criminals are also attracted by the opportunities that conflict presents, and enterprising ones tend to create their own security forces with an eye to protecting assets and warding off competition. To wit, none of these groups wear uniforms or are easily identifiable, and when conflict ends it is not always clear who should be demobilized. Weapons are equally difficult to impound given that they are controlled by multiple parties and stored in disparate locations.

The protracted nature of low-intensity conflict also tends to create inveterate fighters. Being a guerilla or paramilitary is dangerous, but it is also a way of life. For those who manage to ascend the ranks, it can be an attractive one. The lifestyle affords power, status, and security and includes added perks such as easy access to sex, free drinks in pubs, and personal cuts on rackets, among other strokes to ego and pocketbook (Kaplan 1994; Mueller 2004). Although some inveterate fighters resist peace on ideological grounds, many simply refuse to give up the benefits associated with the lifestyle (Kaldor 1999; Mueller 2004). Others fear that peace will bring prosecution, so they soldier on. Whatever an individual's motivations, inveterate fighters tend to clash with their comrades who support peace. These clashes can result in the formation of splinter groups or devolve into internecine feuding.

---

seven trying to stave off defeat in Algeria. . . . Even the South Africans, who held out longer than anybody else, ended up by agreeing to withdraw from Namibia" (1991, 22–23). Other scholars, such as Kitson (1991), point to Cyprus and Kenya as examples of successful counterinsurgency campaigns.

Internment involves the roundup and imprisonment of people who fit a profile considered dangerous (for example, Japanese Americans during World War II). Draining the swamp is a euphemism for destroying a village or neighborhood where guerillas hide out. Collusion involves state forces working covertly with paramilitaries to circumvent the law.

The horizontal structure of guerillas and paramilitaries also makes it difficult for leaders to enforce cease-fires and stand-down orders. While some guerilla and paramilitary groups have relatively hierarchical chains of command, most are horizontally organized. Brigade commanders purchase and store their own weapons, control their own rackets, and organize their own recruiting. They are operationally independent and can resist a stand-down order if they so choose.

None of this precludes an eventual return to peace and stability. Low-intensity conflicts have ended in places as diverse as Sierra Leone and El Salvador. For all intents and purposes, the conflict in Northern Ireland has come to an end as well. Peace, however, only tends to root firmly once armed parties have been fully demilitarized. In Northern Ireland demilitarization has proceeded slowly, and the results have been predictable—continuing violence.

DEMILITARIZATION AND THE BELFAST AGREEMENT

In Northern Ireland the government approached demilitarization narrowly by concentrating on decommissioning. The narrow focus was signaled early on, in 1994, when the IRA announced its cease-fire. Although the group called a cease-fire on the understanding that doing so would lead to formal talks with the British government, the then secretary for Northern Ireland, Patrick Mayhew, abruptly changed course and announced he would only hold talks with the IRA's political wing, Sinn Fein, if the IRA met three new conditions. Mayhew laid out these conditions, the so-called Washington 3, in a speech he gave in Washington, D.C., in March 1995 (Taylor 1999a). The IRA would have to agree to "to disarm progressively," accept guidelines on how and when decommissioning would take place, and engage in a round of decommissioning *before* talks to demonstrate its commitment to peace (Hennessey 2001; Taylor 1999a).

The IRA believed the new conditions were unreasonable (Taylor 1999a). No agreement had been reached, and one might not be reached, so it was premature at best to require the group to decommission. A pre-peace arms dump was also symbolically untenable for the IRA. The IRA and the British state were at a stalemate in 1994, and both knew it (Taylor 1999a). A public decommissioning, however, would send the message that the IRA had surrendered, and not surprisingly its Army Council rejected the condition out of hand.[10] The IRA broke its cease-fire the following February with a spectacular at London's Canary Wharf.[11]

---

[10] Even people in the security apparatus thought the condition was unrealistic. Peter Taylor (1999a) reports that Sir Hugh Annesley, then chief constable of the Royal Ulster Constabulary, advised the prime minister that the IRA would not decommission its arms before peace was established.

[11] A spectacular is a euphemism for an attack aimed at a high-value target or designed to produce eye-catching destruction. The term entered the popular lexicon in the early nineties

The IRA returned to the cease-fire in July 1997 after the Labour Party swept the elections that spring. Prime Minister Tony Blair's government agreed to negotiate with the IRA, and he took the Washington 3 off the table. Little progress was made on the issue in the run-up to the agreement, however. Indeed, the two sides were miles apart on the issue. Republicans believed that decommissioning should follow the agreement's implementation. For them, implementation would signal Unionist good faith and secure rounds of decommissioning. Unionists, for their part, saw decommissioning as a confidence-building measure that would move implementation along (CAIN 2006d; Trimble 1998).

Although decommissioning was a chief concern for many Unionists, they eventually agreed to accept general wording on the issue in the final agreement. Save for timing (decommissioning was to be completed within two years of signing), the agreement failed to stipulate who would oversee the process, where it would take place, and how it would be verified. Unionist concerns over decommissioning were placated temporarily by two measures. The first was the so-called exclusion mechanism in Strand One of the agreement, which stated that "those who hold office should use only democratic, non-violent means, and those who do not should be excluded or removed from office under these provisions" (Multi-party Negotiations 1998). The mechanism, which some Unionists considered weak,[12] was buttressed by a sidebar letter that David Trimble, the chief negotiator for the Ulster Unionist Party (UUP), had requested from Prime Minister Tony Blair. The letter, regarded as a formal interpretation of the agreement, stated that if the exclusion mechanism failed, the prime minister would introduce legislation to strengthen it. David Trimble also persuaded his party that particulars on decommissioning could be worked out in the months between the referendum and actual devolution (Millar 2004).

Although it seems improbable today, Trimble probably believed at the time that he could work out the difficulties. Indeed, he hinged his party's 1999 election campaign on a "no guns, no government" policy.[13] The IRA refused to decommission before devolution, however, and Trimble was left

---

when the IRA launched its England campaign. The IRA bombing at Canary Wharf left a gaping hole in a row of glass high-rise buildings in city center London and caused £150 million in property damage (Harnden 1999).

[12] David Trimble told Frank Millar of the *Irish Times* that the wording in Strand One was less forceful than Tony Blair had led him to believe it would be. However, when Trimble reviewed the proposed text and asked for stronger wording, Blair purportedly replied, "Look, I can't unravel this now, everybody is . . . you know . . . this is where we are, we can't change this document now" (Millar 2004, 69).

[13] The "no guns, no government" phrase is tricky to interpret given that it seems to suggest that guns were a prerequisite for going into a devolved government. However, according to Grimason, "Ulster Unionists believe when Mr. Trimble said 'no guns, no government,' he meant Sinn Fein could only enter the Assembly Executive if the IRA disposed of its weapons at the same time—'jumping together' as it was called" (1999).

in the awkward spot of having to decide whether to allow the Assembly to open without the promised rounds of decommissioning. He eventually chose to participate in the Assembly, but he would suspend it six weeks later after intense pressure from Unionists. Although Trimble had detractors from within his own party, his harshest critics came from his right flank. Indeed, the Democratic Unionist Party (DUP) made IRA decommissioning a daily battle cry and used Trimble's awkward spot to highlight what it saw as IRA duplicity. The party would go on to capture a majority of seats in the 2003 Assembly elections, dislodging the UUP from its status as majority party. Once in the majority, the DUP made full IRA decommissioning a prerequisite for an operating Assembly, even adding demands that IRA arms dumps be photographed. As the party's founder Ian Paisley explained, "if you sin publicly, you have to repent publicly" (Left 2004). The IRA refused the terms (BBC 2004b), and the Assembly failed to reopen. It remained shuttered until 2007.

These rows have been well documented elsewhere, and it is not my intention to referee them here. What is important to the topic at hand is what was missing from the protracted debates over decommissioning. Two absences are particularly striking. First, during the varied, often heated debates about decommissioning, little attention was devoted to Loyalist decommissioning. Indeed, the great majority of pressure was applied to the IRA and Sinn Fein. This is not to suggest that Unionists did not want or expect Loyalists to decommission. They surely did, and do. However, the general assumption, especially early on and among Unionists, was that Loyalist decommissioning would follow naturally from IRA decommissioning.[14] This assumption is not an illogical one to make. In low-intensity conflicts, paramilitaries tend to be reactive (Bruce 1992). They enter the fray only after a state has proven itself unable or unwilling to defeat guerillas or protect civilians from them. Once the threat dissolves, so, theoretically, do they. In reality, Loyalist paramilitaries have behaved contrary to expectation. Neither the UVF nor UDA responded in kind to three rounds of IRA decommissioning in October 2001, April 2002, and October 2003. And when the IRA finally announced a formal end to its campaign in July 2005, both groups engaged in saber rattling (McDonald 2005b).

The debates on decommissioning have also failed to address the wider issue of demilitarization, which entails not only decommissioning but dismantling paramilitary structures and reintegrating combatants. Conflict resolution scholars refer to this wider process as demobilization, disarmament, and reintegration, or DDR for short (Gamba 2006). Decommissioning

---

[14] Republicans did not make this assumption. They have long complained that Loyalist decommissioning has been ignored by the British government, Unionist politicians, and the media (Lane 2001). However, Sinn Fein was unable to use the absence of effective Loyalist decommissioning as a bargaining chip in the Assembly because Loyalist political parties had only negligible representation in the body.

is certainly an important part of any transformation to peace, and reasonable people can debate whether it should occur before, during, or after a peace accord is implemented. However, it is a mistake to assume that decommissioning alone will lead to the dissolution of paramilitaries. Evidence from other conflicts suggests that paramilitary members will turn to (or remain in) criminality even after standing down if there are no formal mechanisms to reintegrate them. Most experts agree that effective conflict transformation must include carrots and sticks to entice/bend combatants to peace (Darby 2006; Gamba 2006). Combatants who are willing to stand down must have viable economic and social opportunities in a post-conflict society; those who refuse to do so must be aggressively policed. In Northern Ireland the state has done little to formally demilitarize its armed groups. Paramilitaries were allowed to organize their own decommissioning, establishing the timing, quantity, and verification process for each weapons dump. Most policy makers also assumed that the voluntary sector would provide the majority of reintegration assistance. However, the voluntary sector is too small to effectively reintegrate the thousands of men in need of assistance. It also lacks the muscle to prevent paramilitary recidivism or to punish those who return to the lifestyle.

Paramilitary Violence since 1998

The limited scope of the province's demilitarization efforts had a predictable effect. While overall numbers of political murder, bombing, and the like are down, paramilitary violence continues to occur in the province. Its character has changed though, with paramilitaries turning their attention inward, "policing" their own communities in often brutal ways. Northern Ireland secretary Mo Mowlam once infamously referred to such violence as "internal housekeeping" (Mackay 1999). The event that prompted her unfortunate turn of phrase was an IRA murder of a Catholic civilian, Andrew Kearney, a few months after the Belfast Accord was signed. The victim's "offense"—to brawl with an IRA man at a bar—had nothing to do with politics, but he would pay for it with his life. Indeed, a North Belfast IRA unit planned and executed his murder with military precision. His attackers slashed the phone lines and shut down the elevator in his high-rise apartment block to delay police and ambulance (BIRW 1998; Oliver 1999).

Mowlam's position was a difficult one. She had to decide if the murder constituted a breech of the IRA's cease-fire. If she determined yes, the agreement could collapse. If no, a young man's death would go unpunished. In the end she decided that the IRA was not in breech of its cease-fire, reasoning that the death, while tragic, was not a traditional military operation. Her decision would send a message to paramilitaries on both sides of the divide that internal violence would not put cease-fires or their attendant advantages in jeopardy (Mackay 1999). The decision would also spell trouble for civilians on both sides of the divide.

Although it may seem odd to an outsider that paramilitaries would want to use violence against their "own," Republican and Loyalist paramilitaries have long policed their respective communities (Boulton 1973; Hillyard 1985; Monaghan 2005). For much of the Troubles they did so out of necessity. The police, who were often engaged in military-style operations (investigating bomb plots, diffusing bombs, or cleaning up their aftermath), had little time for community policing. And their use of aggressive counterterrorism tactics afforded them little goodwill to do so (Monaghan 2005; Taylor 1999a, 1999b). The advent of peace in 1998 was supposed to normalize policing and, as a consequence, limit paramilitary forms of "justice."

Paramilitary policing has continued, however, and in many cases increased. To be fair, some of the increase is relative. That is, as paramilitaries started to wind down their military operations after 1994, internal violence took up a greater percentage of their violence. Between 1969 and 1994, for example, Republican and Loyalist internecine murders accounted for 8.8 percent and 7 percent of their total murders, respectively; between 1995 and 2001 the percentage of internecine murders increased to 13.6 percent and 36.4 percent, respectively. The actual number of internecine killings per year did not increase dramatically after 1994, however. Indeed, for Republicans the average number of internecine murders actually dropped, from 6.7 a year to 1.4. For Loyalists, it rose only slightly, from 2.5 to 3.4.

Evidence indicates that some forms of paramilitary policing have increased in real terms, however. So-called punishment attacks are a case in point.[15] Traditionally, paramilitaries have levied these punishments—both shootings and beatings—for socially deviant behavior, including rape, theft, joyriding, and drug use (Hillyard 1985; Monaghan 2005). Some victims are kneecapped. Others are beaten with bats or planks of wood, and often around the face for maximum visual effect. A particularly macabre punishment nicknamed the six-pack entails having one's ankles, knees, and elbows shot (Hall 1997). Punishment attacks are designed to keep victims alive but disfigure or otherwise disable them. In the tight-knit communities in which punishments attacks usually occur, the bodies of victims become message boards, reminding a community who is in charge and what can happen to those who step out of line.

In 1995, total punishment beatings (Republican and Loyalists) increased

[15] The Independent Monitoring Commission rejects the term "punishment beating" to describe these attacks. As they note, the term "lends a spurious respectability to the perpetrators, as if they were entitled to take the law into their own hands. And it has the ring of a deserved chastisement when the reality is often extreme cruelty and lasting physical and psychological injuries" (2004, 17).

134 percent. Although the increase in beatings was offset that year by a sharp decline (94 percent) in punishment shootings,[16] the overall trend was upward. The total number of attacks (beatings and shootings) was greater in 1995 than in 1994, and the numbers would remain higher in the years that followed. The increase in punishment attacks is especially notable on the Loyalist side of the conflict. Indeed, Loyalist punishment beatings sky-rocketed after 1995, from an average of 31 beatings per year before 1994 to an average of 91 beatings a year afterward. Republican beatings increased less sharply, from 36 to 79. The average number of Loyalist punishment shootings also increased, from 59 per annum to 62. Republican punishment shootings actually declined during the period.[17]

Paramilitaries also appear to have relaxed the rules regarding when to use punishment beatings. Although "punishments" are still meted out for traditional offenses, they are increasingly used to settle personal scores, consolidate neighborhood power blocs, and quash dissent. The expanding list of "punishable offenses" is related in large part to increasing criminality in paramilitary ranks. Both the Independent Monitoring Commission (2004, 2005, 2006) and Human Rights Watch (Hall 1997) have documented cases in which paramilitaries order punishment beatings for rivals in criminal enterprise.[18] The state's tolerance for such crimes—signaled by Mowlam's unfortunate phrasing—has also contributed to an anything-goes mentality. Liam Kennedy (2001) notes, for example, that punishment beatings of children increased markedly after the agreement was signed.

Paramilitaries' refusal to give up internal policing, and in some cases even increasing it, was matched by an uptick in internecine feuding, particularly among Loyalist paramilitaries.[19] Indeed, at times the feuding only seemed to beget more feuding. When Loyalists ended these feuds, they usually returned to their respective corners to begin recruiting new members. Ostensibly such efforts were designed to keep Loyalist lads from joining the "wrong" paramilitary—the definition of which depends on the particular paramilitary you ask. However, the opportunity to increase manpower for future feuding was an obvious motivation.

[16] Winston (1997) and Monaghan (1995) argue that paramilitaries moved from shootings to beatings because they reckoned that beatings would be less likely to endanger their cease-fires than shootings would.

[17] The figures in this and the previous paragraph were calculated using police data on paramilitary attacks between 1988–89 and 2002–3. The fiscal year begins in April, so data are not collected by calendar year. The data are archived on the CAIN Web site (2006k).

[18] The Independent Monitoring Commission was established in January 2004 to track the degree to which parties to the 1998 accord are following the standards set forth for them in the accord. A primary concern of the commission has been tracking paramilitary activity.

[19] Republican internecine feuding reached its peak in the mideighties with bloody feuds between the Irish National Liberation Army (INLA) and the PIRA, and internal feuding within INLA. By contrast, Loyalist feuding was minimal during the Troubles: the UVF and UDA engaged in only one feud, and it was early on in the conflict, in 1974.

The importance of ideology to paramilitaries on both sides of the divide has waned as well. Although paramilitaries have always engaged in illicit activity, like racketeering, to fund their operations, such income generation was highly regulated during the Troubles (Bruce 1992). Regulation was rooted in pragmatism as much as anything else—paramilitary leaders could keep better tabs on the proceeds when they limited who could extort money and from whom—but it nonetheless helped leaders quell internal gripes about money and keep the political goals of their operations front and center. Since the 1998 accord, however, criminal activity among the paramilitaries has increased, and evidence suggests that proceeds are largely used for personal enrichment. In his 2001 book *Godfathers* (2001), for example, Jim McDowell details the emergence of paramilitary "godfathers" who wear designer clothing, take lavish vacations, and purchase luxury homes.[20]

Although 1998 signaled a formal end to the hostilities, violence remains a part of the post-conflict environment. It is the inevitable consequence of a militarized peace in which paramilitaries on both sides took their time standing down. Within the Loyalist fold, the foot-dragging is connected to the fault lines that rumble beneath its surface.

Why Loyalists Remain on the Battlefield

The continued existence of Loyalist paramilitaries and by extension Loyalist violence must be understood in a wider context. That is, dynamics both internal and external to Loyalism help explain the paramilitaries' decision to stay put, and for so long, after formal peace arrived. In this book I make five interconnected arguments about the nature of Loyalist paramilitarism after the peace. Each is presented separately here, but in essence they form a hierarchy of assertions that taken together explain the Loyalist failure to stand down in a timely manner.

PEACE RIPS APART

The 1994 Loyalist cease-fire was regarded by many as a high-water mark for Loyalist paramilitary unity (Finlayson 1999; Taylor 1999b). Indeed, it was negotiated and announced by the Combined Loyalist Military Command (CLMC), an umbrella group of leaders from the Ulster Defence Association (UDA) and the Ulster Volunteer Force (UVF). In reality, however, the 1994 cease-fire, and the peace it portended, created seismic breaks within Loyalism. The coming peace forced Loyalists to redefine themselves, and not surprisingly it spurred sharp internal debates within its ranks. Some

---

[20] McDowell (2001) suggests that Republicans, who are more concerned about image than Loyalists, tapped into the drug trade by "taxing" it. Loyalists by contrast, became active participants—running, distributing, and selling the drugs.

Loyalists supported peace and were willing to negotiate the terms. Others resisted the peace and lashed out not only at Catholics but at their pro-peace peers. This is not to suggest, of course, that Loyalist paramilitaries were a particularly unified lot before. The CMLC was only formed in 1991, and it has been dormant for much of the time since. As Steve Bruce observes, "like any two competing organizations, the UDA and the UVF have rarely been on good terms for long" (1992, 124). Today's divide is, however, more trenchant and violent than previous ones.

The first inkling of trouble came in 1996 when the mid-Ulster brigade of the UVF murdered two Catholic civilians. The murders were unprovoked and in blatant violation of the UVF cease-fire (Anderson 2002). The division's leader, Billy Wright, ordered the attacks ostensibly to send a message to the UVF leadership, based on the Shankill Road in Belfast. That message was simple—mid-Ulster says no to peace. The leadership responded with an unprecedented step, standing down the entire division.[21] Wright went on to form a new paramilitary, the explicitly anti-peace Loyalist Volunteer Force (LVF).

The argument between Wright and his former peers in the UVF leadership did not subside with time. Indeed, although Wright was murdered in prison by members of the Irish National Liberation Army (INLA) before the Belfast Agreement was signed, acrimony from the split continued to fester.[22] Indeed, the splintering provided grist for almost a decade's worth of internecine feuding. Since 1998 Loyalist paramilitaries have been involved in three large, internecine feuds, and each revolved at least in part around the legitimacy of the LVF. These feuds have been bloody and destructive, leading to mass expulsions, burned-out properties, and widespread anxiety in Loyalist neighborhoods. In the years since the Belfast Agreement, the two sides have developed competing visions for the Loyalist future. These visions rest in large part on defining what it means to be a Loyalist in the post-agreement era. The carving up of Loyalism along pro- and anti-peace lines has presented everyday Loyalists with a stark political choice and little room for middle ground between them. I label these visions, also known as identity politics, political and revanchist Loyalism, respectively.[23]

[21] In my interview with David Ervine, he suggested that Wright had also run afoul of the UVF leadership on two other counts. In the first, Wright's men were found to be dealing drugs in a Banbridge nightclub with an INLA unit. In the second, Wright's unit had lost approximately thirty weapons to the security services.

[22] INLA was formed in 1974 by men forced out of the Official IRA (see chap. 2, n. 10, for details on the OIRA). Both groups are small in comparison to the IRA, although INLA has proven itself capable of systematic violence (CAIN 2006a).

[23] I use the term "political" to describe pro-peace advocates because this is how they identify themselves. In so doing I do not intend to suggest that revanchist Loyalism is apolitical. Revanchism is certainly unpalatable, but psychologizing its advocates as irrational or atavistic (that is, apolitical) underestimates not only its power on the street but the resonance of its message there as well. Defining revanchists with terms used to describe mental disorders also

Political Loyalism was nurtured in the UVF prison compounds at Long Kesh under the tutelage of Gusty Spence. For most of his tenure at Long Kesh, Spence was the commanding officer of the UVF wing at the prison, and by all accounts he ran a tight ship (Garland 2001). He required his men to follow a strict exercise regimen, keep their compound immaculate, and participate in parades. Spence also encouraged his men to educate themselves. He persuaded them to read books in the prison's library, enroll in college courses offered by the Open University, and engage in political discussions. As I document in chapter 2, Loyalist prisoners at Long Kesh began to view the conflict, and their participation in it, from a critical perspective. And when they left prison, they decided to develop a political path forward for Loyalism. Political Loyalism's flagship endeavor—the Progressive Unionist Party (PUP)—maintains a socialist approach to economic issues and a liberal take on social ones.

By contrast, revanchist Loyalism is explicitly anti-peace. Its supporters tend to be young turks who climbed paramilitary ranks during the late eighties and early nineties. These new members are credited with reinvigorating Loyalist paramilitary structures by embracing more aggressive tactics (Crawford 2003). Unlike their predecessors, who had links to Unionist and Protestant civic groups (trade unions, Orange orders, and churches), the young turks were from more lumpen sectors of society (Langhammer 2003). They tended to be unemployed, to have criminal records, and to sustain limited connection to civic groups. Not surprisingly, revanchists view the peace accord as a form of capitulation. The war will only end, they argue, with the unconditional surrender of the PIRA or its complete destruction.[24] Indeed, revanchists believe that Ulster is a Protestant place and that Catholics are an inferior people. Not surprisingly, they regard pro-peace Loyalists with special disdain. Such Loyalists are depicted as worse than Catholics because they "ought to know better." Revanchists have also directed their ire toward immigrants in the province, declaring them an evil on par with the IRA. Evidence also points to revanchist involvement in criminality, particularly the sale of illicit drugs (Lister and Jordan 2003; McDowell 2001). The combination of bigotry and criminality leads many commentators to suggest that revanchist Loyalism is nothing more than a cynical attempt to provide political cover for illegitimate activity (Langhammer 2003).

---

forecloses any role for countermobilizing them. A similar argument has been applied to analysis of the right wing in the United States. Early scholars borrowed liberally from psychological terminology to define right-wing adherents as paranoid and anxious (Lipset 1963; Hofstadter 1965). However, as McGirr (2001) rightly observes, early scholars' dismissive attitudes prevented them from predicting the right-wing resurgence that was then percolating.

[24] Although the IRA announced a formal end to its armed campaign in 2005, revanchists argue that the IRA has not decommissioned all of its weapons and still poses a threat to the Union.

A House Divided

The divide between political and revanchist Loyalism splits the Loyalist house in a variety of ways. It cuts within, between, and across Loyalist paramilitaries. To most observers, political Loyalism is associated with the UVF, whereas revanchism is connected to the UDA. This view has some basis in reality (Crawford 2003; McCann 2000). An internecine Loyalist feud in 2000, for example, began when members of UDA C Company attacked a UVF bar, claiming the group's leadership had gone soft.[25] However, while the UVF supported the Belfast Agreement, it has revanchists within its ranks as well. In the winter of 2004, for example, a UVF company in the Donegall Pass area of South Belfast launched a series of attacks against immigrant communities in Belfast. In a flyer distributed throughout the neighborhood to justify the attacks, immigrants were described as "a yellow invasion" and a threat tantamount to the IRA.

It is equally common to find individual paramilitary members who espouse revanchist positions on some issues and progressive stances on others. Frankie Gallagher, a spokesman for the UDA's political wing, the Ulster Political Research Group (UPRG), marched in an anti-racism rally in South Belfast to protest paramilitary attacks against immigrants. However, Gallagher also views the changing demographics of Belfast city as a zero-sum game in which Catholic gains necessarily equal Protestant loss.

The battle between revanchist and political Loyalists is also echoed in interactions between cultural boosters in the Unionist establishment and pro-peace elements in the paramilitaries. Playing against (stereo)type, political Loyalists find themselves opposing Unionist "cultural" boosters who want to define the differences between Catholics and Protestants in rigid terms. Indeed, some of their harshest detractors come from within political Loyalism's ranks.

The Criminal and the Political

Loyalists increasingly use violence to consolidate criminal enterprise and the personal power necessary to sustain it (Lister and Jordan 2003; McDowell 2001). When the LVF moved into the drug trade in the late nineties, for example, it proved itself willing to defend its "business" interests by killing those who threatened it, even if they were Loyalists. In the winter of 2000 the LVF murdered Richard Jameson, a UVF commander in Portadown, for speaking out against the group's drug dealing (McDowell 2001). This sort of violence has nothing to do, either directly or tangentially, with securing the province's union with Great Britain.

---

[25] A C Company parade held just before the attack included banners with anti-peace slogans, one of which read, "The Ulster conflict is about nationality. IRISH OUT!" (Pat Finucane Centre 2005).

Such violence has also led many commentators to denounce post-peace Loyalism as politically empty, a flimsy pretext for self-serving violence. Commentators routinely describe Loyalist paramilitaries as thugs, godfathers, and bosses, and they regularly use colorful nicknames to refer to them, including King Rat, Mad Dog, and the Brigadier of Bling (Sharrock 2005).[26] The implication is that Loyalist violence has devolved into a struggle for control of criminal assets (Freedland 2000; McDowell 2001)

Although there are certainly criminal elements within Loyalism (a phenomenon I document extensively in this book), not *all* contemporary Loyalist violence is criminal. A good portion of the Loyalist internecine paramilitary violence that has manifested itself since 1994 is traceable to the split between pro- and anti-agreement forces heralded by Billy Wright's expulsion from the UVF. This is not to suggest, of course, that political and revanchist Loyalists are still fighting over the actual agreement. Even the most devout pro-peace Loyalists are ambivalent about the accord today. Nor does the history of this split imply that criminal motivations are not part of the motivational mix. They certainly are. However, it is incorrect to suggest, as some commentators have (Freedland 2000; McDowell 2001), that Loyalist violence is nothing more than a gangland war over criminal assets.

The violence between revanchist and political Loyalists suggests a more complicated story. Revanchist Loyalists, for their part, have used their muscle not only against their criminal rivals but against political Loyalists—many of them in the UVF's political wing, the Progressive Unionist Party, who have no involvement in criminal activity. Although one should be careful not to over-ideologize such attacks—Bruce (2004) argues, for example that Billy Wright was driven by megalomania rather than politics—the anti-peace rhetoric in which such attacks are cloaked has a wider political impact. Revanchist smears (such as Lundy, or Fenian lovers) tend to silence political opposition.[27] Who, after all, wants to be called a traitor by one's own community? The stakes are even higher for persons living in areas under revanchist control, where dissent can invite a punishment beating, expulsion, or even death. As such, while revanchist leaders may have little personal interest in politics, their actions help frame people's political choices. The extant unease many Loyalists have with the peace accord only buttresses their cynical use of political rhetoric.

For their part, political Loyalists have also engaged in violence. Their violence is driven, however, by political considerations and usually falls into

[26] Billy Wright was given the nickname King Rat. Johnny Adair, a UDA brigadier I discuss in chapter 6, is known as Mad Dog. Jim Gray, a former UDA brigadier gunned down in 2005, was often called the Brigadier of Bling.

[27] In Protestant circles the term Lundy is shorthand for traitor. It refers to Robert Lundy, the colonel who surrendered to James II, a Catholic king, during the siege of Derry (CAIN 2006g). Fenian is a derogatory term for a Catholic.

one of two categories. The first is defensive violence. In the 2000 feud, for example, political Loyalists only used violence after they had been attacked, and they argued it was necessary to protect the pro-peace Loyalism they had helped craft in 1994 and 1998 from revanchist assault. On occasion political Loyalists also use violence as an offensive tactic. In 2005, for example, the UVF started a feud with the LVF, purportedly to clean up the criminal element once and for all (*Sunday Life* 2005). This violence is neither pretty nor mistake free. In many respects it has been counterproductive. And, to be certain, political and criminal motivations can and do jumble together for some fighters. However, it is clear that political Loyalism's violence was not driven by economic motives alone, or even in large part.

None of this is to imply that political Loyalists are angels. They have their fair share of problems, as my analysis shows. The largest and most obvious is the hypocrisy that surrounded them for almost a decade after the peace accord was signed—talking nonviolence while "the stench of gunfire [hung] in the background."[28] Political Loyalism does, however, have a progressive platform, and its genesis in paramilitary structure should not diminish its viability. Indeed, now that the UVF has formally stood down, both governments should work with political Loyalists to ensure that everyday Loyalists reengage the peace process.

The Belfast Agreement Gives Revanchists the Upper Hand

As ironic as it may sound, the post-conflict environment has tended to favor revanchist over political Loyalism. The primary reason is not, however, as many suggest, the consociational form of the agreement.[29] Indeed, while critics often argue, as Eamonn McCann (2000) does, that the accord has "structured paramilitarism into political and public life," they rarely note that the advantages that accrue from this structure are not evenly distributed within the Loyalist paramilitary fold. I argue here that the primary problem with the agreement is not its consociational format but rather its "one size fits all" model for bringing paramilitaries into the political fold. The Belfast Agreement was designed to bring paramilitaries out of violence by bringing them into politics. However, the agreement's system of carrots and sticks has worked better for Republicans than Loyalists. The IRA's political wing, Sinn Fein, was well established to compete for Assembly seats, but Loyalist political parties were not so advantageously positioned. There

---

[28] An anonymous source who helped establish the Independent Monitoring Commission explained the difficulty of working with the PUP. "I liked those fellows [David Ervine, Billy Hutchinson], but it was hard to work with them because the stench of gunfire hangs in the background."

[29] Consociational governments usually include mechanisms to ensure that each community's rights are protected. Governmental mechanisms include executive power sharing, autonomy, proportional voting, and veto power. See McGarry and O'Leary (2006) on Northern Ireland.

are structural reasons for Loyalist flat-footedness. As pro-state groups, Loyalist paramilitaries have always had less incentive to create an alternative political agenda than their anti-state counterparts in Republican paramilitaries. Indeed, the state already provides a political agenda; Loyalists saw their role as protecting it (Aughey 1989; Bruce 1992). Although paramilitaries usually go on to form their own political parties (paramilitary and state interests often diverge over time), they have more competition than their anti-state peers, who are often the only political game in town. Indeed, in Northern Ireland Loyalist paramilitaries have to compete for votes, allegiance, and "airtime" with the Unionist political establishment. And they have to explain to a constituency wedded to a law-and-order ethos why their paramilitary past should not work against them.

Not surprisingly, Loyalist political parties have failed to develop into sustainable parties. The upshot of this state of affairs is that the Loyalist paramilitary leaders who helped negotiate the Belfast Agreement have had little say in its implementation since, which has led to political alienation among Loyalists more generally. It has also given revanchist Loyalists a stick with which to beat their political Loyalist foes. Every glitch or compromise in the accord's implementation has been laid at the feet of political Loyalists: "You got us into this mess and what have you to show for it?" the mantra goes. Given political Loyalists' minimal representation in the power-sharing Assembly, there is little they can say in response. Revanchists' bonafides so established, they are free to run amok, their criminal endeavors legitimized by their "steadfast" defense of Loyalism. This dynamic will likely continue even in the wake of the UVF's stand-down order, with revanchists accusing the group's leaders of a final capitulation.

The structure for the distribution of European Union peace monies has also unwittingly contributed to revanchist Loyalism's dominance over political Loyalism. As I demonstrate in chapter 5, funding has often gone to single-identity cultural programs sponsored by revanchist groups in the community sphere. These programs have often helped create what one informant calls "better bigots," who use capacity-building schemes to present sectarian views in more articulate, palatable ways. Single-identity work is an important avenue for funding, but granting agencies must be careful not to unwittingly fund single-identity work that contributes to antagonistic forms of Loyalist identity politics.

The paramilitary-cum-politician transformation will not draw most Loyalists out of violence, nor will a decentralized, informal approach to reintegration. Northern Ireland needs a formal, state-led demilitarization program that helps paramilitary members reintegrate into society. Such a program should emphasize restitution, but it must also ensure that those who want to leave the paramilitary life have a sustainable way to do so. This is especially important in light of the UVF's recent stand-down order. The UVF's rank and file will now have to decide whether to continue illegal activity under new banners of allegiance or leave the violence business altogether. The presence of meaningful alternatives will certainly make "retirement" a more attractive option.

BETWEEN A ROCK AND A HARD PLACE—POLITICAL LOYALISM

Political Loyalists have spent the last decade on shaky ground. Some of their problems stem from the structure of the Belfast Agreement and EU peace funding, but it is fair to say that political Loyalists have also been boxed in by the structure within which they operate. Working inside of, or in concert with, a paramilitary group clearly has benefits—being on the inside provides access and room to influence that being on the outside never can. However, peace makes this position an unstable platform from which to launch a formal politic.

These contradictions are mirrored in the schizophrenic reaction that politicians, commentators, and citizens alike display toward Loyalist violence. Commentators routinely excoriate Loyalist paramilitaries for their continued violence. Yet when Loyalist foot soldiers run amok, people often avoid calling the police, turning instead to paramilitary leaders and demanding that they "do something." However, when paramilitaries "do something" with the tools at their disposal—guns, bats, physical force—they are condemned for thuggish behavior and enjoined to submit to the rule of law. I explore these contradictions more fully in the conclusion by analyzing the aftermath of a Loyalist internecine murder in 1997. Suffice it to say here that while critics repeatedly called on paramilitary leaders to "do something" about the purported killer in their ranks, they were less than happy with the group's response—to shoot the man believed responsible.

Responsibility for the decision to serve as police, judge, and jury in the wake of formal peace rests squarely on the shoulders of Loyalist paramilitaries. Although the role was embraced out of necessity during the Troubles, it is neither warranted nor necessary today. To be fair, however, the Police Services of Northern Ireland (PSNI) also bears some responsibility for this state of affairs. It has not done nearly enough to resume normal policing in Loyalist communities. Until it does, paramilitaries or their remnants will continue to fill the policing void. A number of reasons explain the PSNI's neglect, including the pernicious effects of collusion and the legacy of distrust that lingers from the Troubles. However one apportions the blame for the PSNI's meager efforts to police Loyalist criminality, it is safe to say that political Loyalists were not capable of doing the job. Indeed, when political Loyalists took care of their criminal elements in-house, they invited charges of dirty hands; when they left the job to the PSNI, they were accused of harboring criminals. Aggressive policing of Loyalist criminality must continue until Loyalist paramilitary structures are fully dismantled.

Moreover, the potential for revanchist gangs to form out of the remnants of Loyalist paramilitary units must be prevented with due diligence.

Some Theoretical Considerations

Although this book is primarily about Northern Ireland, my findings have relevance to wider, theoretical debates about low-intensity conflicts. In particular, my research counters two widely held assumptions in the political violence literature—that particularism undermines peace and that paramilitaries are driven primarily by economic motives. Here I outline these assumptions and suggest how my analysis calls them into question.

Particularism versus Cosmopolitanism

With the rise of ethnic and religious conflicts after World War II, political violence scholars turned their attention to so-called identity politics. Indeed, traditional explanations, which put internal conflict within states (as many of these conflicts were) down to a competition between classes, did not adequately capture the flavor of civil wars or the emotions that drove them. Scholars who used Marxism to explain the conflict in Northern Ireland, for example, still tended to arrive at distinctly "green" (Republican) or "red" (Unionist) solutions, thus highlighting, if unintentionally, the depth of ethnoreligious attachments among even the academic set (see McGarry and O'Leary 1995 for an extended overview).

Identity is, however, a broad term. To make it sufficiently useful for analytic purposes, scholars tend to differentiate between particularist and cosmopolitan variants of identity politics (Kaldor 1999; LaClau 1992; Mouffe 1995; Shelby 2005). Groups or movements that espouse particularist identities tend to believe that as a group they are singular, that their differences from other groups in a polity are far greater than their similarities. Particularist groups also view their culture and way of life as fragile and in need of protection. So construed, difference can be frightening, even threatening. A variety of movements and armed groups have embraced particularist identity politics. Segments of the black power movement in the United States, for example, posit the black experience as singular and black self-reliance as de rigueur (Shelby 2005). During the Bosnian civil war, Serb leaders justified ethnic cleansing by arguing that Serbians needed their own state to fulfill their destiny (Neuffer 2001). In Mexico, the Zapatista Army of National Liberation has made autonomy a central plank of its political platform, arguing that indigenous people can only develop in isolation from the rest of Mexico (Gallaher and Froehling 2002).

In contrast, cosmopolitan identity politics tend to emphasize connections between identity groups and cultures—a focus on the greater unity of humankind. Such politics acknowledge difference, but its advocates are neither threatened by it nor frightened of it. In some cases they even celebrate it. Cosmopolitan identity politics include both liberal and socialist variants. Liberal calls for a colorblind society, for example, are based on the notion that differences can be overcome by force of will. For their part, socialists argue that ethnic and religious attachments should not keep working-class peoples from coming together to protect their common class-based interests.

Many conflict scholars eschew particularist politics, especially in newly peaceful societies. They argue that particularism feeds conflict, that its presence in post-conflict societies can destabilize fragile societies and lead to a resumption of war. These scholars argue that peacemakers should support "cosmopolitan" identities, which are broad based, and avoid ethnic or religious grounds (Kaldor 1999; Wilson 2005). Not surprisingly, advocates of cosmopolitanism tend to dislike consociational approaches to peace because these approaches concretize difference in political structures. Advocates argue that consociational agreements can further entrench conflict identities and lead to resumption of hostilities (Lustick 1997; Kaldor 2001).

Other scholars argue, however, that cosmopolitanism is an elitist approach to conflict resolution (Calhoun 2003; Chandler 2003; Elshtain 2001). Elshtain (2001) remarks, for example, that only "jet-setting elites" can afford to rise above the "long-standing loyalties" that structure most people's lives in divided societies. Critics also complain that cosmopolitanism is naïve. In low-intensity conflicts like that in Northern Ireland, states are unable to militarily defeat guerillas, so concessions to the ethnoreligious blocs they represent are necessary to end the bloodshed. Moreover, most divided societies are unable to produce the social infrastructure (or changing social relations) necessary to create a solid base for cosmopolitan political parties, civic groups, and the like. Middle-class opportunities for *all* citizens can provide such a base, but these opportunities often require stable peace and time to develop.

In Northern Ireland this debate has played out in reference to the structure of the Belfast Agreement (see McGarry and O'Leary 2006 for a good overview). The Belfast Agreement was a consociational agreement;[30] it sanctioned ethnoreligious political parties and requires Protestant and Catholic

---

[30] Horowitz (2002) identifies two nonconsociational exceptions within the agreement. The first concerns Assembly vetoes. Although consociational agreements assume that political parties represent specific ethnic blocs, they are not required to do so. In the Belfast Agreement, however, vetoes require parallel consent or weighted majority, both mechanisms that, according to Horowitz, require Assembly members "to declare themselves to be 'nationalist, unionist or other'" (2002, 194). Also, Horowitz notes that the single transferable vote does not fit the general consociational model, which "prefer[s] list-system proportional representation" (195).

representation on government boards in proportion to each group's share of the population. When the agreement was being negotiated, participants from both ethnoreligious camps largely accepted the format as the only viable alternative.[31] However, problems in implementing the agreement have prompted critics from both communities to question whether it has actually worsened sectarian tensions (Farry 2006; Hyland 2002; Langhammer 2003; McCann 2005). Wilson argues, for example, that the Belfast Agreement has "crowd[ed] out any debate on the public interest or the common good." It has "reproduce[ed] communalist mindsets and entrenche[ed] division" (2005, 18). He calls for a new agreement built on "civic cosmopolitanism":

> An integrationist project for constitutional reform would in essence be the opposite of joint authority. Bottom-up rather than top-down, it would seek to corrode, rather than entrench, the "logic of the blocs" between unionism and nationalism. It would argue for civic allegiance to a neutral "state" in Northern Ireland, based on an egalitarian system of power-sharing which had the capacity to evolve over time toward a "normal" left-right divide. It would comprise a cosmopolitan, "both-and," rather than an "either-or" approach to the wider Irish and British (and European) contexts. (17)

In a similar vein, borough-level councillor Mark Langhammer argues that the Northern Ireland Assembly—the agreement's key power-sharing mechanism—is counterproductive:

> I'm a busy politician at local council level.[32] I get constituency complaints about all manner of things—from housing benefits, from consumer affairs to neighbor disputes, thousands in the course of any given year. But not one person has raised the need for Stormont. Ever! It's not wanted. It's not needed. It passed no laws that wouldn't have been passed by a Direct Rule Minister. . . . Its sole significant contribution has been in raising political temperature needlessly, stimulating communal antagonism and stoking up sectarian enmity. (2004)

Although the persistence and in some cases growth of sectarianism are disturbing trends and may stem in part from the structure of the agreement, I argue here that the consociational nature of the agreement is not the pri-

---

[31] Horowitz suggests that specific historical contingencies led both sides to adopt a consociational model. For Nationalists, "history showed that failure to include the extremes would render accommodation impossible, and it showed that only a carefully contrived web of guarantees would be sufficient to produce a durable accommodative dispensation" (2002, 203–4). For Unionists, history "provided a sense of a ticking clock." "Demography, voter turnout, and support from the British government" are not trends moving in Unionist favor (204).

[32] Langhammer was a borough-level councillor (Labour) for Newtonabbey between 1993 and 2005.

mary problem plaguing post-peace Northern Ireland. In so doing I follow scholars like Tonge (2003), McGarry and O'Leary (2006), and Gilligan and Tonge (2003), who "acknowledge the communalism underpinning the deal" and see it "as a part of a necessary realism" (Gilligan and Tonge 2003, 4). None of this is to suggest that the current agreement is the only option for peace. The problems implicit in its implementation clearly give reason for pause, and a different political structure might certainly dampen sectarian attitudes. However, it is unrealistic to think that the structure of the Belfast Agreement, or any other form of agreement, will by itself erase the depth of ethnoreligious (that is, particularist) attachments. This research suggests that the more salient question to the topic at hand is not which agreement style will work best, but which of the currently available Loyalist identity politics will allow Loyalists to reach a place where cosmopolitanism can become an attractive option.

At present, both variants of Loyalist identity politics are particularist. Indeed, revanchist and political Loyalists both believe that Ulster Protestants are a singular people—that their differences from Catholics in the province and in Ireland are far greater than their similarities. There are, however, important distinctions between political and revanchist Loyalists, particularly regarding their views of Catholics. Revanchist Loyalism offers an antagonistic reading of Catholicism as inferior, dangerous, and worthy of destruction. Political Loyalists take an agonistic approach.[33] They believe that Catholics and Protestants can share the same political unit, and the same rights therein, even if they lead largely separate lives.

Despite these differences, many commentators dismiss Loyalism wholesale. Indeed some make no effort to distinguish between Loyalism's political and revanchist elements. And even those who do make the effort tend to dismiss political Loyalism as anachronistic or inconsequential. This is a grave error. Peace and stability in Northern Ireland require the participation of all of its former combatants, Loyalists included. Loyalists cannot be dismissed out of hand, no matter how repugnant some may find them. As such, it pays to recognize and acknowledge the different options within the Loyalist fold (particularist though they may all be). Political Loyalism, though long couched in a paramilitary structure, is poised to offer a nonviolent and progressive path forward for the province's Loyalist population. Whatever form of government Northern Ireland eventually chooses, it must provide mechanisms for the inclusion of political Loyalists.

---

[33] In political theory, agonism is contrasted with liberalism and idealism. Unlike liberals and idealists, who believe people can learn to be blind to difference, agonists argue that conflict stemming from difference is natural and a permanent part of society. Conflict over difference can, however, be channeled positively. Indeed, different social groups do not have to like each other or spend much time together; they simply have to respect the right of "the other" to exist in the same polity (Mouffe 2000). For an accessible overview of the differences between agonism and liberalism/idealism, see the Wikipedia listing for agonism (2005a).

THE CRIMINALITY THESIS

A recent axiom in the political violence literature holds that low-intensity conflicts are criminal by nature—that their combatants are motivated by criminal rather than political concerns (Kaplan 2001; Münkler 2004; van Creveld 1991). Martin van Creveld argues, for example, that criminality is part and parcel of the structure of low-intensity conflict: "once the legal monopoly of armed force, long claimed by the state, is wrested out of its hands, existing distinctions between war and crime will break down" (1991, 204). Mueller notes that "warfare has been reduced to its remnants—or dregs—and thugs are the residual combatants" (2004, 2).[34] Enzensberger explains that contemporary combatants fight merely to fight, and as such, contemporary warfare is "about nothing at all" (1993, 30). Collier and Hoeffler (2002) argue that civil wars tend to emerge in developing countries that have large resource bases; they conclude that greed, rather than grievance, is the primary motive behind civil war. Mary Kaldor (1999) argues that contemporary demilitarization is so difficult because combatants are criminals who cannot be enticed by political concessions to stop fighting.[35] Indeed, most such combatants find war the preferred setting for plunder. Although few political commentators in Northern Ireland reference this literature directly (see Wilson 2005 for an exception), the criminal trope is widely used to describe Loyalist paramilitary violence.

There are, however, a variety of reasons to reject the equation of low intensity conflict with criminality. This is not to suggest that criminality is not part of the mix, for surely it is. Kalyvas (2001) is correct to remind us that criminality was also present in more traditional, state-on-state wars. All armies, state or private, have to deal with looting and other criminal behavior by their conscripts. The difference is not that looting exists in some conflicts and not in others but that traditional armies are better equipped to thwart it.

The motivations of those who make such claims also deserve scrutiny. Many tend to be elites who have a vested interest in eliminating guerilla or paramilitary groups. Indeed, these groups tend to target elites in large part because they have political and economic power. Elites are certainly within their rights to criticize such groups, but it is hardly fair or accurate to

---

[34] Although both van Creveld and Mueller agree that contemporary warfare is often criminal in nature, they differ on how to define such wars. Van Creveld sees low-intensity warfare as something new, whereas Mueller believes that low-intensity warfare is merely the remnants of state-on-state war, which is in serial decline.

[35] Unlike some scholars of contemporary warfare, Kaldor makes a distinction between guerilla warfare and what she labels "new wars." In her seminal work *New and Old Wars* (1999), she argues that guerillas sought to win hearts and minds, whereas new warriors endeavor to create fear and hatred. In this work Kaldor depicts the fall of the Berlin wall as the event that marked the change from guerilla to new warfare. In other work, however, she has implied that the conflict in Northern Ireland is emblematic of a new war (2001).

define an armed group's motivations purely from the perspective of their targets.

Likewise, dismissing contemporary warfare as criminal can obscure the role that internal divisions play in fostering violence. Like other organizations, guerilla and paramilitary groups have their internal politics. Differences can be personal, the result of petty jealousies and vain pretensions, or ideological, rooted in different worldviews. At times they can overlap or become entangled. To reduce guerilla and paramilitary motivations to one variable—criminal competition—obscures a realistic assessment of paramilitary organizations and, as a consequence, policies aimed at dismantling them.

In this book I do not discount the existence of criminal motivations behind some Loyalist violence. However, as my description in the last section makes clear, Loyalist violence is driven by far more than competition over criminal assets. Indeed, the data I present here demonstrate that much of the post-accord Loyalist violence stems from differing opinions of the accord itself. Other layers of discord certainly overlay this divide, but they do not erase its formative or continuing impact. This recognition should propel government and voluntary-sector peacemakers to support the efforts of political Loyalists over and against their revanchist peers.

Methods and Organization of the Book

The majority of data used in this book were derived from interviews with political Loyalists affiliated with the UVF. My decision to focus on the UVF, rather than the UDA or LVF, is largely a matter of happenstance. I began this project at the Linen Hall Library in Belfast, digging through its political collection. One of the first things I stumbled across was an article by a UVF prisoner, Martin Snodden, in a quarterly titled *Journal of Prisoners on Prisons* (1996). In the article "Culture behind the Wire," Snodden recounted his experience in the UVF compound at Long Kesh. His story came alive as I read the article, and I rang him up the next day to see if I could arrange an interview with him. Fortunately, he obliged my request.

When we met a few days later, I was impressed with Martin Snodden and not a little chagrined by my own preconceptions. I had expected him to be a "hard" man—gruff and dismissive. He was nothing of the sort. He was frank—telling me about the crime that led him to jail—and engaging; he answered my nosy, often convoluted questions with patience and charm. In my interview I discovered that when Martin was released from prison, he helped form the Ex-Prisoners' Interpretive Centre (EPIC), which aids political prisoners associated with the UVF in their reintegration into society. The organization also conducts research relevant to ex-prisoners and their families. After several years at EPIC, Martin left to form the Multi-Agency

Resource Agency (MARC),[36] an organization that helps Troubles-related trauma victims move on with their lives. It was, I thought, a redemptive approach to post-prison life. After my interview I wanted to talk to more people like Martin Snodden, and inevitably I did. Although my interviews often led from one UVF person to the next, I did speak to a few people associated with the UDA.

My interviews for this book are also largely confined to ex-prisoners rather than active combatants. When I began this project in 2002, I had hoped to interview a cross section of members (new and old, high ranking and foot solider), but as I progressed through my research I encountered two barriers. First, identifying who belongs to a paramilitary organization was more difficult than I had imagined. Given that paramilitary membership is officially illegal, few people will actually admit, "I'm in the UVF." More importantly, many lower-level foot soldiers are involved in criminality. I realized that such men would have little motivation to tell me the truth about their endeavors. Nor did I relish sorting through the spin they would likely foist on a visiting foreigner. This is not to suggest I had no spin to contend with—I did—but it was in manageable doses and more readily fact-checked, given that ex-prisoners and other paramilitary cum peacemakers have produced a written record to draw on. I was also acutely aware that interviewing criminal elements inside paramilitary structures posed its own, more dangerous risks. These were not risks I was willing to face, given that my interest was, at the end of the day, in efforts to remake rather than destroy Loyalism. My focus does, however, make this work a partial rather than comprehensive take on Loyalist paramilitary structure.

Because interviews were my primary method of data collection, I draw quotations extensively from them throughout the book. Unless otherwise noted, all personal quotations here forward are from these interviews. Presenting interview data in this way allows me to avoid repetitive citation in the body of the text, even though it may suggest that interview data are less central to the book than they really are.

This book is divided into three parts. In the first, which contains the introductory material found in this chapter and the next, I detail the Loyalist prison experience. Although most Troubles-related prison sentences ended in 1998 (before the temporal focus of this book), political Loyalism was largely nurtured in prison. Understanding this period is crucial for understanding political Loyalism today. In the second and third sections of the book I examine how the divide between revanchist and political Loyalists plays out on the ground in Loyalist communities. Given that my research was conducted between 2002 and 2006, my focus is primarily on the dynamics of this divide before the UVF issued its stand-down order. The second section covers what

---

[36] MARC has since changed its name to the Conflict Trauma Resource Centre.

are largely peaceful manifestations of this divide. In chapter 3 I compare revanchist and political versions of class politics. In chapter 4 I examine Loyalist efforts to create a cultural repertoire around the Ulster Scots "language" and the theory of the Cruthin. In chapter 5, the final chapter in this section, I discuss the funding mechanisms by which such work is carried out. In the third section of the book I examine the violent manifestations of the revanchist/political split within Loyalism. In chapter 6 I examine Loyalist internecine feuding, and in chapter 7 I chronicle UVF attacks against immigrants and political Loyalists' attempts to stop them. I conclude the book with chapter 8, in which I assess the battle for ascendancy in Loyalism and its impact on the wider Loyalist community. I also proffer tentative prescriptions for Loyalist demilitarization and discuss the ramifications of the UVF's decision to finally stand down.

2 *The Loyalist Prison Experience*

During the Troubles, thousands of men and women from both communities went to prison for committing terrorist offenses. The Republican experience in prison has been well documented. The story of Bobby Sands and the hunger strikers, for example, is now firmly part of Republican lore. Sands's grave in Belfast is a shrine to the Republican struggle, and his image has become iconic. Indeed, his young face smiles above pedestrians in a number of murals along the Falls Road, the heartland of Nationalist West Belfast (see fig. 2). In one mural Sands is even depicted as a Jesus figure, hanging from an H, the shape of the jail in which the hunger strikes were held (see fig. 3). Republican prisoners are also well regarded in Nationalist communities, especially those who were involved in any of the movement's formative protests of the early 1980s, which began with the blanket protest, progressed to the dirty protest, and culminated in the hunger strikes. Many of these prisoners are now community workers and politicians in Sinn Fein. More recent prisoners are also honored in murals along the Falls Road. There are even murals honoring the special forms of humiliation Republican women faced in prison—no small feat given the macho nature of many resistance groups.

The Loyalist prison experience, by contrast, has been little commemorated. There are few murals honoring the Loyalist prison experience (most just call for the prisoners' release), and ex-prisoners are not usually well regarded in Unionist circles. Indeed, there is little love lost between Loyalist ex-prisoners and their Unionist brethren, the reasons for which I document later in the chapter. As I also demonstrate, however, the Loyalist prison experience was formative for pushing Loyalism advocates toward the peace table. Key negotiators in the 1998 peace accord were Loyalist ex-prisoners, and Loyalist ex-prisoners play an important role in fostering progressive notions of Loyalism in the post-1998 environment. Indeed, the most progressive

Fig. 2. Mural of Bobby Sands, West Belfast.

political party currently representing the Protestant side of the polity, the
Progressive Unionist Party (PUP), was built by two UVF ex-prisoners—
David Ervine and Billy Hutchinson. Despite the formative place of the Loyalist prison experience, the story itself is largely untold. As Tom Roberts, a
former Loyalist prisoner and the current director of EPIC succinctly put it
in our interview, "it is not a period that's been told. You know, there's a lot
of people who wouldn't be aware that Loyalist prisoners were [even] on
protest for a period of almost two years."

I begin this chapter, therefore, by explaining why the Loyalist prison experience has remained untold even as the Republican experience has been
memorialized in song, verse, and public celebration. I then give a brief
overview of the prison system as it existed in Northern Ireland during the
Troubles. I do so not only to acquaint the reader with the wealth of terms
used to refer to the different places where people were imprisoned during
the Troubles (Long Kesh, H Blocks, the Maze, the "cages," and the like) but
also to describe the key changes made regarding the accommodations of
prisoners during the height of the Troubles. These changes were initiated by
a Labour government in 1976 but were famously carried to fruition under

Fig. 3. Mural of the IRA hunger strikes, West Belfast.

the prime ministership of Margaret Thatcher. They were integral to the Republican protests mentioned previously and, as I demonstrate later, to Loyalist protest and politicization as well. In the third section I detail the prison experiences of Loyalists in both the Maze and the H Blocks. These prisons were quite different and led to different forms of interaction and political protest. In the fourth section I overview the release of political prisoners through provisions laid out in the Belfast Agreement. In this section I also discuss problems prisoners face with reintegration. In particular, I focus on employment problems because the barriers prisoners have faced (and continue to face) help explain their eventual turn to the voluntary sector in search of employment. I conclude the chapter with a short section about the differences within political Loyalism, especially as it relates to Loyalist community work.

A Sense of Abandonment

There are a variety of reasons why Loyalist ex-prisoners are treated so differently than their counterparts in the Republican community. One of the reasons is the fundamental divide between Loyalism and Unionism.

Although both terms identify someone as Protestant (in an ethnic sense) and as supportive of continued union with Great Britain, the divide between them captures important lines of difference within the Protestant population. Two are especially important: class positioning and tolerance for violence. Generally, the term Loyalist places someone as working class, while the Unionist label positions someone as middle or upper class. The working-class connotation of the term Loyalism does not, however, have a derogatory association. Unlike their counterparts in the United States, working-class people in both Ireland and Great Britain are usually comfortable with terms that denote class. Indeed, Loyalists would not be offended to be called working class by someone from a higher class. They are intensely proud of their working-class roots and not a little suspicious of their better-off counterparts. When I asked William "Plum" Smith, an ex-UVF prisoner and a caseworker at EPIC, to describe the difference between a Unionist and Loyalist, for example, he responded: "Unionism to me is the middle-class Protestants using culture and prayer and things for their own ends. Working-class Protestants, you know, to me are Loyalists."

The term Loyalism also denotes a greater tolerance toward violence. Generally, a person is called a Loyalist if he or she belongs to, supports, or lives in territory governed by a paramilitary organization. Indeed, it is telling that of the three largest paramilitaries on the Protestant side of the conflict, none contains the term Unionist in its name (this applies to both official titles and noms de guerre). It is equally notable than when Billy Wright's unit splintered from the UVF in the run-up to the 1998 peace accord, it named its new force the Loyalist Volunteer Force (LVF), a name meant to symbolize the group's conviction that Unionists had sold out the Protestant people. None of this is to imply that working-class people are somehow more atavistic than their middle- and upper-class counterparts in the Unionist establishment. There are logical reasons why people in Loyalist working-class neighborhoods would tolerate more violence than people in Unionist areas. In large part, they had no choice: the IRA was centered in Catholic working-class areas. (At the start of the Troubles there were few middle-and upper-class Catholic areas.) And when the IRA engaged in spontaneous or otherwise unplanned violence toward Loyalists, it was usually within spatially proximate areas. Indeed, middle- and upper-class Protestants could afford to buffer their estates in ways that neither the Catholic nor Protestant working classes could. The result was that it was easier for hatreds to spill across borders in working-class areas, where there were more borders and fewer buffers. In this context, Loyalist violence was often sanctioned as a form of protection and defense for the community at large (Mulholland 2002).

Unionists have, however, always held the political reins in the Protestant community, as they have for the whole of Northern Ireland. And unlike their Loyalist "cousins," Unionists have tended to oppose Loyalist violence, or at the very least to keep it at arms length. There are three reasons for their rejection of violence. First, at a personal level many Unionists oppose paramilitary violence on religious grounds (just as many Nationalists do on the Catholic side of the conflict). Second, Unionists' critiques of the IRA hinge on the illegality of its actions. The PIRA, it is argued, have stepped outside of the legal and proper boundaries for enacting social change. Unionist public support of Loyalist violence would undermine this position. As Martin Snodden explained it to me, "the Unionist family, by and large, is very much a grouping that would subscribe to law and order." Indeed, these sentiments often applied even to legitimate forms of protest *within* Unionism. Tom Roberts noted, for example: "I can remember my father—he worked in the Linen Mills at that time, you know. Pretty hard difficult work. And, he would have been reluctant even to be a member of the trade union because that would have been seen as being revolutionary if you like. As challenging the state."

A third reason is that Protestants, by virtue of their dominant position in Northern Irish society, had a number of legitimate outlets for fighting the PIRA. Young men who wanted to defend Ulster from Republicans, for example, could join the Royal Ulster Constabulary (RUC), the B Specials,[1] or the British armed forces, which included a number of forces that recruited from and were stationed in Northern Ireland. It is important to note that Unionists and Loyalists alike shared the sentiment that young Protestant males had legitimate outlets for their patriotism. As such, some young men did not share their involvement in the paramilitaries with their parents or other family members. Martin Snodden told me, for example, that his parents only discovered he was in the UVF after his arrest.

The message coming from the Unionist (and Protestant) leadership was not, however, always so clear-cut in its opposition to the use of violence to protect the union. Indeed, while Unionism (in contrast to Loyalism) has always been associated with law and order, a number of key leaders within its ranks have been accused of tacitly supporting violence by whipping up fear and sectarian tension (Brewer 1998; Taylor 1999b). Perhaps the most infamous example is a speech that William Craig gave to a rally of nearly a hundred thousand people on 18 March 1972, the worst year of the conflict. In his speech Craig called on Loyalists to "build up a dossier of the men and the women who are a menace to this country because if and when the politicians fail us, it may be our job to liquidate the enemy" (as quoted in Taylor 1999b, 96).

---

[1] The B Specials were a part of the Ulster Special Constabulary (USC), which was formed in 1925. The USC was comprised of three supplemental paramilitary forces. The B Specials was a part-time defense unit. Its members were all Protestants, and its relationship with the Catholic population was always particularly contentious and mistrustful. After a series of offenses by its members, the B Specials was replaced by the Ulster Defence Regiment (CAIN 2006j).

Ian Paisley has also been criticized for flirting with militancy in its rhetorical forms. Bruce (2005) observes, for example, that Paisley came "close, in rhetoric at least, to rejecting the state's monopoly of violence." In 1981 Paisley created a so-called third force to protect Protestant civilians. He even invited journalists to witness a secret gathering of the group. They were treated to a show of "500 men in combat jackets wav[ing] what were purported to be certificates for legally-held firearms" (Bruce 2005, 14). In another example, in a speech the same year, Paisley intoned: "We have a choice to make. Shall we allow ourselves to be murdered by the IRA, or shall we go out and kill the killers?" (as quoted in Bruce 2005, 14).

There is, of course, no evidence that either Craig or Paisley committed violence or sanctioned specific plans for violence by others (Bruce 2005). For his part, Paisley has often been a strident critic of Loyalist violence.[2] His rhetorical "bombs" across the ethnoreligious divide have, however, led many commentators to accuse him of hypocrisy (Brewer 1998; Cooke 1996). Ex-prisoners feel the same way. As Tom Roberts noted in our interview, "There's a great deal of hypocrisy. I would call it, within 'middle Unionism.' Whereas a lot of these people created the environment where violence is inevitable, they don't necessarily accept the people who engage in the violent conflict." Michael Atcheson, another UVF ex-prisoner and a worker with the voluntary-sector group called Local Initiatives for Needy Communities (LINC),[3] expressed a similar sentiment: "You know, this whole conflict came [from] middle-class/upper-class Unionism. But it was working-class Unionists who were co-opted. You know, it's the same middle-class leaders who called for young men of Ulster to come and defend their country, their religion, and their community, and now condemn these young men as scumbags."

As Michael Atcheson's comments suggest, Loyalists often felt abandoned by their community when they went to prison. And many of them continue to feel abandoned after release. Martin Snodden, for example, described the experiences of ex-prisoners he catalogued while doing research for EPIC:

> I know, we done research whenever I was the director of EPIC, and I know of some people who experienced being ostracized from their own community. They weren't allowed to enter into the local pubs that were run by Unionist people. That occurred in the Enniskillen area. That's a fact. Now, pub culture is major [here]. If you don't have access to a local pub, you don't have access to the local community. Because it's hugely [built] around [the pub], the nucleus of socialization takes place there.

[2] Bruce (2005) also states that paramilitaries have never had much success drawing recruits from the ranks of Paisley's Free Presbyterian church.

[3] LINC describes itself as a "Nazarene Compassionate Ministry Working for Peace, Reconciliation, and Social Justice in Northern Ireland" (LINC Resource Centre 2005).

If you cannot go to the pub, Martin concluded, "you're screwed, marginalized, stigmatized as a result."

Ex-prisoners find such treatment especially galling. Many feel that respectable Unionists—politicians, preachers, business elite—tacitly encouraged violence from the sidelines even as they kept themselves at arms length from it.[4] Indeed, Tom Roberts sees it as part of the Unionist strategy. Unionists were, he reflected, "always quite happy to use the veiled strategy of 'If you don't deal with us, there's these bogeymen in the background who will do what they do.'" Not surprisingly, Loyalist ex-prisoners were scornful of these tactics and those they believe used them. Martin Snodden, for example, was blunt in his assessment of the Unionist leaders in power when he went to prison. "The so-called leaders had their heads up their arses," he told me. When I asked which leaders he was talking about, he responded, "Well, you had the big dinosaur himself, Mr. Paisley. And, you had William Craig, who was the leader of the Vanguard Group, and former home office minister with the Stormont Government."

As Martin's comments suggest, ex-prisoners have little respect for the Unionist leaders of their youth. Perhaps not surprisingly, the feeling is mutual. Indeed, when veteran journalist Peter Taylor asked Paisley to comment on the Loyalist ire that is often directed his way, he retorted:

> Oh yes, they do blame me. They say I got them put into prison and I've heard them all and I read their magazines. Their slanders are outrageous, and all I can say is they're not worthy of comment because if they had been worthy of comment the vast majority of the electorate of Northern Ireland wouldn't have voted for me the way they do. There's no one that's stood more abuse from the paramilitary elements that I have stood, and you can go back and look at their magazines and I was bad man number one. (as quoted in Taylor 1999b, 98)

Although my interview sample is admittedly small, I did not get the sense that ex-prisoners blamed Paisley for their crimes. The men in my sample assumed responsibility for their crimes. Indeed, a good number still think their crimes were legitimate acts of war. Their problem with Paisley is not that he led them to war but that he failed to stand firmly behind his militaristic rhetoric. Steve Bruce (2005) makes this point in his work on Loyalist paramilitaries. As one of his informants explained, in reference to Paisley's

---

[4] Loyalist paramilitaries are not alone in making this assertion. Stephen Farry of the Alliance Party expressed a similar view in our interview. "The Unionist leadership have always kept themselves at arms length from paramilitaries. I mean, they have never been involved, directly involved in the paramilitaries. But, there's been a symbiotic relationship there between the main Unionist political parties and the paramilitary muscle on the street." As an example, Farry cited the Unionist demands about the Drumcree march in 1996: "They tacitly used the threat that Loyalist paramilitaries were posing to shoot Catholics to get their way. They just said, 'because this threat exists, you have to give in.'"

"third force" movement, "waving fuckin fire arms dockets! Fuckin joke. That boy was just an embarrassment" (2005, 15).

Other men in my sample regret their crimes, but they wish cooler heads had prevailed among Unionist leaders of the day. Martin Snodden provides a good example. When Martin was nineteen, he and two other volunteers, Eddie Kinner and George Brown, signed up for a UVF mission. They were asked to bomb Conway's Bar on the Shore Road. Conway's was selected, Martin explained, because "our [intelligence] operation at that time said that it was an IRA headquarter, and the IRA were using it. So, it was a very clear act, as far as I was concerned, at that time, an act of war by the IRA." The trio's bomb did not go off as planned, however, and two people were killed—Martin's fellow bomber George Brown and a Catholic woman named Marie Doyle. That one of the victims was a woman seemed to tear at Martin the most. "I was horrified to learn a woman had died. It was not what I had ever wanted or planned."

Although Martin regrets his crime, he also told me he believes Unionist leaders contributed to the volatile climate that provoked paramilitarism in those early days. And as a paramilitary cum peacemaker, Martin believes that true conflict transformation will only occur if the entire society confronts its bigotry. As he explained, "You know, we're [MARC] very particular with the words we use because a lot of people abuse the expression 'innocent civilians.' However, in an environment that we've had, a conflict so protracted, it's not an appropriate term. Civilians can contribute to the conflict without being protagonists within the conflict."

Although Loyalists felt abandoned in prison and rejected after their release, the Loyalist prison experience was nonetheless a deeply formative one for the advent of political Loyalism. Ex-prisoners not only played an integral role in the Belfast agreement, but many of them continue to do the hard work of conflict transformation on the ground in Loyalist communities. Before turning to the specifics of the Loyalist prison experience, I present a brief overview of the prison system in Northern Ireland during the Troubles.

The Prison System in Northern Ireland

One of the primary battlegrounds of the Troubles—a conflict that for the most part lacked clearly demarcated battlefields and fronts—was prison (McEvoy 2001). The combat there was mostly symbolic. It was a battle over the terms of imprisonment and its meaning. Republican and Loyalist prisoners argued that their offenses were political. They had killed, bombed, and maimed for political reasons. They were no ordinary criminals. The state disagreed, preferring the label "terrorist" and standard criminal treatment. Because it was the state that defined crimes and administered the punishment, most of the battles on prison terrain were between the paramilitaries and the state rather than among the paramilitaries. Indeed, this was even the case in facilities in which prisoners were not segregated by paramilitary membership.

During the period of the Troubles, seven prisons were in use in Northern Ireland—a substantial number for a small country whose population is just over 1.5 million. Given the advent and durability of the Troubles, however, the state required a large prison system. It had to hold two distinct types of prisoners: "ordinary decent criminals" (ODCs), whose sentences were often relatively short, and paramilitary members, whose crimes were terrorist offenses and whose sentences were usually long (McEvoy 2001). After the Troubles began, the number of persons imprisoned increased rapidly. At its largest in the late 1970s, the prison population totaled almost 3,000, up from 600 in 1969. The numbers leveled off in the 1980s and have dropped sharply since 1998, when many long-term prisoners were released under the terms of the 1998 Belfast Agreement (McEvoy 2001).

During the early years of the Troubles (before 1976), a person who was convicted for actions undertaken on behalf of a paramilitary was labeled as either "conforming" or "nonconforming" and housed accordingly. Conforming prisoners agreed to abandon their paramilitary attachment (while in prison) and to obey prison rules. Conforming prisoners were housed with ordinary decent criminals as well as other conforming prisoners from both Loyalist and Republican paramilitaries. Nonconforming prisoners maintained association with their paramilitary and insisted on receiving a political designation for their crimes. They were usually housed only with other members of their paramilitary. In 1972 the decision to not conform was afforded a level of legitimacy when then secretary of state for Northern Ireland, William Whitelaw, granted nonconforming prisoners what was known as special category status. Akin to prisoner-of-war status, special category status allowed prisoners to be housed only with other members of their paramilitary, to wear civilian clothes, to associate with their fellow prisoners in pen areas, and to decline otherwise mandatory prison work schemes (CAIN 2006i).[5]

When the Troubles began to intensify, however, the British government put its special category protocol under review. In 1974 it commissioned a report on the matter. The report, which emerged a year later, recommended the elimination of the newly granted special category status. In March 1976, the government announced that it would thereafter suspend special

[5] In hindsight it may seem odd that the British government would grant paramilitary figures of either stripe the leeway afforded by special category status. In the early days of the conflict, however, the government generally took the approach that some violence between the two communities was both inevitable and acceptable. Indeed, in 1971 then British home secretary Reginald Maudling described conditions in Northern Ireland as constituting "an acceptable level of violence" (CAIN 2006f).

category status for any person arrested for committing a terrorist act. Republican and Loyalist prisoners responded to the change with a variety of protests. The Republican protest, which began with the blanket protest, was followed by the dirty protest and eventually the hunger strikes.[6] Loyalists prisoners also engaged in a variety of protests—most notably the Loyalist blanket protest. They did not, however, launch a hunger strike.

The oldest prison in use during the Troubles was the Crumlin Road Prison. A high-security prison, Crumlin had the worst infrastructure in the system during the Troubles (McEvoy 2001). It housed conforming and nonconforming paramilitary prisoners as well as ordinary decent criminals. Crumlin also included a holding area for prisoners waiting assignment to a prison. In 1996 the prison was closed.

The Maze is the second oldest prison in the Northern Irish political system. Located just south of Belfast, it was originally a British Royal Air Force base. When the Troubles began it was transformed into a prison to accommodate the influx of new prisoners. The site is also known as Long Kesh.

There were actually two distinct prisons on the grounds of the Maze. The first, comprised of prisoner of war–style compounds, housed special-category-status prisoners and was segregated along paramilitary lines. The prisoners in each compound were permitted to elect a commanding officer, who was in charge of running the affairs within the compound. Prisoners slept in Nissan huts and were allowed access to a private prison yard (only accessible to members of the paramilitary) at 7:30 in the morning. The second prison, built later and known as the H Blocks, included eight H-shaped structures. Its construction coincided with the elimination of special category status. Prisoners in H Blocks were required to wear prison garb and to participate in prison work schemes. During some periods of the Troubles, Loyalist and Republican prisoners were housed together. At others, they were segregated. Periods of segregation usually followed protests by one or the other side, or turmoil in integrated wings. The Maze was a high-security prison, and no ordinary decent criminals were housed in any of its structures. It was closed in 2000. Current plans for the site, which is more than 350 acres in size, include a deluxe sports stadium and entertainment venues for shopping and dinning. A Troubles-related museum and conflict transformation center are also planned for the site.

Maghaberry Prison is one of Northern Ireland's newest prison complexes and was only fully opened in 1987. Like the Maze, Maghaberry actually contains two prison structures on its grounds. One houses female prisoners

---

[6] People commonly blame the government of Margaret Thatcher for the renunciation of special category status. Although the policy was enacted by the previous government, she was in power during the Republican hunger strikes in 1981, when prison protest around the issue was at its height.

of all types—conforming, nonconforming, and ordinary decents. The second, a maximum security prison, houses male prisoners who committed conflict-related crimes but who agree to conform to prison rules. Prisoners who chose to renounce paramilitary attachments while in prison were also transferred here. Conditions at Maghaberry are often depicted as among the best in Great Britain (McEvoy 2001), but it has not escaped the sort of internal political battles that have plagued other prisons, like the H Blocks, where Republican and Loyalists prisoners were (sometimes) integrated. In summer 2003, for example, Maghaberry erupted in protest as prisoners from both the Loyalist and Republican sides demanded segregation within the system. Some dissident Republicans began a dirty protest, and a group of Loyalist prisoners took over the roof of the prison for a night in protest (BBC 2003b).

The remaining prisons in operation during the Troubles were Magilligan Prison and the Young Offenders Centre. Magilligan, which remains open, was largely reserved for ordinary decent criminals, although at various times it was used to house paramilitary prisoners whose sentences were relatively short. The Young Offenders Centre was for male criminals of all sorts between the ages of eighteen and twenty-one (McEvoy 2001).

The majority of ex-prisoners interviewed for this book went to prison during the early phases of the conflict. Most were interned in either the compounds or the H Blocks at the Maze. Several, however, spent some time at the Crumlin Road prison. It is to their stories in prison that I now turn.

In the Compounds, On the H Blocks

Incarceration was a transformative experience for Loyalists on a number of fronts. Three are especially important in understanding the eventual politicization that some Loyalists would experience in the years after their release. I discuss each in turn.

DEFINING THEIR CRIMES IN POLITICAL TERMS

Going to jail forced many Loyalists to define the actions that led to their incarceration. At one level this may seem an obvious matter, as simple as saying, "I went to jail for a double murder," or "I went to prison on an explosives charge." As McEvoy (2001) remarks, however, one of the key fronts in the war euphemistically known as the Troubles was definitional—how to define the crimes that paramilitaries on both sides committed during its tenure. And although prisoners on both sides of the conflict had to contend with such definitional battles, they were often harder for Loyalists than Republicans.

Unlike their Republican counterparts, for example, Loyalists had no sweeping narratives through which to situate their violence. Republicans could cloak their murders and bombs, even those conducted with the most sectarian of motives, under the rhetorical garb of "the struggle" and "the quest for freedom." Loyalists had no ready bag of narratives with which to do the same. Their violence was more often presented as sectarian or disorganized. And as I mention earlier, Loyalists could not rely on Unionists to back their actions. They also had more difficulty legitimizing their targets of violence than did Republicans. Members of the RUC and the army, for example, wore uniforms and were easily identifiable as such to the public. Although there would still be an outcry in the Protestant community when members in their ranks were killed, the potential for death was considered a hazard of the occupation (members were, after all, armed in the course of their duties). In contrast, although members of the IRA were engaged in equally dangerous work (and armed as well), they were largely indistinguishable from the civilian population. This ambiguity not only contributed to the larger civilian murder rate by Loyalists than by Republicans (Mulholland 2002); it also eventually led commanding officers in both the UDA and the UVF to decide that the only effective way to address the IRA was to hit the population in which it lived (Crawford 2003; Garland 2001). The wider population, however, always regarded civilian deaths with greater repugnance than military deaths.

Given these constraints, Loyalists often struggled to define their violence. Would they accept the narrative of "middle Unionism," which alternately abandoned them, disparaged them, or refused to sanction their actions? Or would they build a discursive counterpart to Republican mantras about the political nature of their violence? It is, of course, very difficult to truly know the motivations of someone who takes another human's life. And, it is surely true that many people only make sense of their crimes and their motives after the fact rather than before it. Nonetheless, some Loyalist prisoners chose to define their crimes as political acts, just as their Republican counterparts did. And whether or not Loyalists' motivations were political at the time (or post facto), the decision to present their crimes as political allowed them to think about the future of Loyalism in political terms and to formulate views quite different from those espoused by Unionists at the time.

When I asked Plum Smith about his time in prison, he described his crime as a political one: "We weren't common criminals and so we didn't want to be treated like ordinary criminals. Therefore, it was all a struggle of names between the authorities and ourselves . . . the struggle to wear our own clothes—things like that there." Plum also noted the difficulty he and his fellow Loyalists had in getting Unionist leaders to support their claims: "When we got in the conflict situation, first of all we struggled with our *own* authorities in that we regarded ourselves as being political, as prisoners of war." As I remarked earlier, Martin Snodden also defined his crime as a political act. He saw Conway's Bar as a fair target because UVF intelligence suggested that it was "an IRA headquarter."[7]

Naming their crimes as political, however, was a first step for many Loyalist prisoners. Indeed, questioning the nature of their crimes led prisoners to question the conflict itself. As Plum explained:

> During the early seventies, it was myself, Gusty Spence, [name inaudible on research tape], and a number of our people. And, we started thinking about the conflict. How you came to be in the place. You know, what got us to the point where we felt we had to do something to end up in jail. And, so, it was, in the main searching for, well, it was a quest, you know, about the Unionist Party, about being the majority, about all the things that go into Protestantism, and about an all Ireland and all that there. We started questioning these things. Asking questions.

One of the cofounders of LINC, Billy Mitchell, also recalled having lots of discussions while in prison. He saw those dialogues in political terms as well.

> I was in the compounds with Gusty and Eddy Kinner, and a lot of people at that meeting that night [a talk Mitchell gave at the Spectrum Centre, which the author attended]. We engaged in a lot of dialogue and debate and discussion. And the objective of that there was to expand our minds, to engage in dialogue, to develop thought.

The ability of a prisoner to question was no small feat, and it opened up a space for prisoners to ask questions. As Plum Smith noted,

> We created a system in Long Kesh where we pushed education. We pushed thinking. We had progressive political meetings. And, we talked about things we couldn't talk about outside.

While these conversations were important for personal development, they also laid the groundwork for a specifically Loyalist politics. It was a politics that would, as Plum says, carry straight through to the 1998 Belfast Agreement:

> That's where the PUP actually was incarnated. In Long Kesh. And we drew up a paper at that time which was called "sharing responsibility." We didn't like

---

[7] Martin's fellow bomber, Eddie Kinner, was asked by Peter Taylor if he thought the Conway attack was sectarian. Kinner replied that at the time he did not care whether the location was an IRA meeting place or just a Catholic bar: "My attitude was that they are inflicting that on my community. They [Catholics] harbour IRA men that were carrying that out in my community. They didn't expel IRA men from their community that attacked my community" (as quoted in Taylor 1999b, 144).

to use the words "sharing power." We used the words "sharing responsibility." So, by about 1974, the government at that time, they said it was OK to send it to our community. . . . And "Sharing Responsibility," that one was basically the Good Friday Agreement. You know. Most of what we said at that time got into the agreement. So, that's where the seeds of the PUP and politics grew.

The budding politicization of Loyalism was cut short, however, with the government's decision in 1976 to end special category status for political prisoners. As Plum remarked in a different part of our interview:

> That criminalization policy made it worse, right. And, that's where you lost the good steps that we had created within Long Kesh. They were all ruined within five years.

It was also, as Plum stated, the reason most political Loyalism today comes from Long Kesh. "That's why you have that gap" among Loyalist prisoners:

> Most prisoners that come out of Long Kesh came out *without* a chip on their shoulder. But most of prisoners coming out of H Blocks . . . came out hating the system, chip on their shoulder, and a totally different attitude.

Tom Roberts, who was imprisoned in the H Blocks, presented a similar picture of the differing systems. As he described it:

> Well, the compounds were a much healthier system of imprisonment, because there was really only perimeter security if you like. And the prisoners were very much in control of their day-to-day lives. And it was more conducive to a learning environment. I think that was probably due to the influence of Gusty Spence in the compound system. He ran a pretty disciplined organization in there. Because people aren't just sitting in prison degenerating into anarchy, if you like. Whereas some people may have resented a lot of the regime that was exacted in the compound, I think it was a better system.

Although Long Kesh clearly played a formative role in the development of a political Loyalism, its prisoners in the H Blocks were not entirely apolitical. Indeed, many Loyalists in the H Blocks developed a political ethos as a result of their battles to be segregated from Republicans. Tom Roberts recalls protesting in this way:

> When the Republicans were beginning to make our lives intolerable, then what happened is we wrecked the cells and everything that we could. And the tables were turned then. So we were moved into separate accommodation. And we were regarded as protesting prisoners, and we lost all of our privileges as well. But the balance of that was that it brought us all together in the same accommodation. So we could organize ourselves better. And that went on, that protest situation went on for about two years almost until finally it culminated

and we were granted de facto segregation. And they stopped treating us as protesting prisoners. It was all very low key, because I don't think the government wanted to acknowledge the fact that they had conceded to segregation.

As Tom notes, however (in a quote excerpted at the start of this chapter), this story is not one that has been told. While the factors discussed above explain why the loyalist prison experience has been little commemorated, it is important to note that prisoners themselves often held a contradictory view toward their crimes. Indeed, while most were adamant that their offenses were political, many were unable to completely disassociate themselves from the prevalent view within Unionism that legal channels are the (only) way to resolve problems. Many of the ex-prisoners I interviewed, for example, saw prison, and the problems they encountered there, as their cross to bear for breaking the law. Billy Mitchell defined his crimes as political, but when we discussed the issue of protest within the prison system, he expressed reservations about the practice. As an example, he brought up the issue of human rights abuses within the prison system and how Loyalists dealt with them.

> There's a lot of human rights abuses in prison. And an awful lot of human rights abuses in the barracks. The difference between Loyalists and Republicans—we don't go on about it. I think it's a bit rich for anyone who's taken in [to prison] for having shot someone to complain about a policeman beating them. To me, that's a wee bit hypocritical. And that was one thing that Gusty tried to encourage—youse were prepared to kill. You can't go blaming someone else. And you might not like it, but you can fight back. But you go through the prison system, and the legal complaint system.

Given that Loyalist ex-prisoners had such feelings of ambivalence about their crimes as well as a continued attachment to the discourse of law and order, it is not surprising that although Loyalist protest occurred, it was more muted than that on the Republican side of the conflict.

EDUCATION

One of the prevailing stereotypes of the Troubles was that Loyalists left prison as ignorant as the day they arrived, whereas Republicans came out quoting Marx, Tolstoy, and the other greats they read behind the bars. The stereotype is alive and well today. When Andrew Anthony wrote a piece on the Northern Bank robbery in the *Sunday Observer* (2005),[8] he used it as a

---

[8] In December 2004 the Belfast headquarters of the Northern Bank were robbed. Over 26 million pounds were stolen during the heist. Although no one had been arrested for the crime at the time of writing, the IRA or some faction of it is widely believed to be behind the heist, given the precision and organization necessary to carry it off. To date, it is the largest sum of cash ever stolen from a bank in the United Kingdom.

point of contrast to paint a picture of one of his sources, a Republican ex-prisoner named Andy McIntyre: "A large mound of a man with a goatee beard and glasses, McIntyre seemed to confirm the old saw that loyalists leave prison with a tattoo, while Republicans walk out with a degree. He has not only a degree in politics but also a PhD—he wrote his doctorate on the Provisional IRA" (2005, 29). Although it is true that many Republicans came out of prison with an education, it is equally true that many Loyalists did as well. The UVF estimates that 60–70 percent of its volunteers received a degree or other "educational qualification." The UDA estimates that 20 percent of its volunteers participated in prison education schemes (Irwin 2003; Stevenson 1996).

Some Loyalist education was informal, as the previous quotations indicate, but some Loyalists participated in formal programs as well. Several ex-prisoners in this sample, for example, received bachelor's degrees while in prison. Martin Snodden was proud of his university degree, although he viewed it as part of a wider education system:

> You know, I participated in both formal and informal education. My formal education—I did a university degree while I was in prison through the Open University. Curiously enough, I actually studied mathematics and computers. Systems—hard systems, soft systems. That was the formal side of the education. [But] the informal side of the education was much more reading about Irish history, reading about different conflicts, and having dialogue about the conflict.

Tom Roberts also received a bachelor's degree while in prison: "I did a degree, did a first class honors degree in mathematics and computer science." Plum Smith took university courses while in prison as well. He first brought up his degree when I asked him if he thought Peter Taylor's book *Loyalists* (1999b) was a fair take on Loyalism:

> When I was in prison I did university. And one of the things was humanities, the study of humanities. And you have to look at each author to see what their politics are and what they're like. You can't take one thing they say as gospel. [So] there's parts of his book that are good . . . but he could've added to the flavor of it.

Kenny McClinton, an ex-prisoner with the Ulster Freedom Fighters (UFF),[9] also used his time in prison to become educated. When I interviewed him in the summer of 2003, he told me he had just completed his doctorate in theology. McClinton was, like many of his Loyalist peers, proud of the strides he had made:

---

[9] The UFF is a nom de guerre frequently employed by the UDA.

I have been a full-time terrorist, up to my neck in terrorism, UFF terrorism. I have been a full-time life sentence prisoner. Sixteen years maximum security prison. And now I am by the grace of God a full-time pastor. I am now, in fact, Doctor McClinton, Master of Theology. I studied, from being semi-literate going into prison, and came out with an honors degree, Bachelor of Arts Honors degree in criminology in the social sciences. I write my own poetry. I write my own articles. I write my own Bible expositions and send out Bible expositions to 150 recipients every week.

Several prisoners in Long Kesh even took classes on the Irish language while in prison. Their decision to do so was often a way to formally acknowledge the links that Ulster Protestants have with Irish language and culture. As I describe in greater detail in chapter 4, this notion is a controversial admission in the current "cultural" climate of Loyalism.

As Kenny's comments demonstrate, participating in the formal education system gave prisoners a newfound sense of confidence and accomplishment. It also opened prisoners' eyes to the possibility of acquiring professional jobs, which most, as the sons of working-class Protestants from the province's linen mills and shipyards, would not typically have considered. As I demonstrate in the next section, however, ex-prisoners often had difficulty obtaining such employment after their release, and those difficulties explain a lot about the role and place of ex-prisoners in Belfast's staunchly Loyalist estates.

Dialogue with Republicans

Another formative moment in the Loyalist prison experience was the dialogue that some Loyalists established with Republicans. These dialogues included a few formally organized discussions, but most were informal, held between individuals.

While he was in Long Kesh, Martin Snodden struck up a friendship with a Republican prisoner who was a member of the Official IRA.[10] Martin met the prisoner by happenstance one morning when both were using the prison library. He recounted the meeting in an interview he gave the BBC program *Home Truths*.

There was a communal study area. During my period, whenever I was studying for the Open University degree, there was Nationalists that came across and studied there as well. Whenever they first opened I was sitting in a room and this Republican prisoner came into the same room. He was an Official IRA man. He sat down and we both carried on studying. In mid-morning we were, you know,

---

[10] In 1970 the Irish Republican Army splintered over disagreements about policy. The splinter group called itself the Provisional Irish Republican Army. Those left behind were dubbed the Official IRA. The OIRA was led by men with Marxist leanings. It declared a cease-fire in 1972 (CAIN 2006h).

both of us were looking for a cup of tea, but neither of you wanted to offer the other a cup of tea. Neither did we know whether to take a cup of tea if we were offered. So, it was quite an amusing experience. We ended up, we did take tea. And, we talked for many, many hours afterwards about our upbringing, about our experiences, and we realized that we had an awful lot in common. In fact, much more in common than what we had differences. (*Home Truths* 2004)

In our interview, Martin described entering into a dialogue with the OIRA prisoner. They carried on largely an informal set of conversations, although politics came up on occasion. The two eventually became friends. As Martin explained in our interview:

The informal side of our education [involved] reading about Irish history, reading about different conflicts, and having lots of dialogue about the conflict. And, I actually participated in one [a dialogue] with an Official IRA man. And we became great friends. We did a bit of storytelling with regard to our upbringing and our experiences. Within them [Republican prisoners] there wasn't much difference. We had developed a very, very strong friendship. He was in for a life sentence as well, but he was released before I was released.

When I asked Martin if he had kept in touch with the OIRA man, Martin laughed, telling me:

Not only did he keep in touch with me, he actually came to visit me in prison, which was all paired up [segregated by paramilitary affiliation] at Long Kesh, and many of the screws [the police] were scratchin' their heads and saying "What the hell's going on here?" you know. Shortly after he was released he went off to live in Australia, and I've lost contact with him.

Such contacts would prove beneficial for Martin's work at MARC years later. As he put together the board for the group, he was able to use his contacts with Republican ex-prisoners to involve them in MARC's work. Indeed, Martin explained to me that he wanted MARC to be viewed as available to both communities, and one way to do that was to have Republicans on the board. Although his friend had moved to Australia, Martin was able to draw on other OIRA ex-prisoners: "There's other Official IRA men on the street who I still have contact with, that's Republican prisoners. [And] two members sit as members of the board here. So there is this relationship [to the Republicans]."

Billy Mitchell also described talking with Republican prisoners while in Long Kesh. In her biographical sketch of Mitchell, posted on the LINC Web site, Kate Fearon (2002) describes how Republicans and Loyalists used the prison pitch (playing field) to communicate with one another. The pitch divided the Republican and Loyalist compounds, but it was only separated from the compounds by a wire mesh fence, so it was possible to have conversations with the "other side" while on the field. It was also one of the few places where members of the two groups actually came into contact with one another. Usually communications were reserved for strategizing about bettering conditions inside the compounds: success often depended on the two sets of prisoners presenting a united front on an issue. As Fearon explains:

> The football field ran between the two fences that separated the Loyalist and the Republican sectors of the prison so a system had to be worked out [for communication]. Republicans played Gaelic on the pitch, a 15 a side game. Loyalists, who played soccer, an 11 a side game, wanted parity of player numbers. They negotiated with the prison authorities to have the same number of players out on the pitch as the Republicans had. "We even threatened to play Gaelic ourselves if that was the only way to get the extra men out on the pitch," says [Billy] Mitchell. "Eventually we were allowed the extra 'players' as reserves. I was one of the extra 'players' and it was my job to have dialogue through the compound wire with Republicans. It was usually Gerry Kelly (now an Assembly Member for North Belfast) and Hugh Feeny that I talked to. The football pitch ran up to the wire of their compound. I would just have shouted over, or to any of them walking round their compound 'would you send Feeny out?' " So Feeny and Mitchell would discuss prison issues and exchange information about how best the different organisations could achieve better conditions. (2002)

Although most conversations between Republicans and Loyalists were informal, there were some formal conversations organized. These largely took place with the Marxist-inspired Official IRA and centered on class-based issues or the more standard fare of prison concerns. Indeed, the larger constitutional issue was avoided altogether in these talks. The formal nature of the talks was productive for both sides, however. Fearon (2002), for example, describes a joint presentation that members of the UVF and the Official IRA gave to the probation board's welfare office. That meeting eventually led to the creation (and publication) of a Charter of Rights for the prisoners in the compounds.

It is logical to assume that the engagement between Loyalists and Republicans in prison planted the early seeds of peace by allowing enemies to meet one another on neutral terrain and to see their commonalities. The reality, however, is that for most Loyalist ex-prisoners from Long Kesh, their internal conversations with each other were much more formative of their eventual move toward peace than were any conversations they had with the enemy (Fearon 2002). Indeed, Loyalists from Long Kesh will tell you that their baggage—sectarianism, violence, and the like—was as much a product of Unionism as it was ignorance of Republicans.

Despite the limited nature of the links between the Official IRA and the UVF in Long Kesh, connections between the two groups have been reproduced by their ex-prisoners on the outside. However, these links are as much the result of similar economic views on issues, and internal Republican dynamics, as they are the result of abiding attachments built between Loyalists and Republicans during their prison terms. As Billy Mitchell explained in our interview, in reference to current cross-community work between Republicans and Loyalists, the dominance of Sinn Fein makes it difficult to talk to Republican ex-prisoners in its ranks:

> The Republicans who would listen to us would be the Official Republican Movement. And others, like Andy McIntyre [a former Republican prisoner and a vocal critic of Sinn Fein] . . . Mackers [nickname for McIntyre] would be a Marxist, and the Official Republican Movement would be Marxist. They would at least listen to our arguments. Where the Shinners, Sinn Fein, I don't believe Sinn Fein have an ideology, a socialist philosophy. To me they're Catholic Nationalists. And Sinn Fein don't listen. They have what we call the thought police. You know, they have discussions, but the discussion is controlled. Whereas our interaction with McKearney, and McIntyre, and the Official Republican Movement, on issues of human rights and liberty, at least they'll listen to your argument and try and understand where you're coming from. And engage with you. And that's what its about.

As Billy's comments indicate, ex-prisoners are often at the forefront of cross-community work. Much of their involvement can be traced to the politicization I have already detailed. However, the barriers to professional employment that ex-prisoners face upon their release also played a formative role. It is to the subjects of release and reintegration that I now turn.

Release from Prison, Reintegration into the Community

Before the 1994 joint cease-fires and the 1998 Good Friday Agreement, most politically motivated prisoners were released under conditions that were established in 1976 to regularize the release of political prisoners and bring them in line with ordinary decent criminals (McEvoy 2001). Those rules allowed all prisoners with fixed-length sentences to be considered for release midway through their term. In 1989 the government reduced the remission rate by 17 percent for paramilitary prisoners (McEvoy 2001). The result of the government's release policy was that paramilitary prisoners, whose sentences were usually long, trickled out of prison at a slow rate.

Not surprisingly, given the low rate of release, the issue of prisoners figured heavily in the negotiations leading up to the 1994 cease-fires. As McEvoy (2001) argues, the issue was of concern to both sides, but it was of larger concern to Loyalists. Republicans saw the cease-fire as an avenue to redress long-standing political issues such as structural inequality, whereas Loyalists saw the potential cease-fire in more functional terms. It was an opportunity to bring its combatants home now that the union was "safe" for the moment from the IRA's bombs. Indeed, because Loyalists had always viewed their violence as a response to Republican aggression (rather than at the behest of a specific ideology), a wider political agenda did not figure as prominently among their concerns. Political issues would come later.

Kieron McEvoy (2001) has described the British government's response to the cease-fires as "minimalist and begrudging." Indeed, for the first year after the cease-fires, the government had no official response. When it finally acted, its response was regarded as negligible by many. The government reinstated the remission rate for paramilitary prisoners to its pre-1989 level. The government was even unsure how to present its move. As McEvoy notes, the government vacillated between presenting the change as "a simple housekeeping measure," on the one hand, and "a very cautious response to the ceasefires" on the other (2001, 327). Although the IRA did not end its cease-fire because of the government's failure to act on the issue of prison releases, Republican ex-prisoners told McEvoy (2001) that its failure to do so was "symptomatic" of its begrudging attitude to negotiation with the group.

McEvoy (2001) argues that the Labour government of Tony Blair took a more practical approach to the issue of prisoner releases. Early release was not only specifically mentioned in the agreement, but general conditions were outlined for its progress. At a general level, the agreement promised to "put in place mechanisms to provide for an accelerated programme for the release of prisoners, including transferred prisoners, convicted of scheduled offences in Northern Ireland or, in the case of those sentenced outside Northern Ireland, similar offences." The agreement also stipulated that "both Governments will complete a review process within a fixed time frame and set prospective release dates for all qualifying prisoners." And to make sure releases were considered in a timely manner, the agreement required both governments to "seek to enact the appropriate legislation to give effect to these arrangements by the end of June 1998" (Multi-party Negotiations 1998, section 10, "Prisoners").

In Northern Ireland the new Assembly passed the Northern Ireland Sentences Act of 1998 to govern the release of politically motivated prisoners. The legislation created an independent commission to regulate the release of prisoners, and prisoners had to apply for release. There would be no automatic release of any prisoners. Prisoners convicted of terrorist offenses after the agreement date were ineligible for release, as were prisoners associated with groups not party to the cease-fire. Prisoners also had to satisfy the commission that they were neither a danger to society nor likely to return to paramilitarism. The commission organized a schematic for dealing with differential sentencing lengths, cutting life sentences by one-third and fixed terms by two-thirds. Between June 1998 and October 2000, when the early releases were to be completed, 433 prisoners were freed from the prison systems. Although technically free, most prisoners were released on special "light licenses," which allowed the prison system to revoke release (up to the duration of the initial sentence) for those involved in paramilitary or criminal activity. A total of 193 Loyalists were released from prison between 1998 and October 2000 (McEvoy 2001).

A considerable amount of attention has been paid to ex-prisoners in Northern Ireland since the 1998 peace accords. In many ways, this is not surprising. Although the raw numbers—433 freed—are not huge, even per capita, the releases associated with the Belfast Agreement were temporally and spatially concentrated. All requests for release governed under the Belfast Agreement were processed within two years of the agreement, and most prisoners were released in bunches. Ex-prisoners also tended to resettle in the same neighborhoods, normally recognizable areas like Whiterock on the Republican side or the Shankill on the Loyalist side. In Belfast, most prisoners had come from these neighborhoods, so moving back was a logical step. On the Loyalist side, neighborhoods like the Shankill were also popular because Unionist ambivalence (even hostility) made living in other areas difficult, if not intolerable. Tom Roberts, who was from Portadown, explained: "When I first came out of prison I used to come down to the Shankill Road there because I felt more at home. Because there's a high concentration of prisoners here so they're not as easily discriminated against in their own community. . . . In Portadown, for all its image of extreme Unionism, there's no one too keen about former prisoners."

The problems that these ex-prisoners faced upon release have been well documented. Indeed, ex-prisoner groups representing all of the province's major paramilitaries have commissioned research to highlight the problems (Crothers 1998; Ó hAdhmaill 2005). The findings in this literature are well known, and it is not my intention to rehash them here. Suffice it to say that the problems these ex-prisoners face are wide-ranging, running the gamut from personal issues, such as how to relate to a spouse or child who seems like a stranger, to practical matters such as how to apply for a council flat or find a job.

Less remarked on in the literature is how these difficulties have contributed to the prevalence of ex-paramilitaries in the voluntary sector. Indeed, although it is logical that prisoners and ex-prisoners might be involved in peace negotiations, it was not a foregone conclusion that so many ex-prisoners would become community workers in the voluntary sector. The education that many prisoners obtained in prison made professional employment, with its good salaries and job security, a desirable goal.

Many of the ex-prisoners I interviewed, however, found it difficult to find professional jobs after prison. As Tom Roberts explained:

I did an honors degree in mathematics and computer science. I was sort of naïvely thinking that that would help my prospects in employment. But when I came out for a few years I was, due to the discrimination that exists against former prisoners, I was condemned to doing menial laboring-type jobs, which I found very demoralizing. I also had a tremendous feeling of guilt for me own family. I went to prison when my two kids were under two years old. And when I got out they were teenagers. So I would have liked to have had the resources to give them something better because of the sacrifice they had to make.

Michael Atcheson had a similar experience: "I mean, I was away. I served eleven years. I got twenty-two years, I served eleven years. I'm out of jail now, six years, but I'm always going to be a prisoner. And, what am I going to do?" Michael even encountered a glass ceiling effect in the Loyalist neighborhood he lives in. When he considered running for a local political office, for example, after a number of years of community work under his belt, he described encountering resistance from his neighbors: "A woman in the area I was from said, 'you're a great wee boy, and you do those floors and all that there, but I'll never vote for you.' . . . They'll come to you with their housing problems, advice, and stuff like that, but they didn't vote for you."

Plum Smith also suffered discrimination, although he emphasized the structural nature of the discrimination: "Me, as an ex-prisoner coming out of prison, there are restrictions placed on me. Ex-combatants have restrictions placed on them. . . . At the end of the day, it says at the bottom of the [application] sheet, 'have you ever been in prison?' Well, what do you do? You have to say it." Plum also noted that barriers to good employment pushed a lot of ex-prisoners, especially those who had become educated and politicized while in prison, into the voluntary sector. It was one of the few meaningful jobs ex-prisoners could find.

> Once you go out into jobs with the civil service, middle class Unionism, which is bigger than the community work, that's where all the openings are, the jobs are. You know, that's where you hit the wall . . . so, basically a lot of us come out and worked voluntary, in the voluntary sector, sometimes without wages. Some of us found jobs, and a lot of people just went back into anonymity. But the main core of us are involved in this [voluntary sector] to basically help our communities.

As Plum's comments indicate, work in the voluntary sector can be rewarding. His comments, however, belie the difficulty attached to work in the voluntary sector. It is often unpaid and/or dependent on grant funding, so there is little security for either the ex-prisoners or the organizations for which they work. In chapter 5 I cover these issues and analyze the growth and sustainability of the voluntary sector in greater detail.

Should We Care about Ex-prisoners?

For the families of the victims of crimes committed by paramilitaries, the mere hint that anyone worries about the difficulties ex-prisoners face can be infuriating. Indeed, many reject outright the idea that paramilitaries are victims of the conflict. When the Healing through Remembering Project issued a call for submissions from conflict victims, it cast its definition of victim broadly to include not only traditional constituencies, such as those who lost a family member to a paramilitary bombing, but groups not normally considered victims as well, such as ex-prisoners and paramilitary members. One submission, published in the project proceedings, was blunt in its response to the call: "We want no part in any service which places our family in the same vein as the perpetrators of murder. They are not victims but criminals and murderers" (Healing through Remembering Project 2002, 29).

The debate about who should and should not be categorized as a victim is far from settled. Indeed, the project manager admitted as much in the proceedings, noting that the "term [victim] has been a source of conflict, [and the] debate continued to play itself out in the background throughout our work" (Healing through Remembering Project 2002, 15). While I support a broad definition of victimhood, I recognize that there are real dangers in focusing on the perpetrators of violence in a post-conflict society, not the least of which is the potential to venerate perpetrators of violence for their presumed redemption. Approbation, even of an unintended sort, can make the families of paramilitary victims feel as if their loved ones, and the crimes against them, no longer matter. It can be salt on an already very raw wound.

There are, however, important reasons for studying ex-paramilitaries. Although it would be a mistake to depict all, or even most, ex-prisoners as radically transformed by their prison experience, it is clear that Long Kesh graduated a special class of Loyalist prisoners who became politically motivated to work for peace upon their release.

While Martin, Plum, Tom, Billy, and Michael are prisoners of the same era, it would be unfair to suggest that they are a monolithic group working together seamlessly to transform Loyalism. Indeed, real differences of opinion and approach exist. Billy Mitchell told me, for example, that he found the "psychological" approach troublesome:

> There's a whole industry being created here on trauma counseling. There's problems with a lot of this trauma stuff—this so-called post-traumatic stress disorder. There are these people who seem to believe that everyone who's been through the Troubles here, who's been to prison, have hidden problems they refuse to deal with. And that all of us need help, that we need people to come and help us to bring it out in the open. We just see it as an industry for *them*, not for *us*. I personally don't believe it.

Billy also told me that one of his close friends, a fellow ex-prisoner named Billy Giles,[11] had committed suicide after participating in a trauma workshop held in South Africa for ex-combatants.

---

[11] The first chapter in Peter Taylor's *Loyalists* (1999b) highlights Billy Giles. Taylor explains Giles's suicide as the result of persistent guilt he could never overcome and to which he eventually succumbed. When I asked Mitchell about Taylor's interpretation, he responded that Taylor was unaware of Giles's trip to South Africa.

They [the psychologists] took him back [to the past]. Well, what I believe, and what Billy had said to us [my wife and me] was, it took him into a dark hole and he had no way to get out.

Some ex-prisoners were also suspicious of the Loyalist-cum-preacher transition of McClinton. One ex-prisoner, who did not want to be quoted, stated: "You know, particularly in Northern Ireland, the title pastor is rather loosely thrown about. You know, there seems to be pastors on every street corner." When I asked him later what he though of Loyalist efforts to establish connections to extremist groups in the United States,[12] he implicated paramilitary cum preachers: "You can find these links. Some of these dubious [ex-paramilitary] pastors would be involved in that type of thing."

Differences aside, political Loyalists share several things: they support peace, and they hope to push Loyalism in another direction.[13] And increasingly they serve as a bulwark against revanchist efforts to hijack Loyalism for purely criminal purposes. In the next two chapters I explore political Loyalists' efforts (and those of their adversaries) in relation to class-based themes (chapter 3) as well as cultural ones (chapter 4).

---

[12] Loyalists and other Protestants have periodically tried to develop a support base in the United States to blunt U.S. supporters of the IRA. Most of these attempts, however, have focused on fundamentalist or extremist groups in the United States. Ian Paisley, for example, has connections to Bob Jones University in South Carolina. In 2000 the Bob Jones University Web site described Catholicism as a cult and prohibited interracial dating (Broder 2000). Paisley received an honorary doctorate from the university in 1996. Supporters of Ulster independence have also tried to establish connections to separatist groups in the United States. David Kerr, editor of the Loyalist magazine *Ulster Nation* and a former member of the National Front, has likened the Ulster Protestant cause to neo-Confederate groups in the United States. As he explained in an essay on the *Ulster Nation* Web site, "Ulster-nationalists and Southern-nationalists have much in common. We share similar cultural and ethnic roots. We think in much the same way and we both stick in the throats of the liberal-leftist powers-that-be. We look forward to the day when a reborn Confederacy enjoys full diplomatic relations with an independent Ulster" (Kerr 1997). In my interview with Kerr, he told me that his group supported neo-Confederate groups in the United States but that there were no formal links between them.

[13] Kenny McClinton told me he does not support the Belfast Agreement but does support an end to the hostilities. Several ex-prisoners I spoke to were skeptical of McClinton's commitment to peace, pointing to his connections to Billy Wright and the LVF. Journalist Martin Dillon, in his book *God and the Gun*, also adopts a skeptical pose: "The 'born-again' Kenny McClinton is preferable to the murderer but he has not rid himself of the sectarian values that have caused so much death and destruction on both sides" (1990, 54). In this book I categorize McClinton as a revanchist, although I believe he is opposed to continued paramilitarism. In our interview McClinton presented his faith as instrumental in helping him turn his life around. However, his opposition to paramilitarism is probably influenced by personal considerations as well. McClinton continues to receive death threats from Loyalist paramilitary men. When I visited his home in 2003, he recounted an assassination attempt on his life in 1997 and told me he had had bulletproof windows installed in his home.

3 *Class Matters*

One of the most striking aspects of walking across Belfast's sectarian divides is how structurally similar Protestant and Catholic working-class estates actually are. Both sides are dominated by terraced council houses operated by the Northern Ireland Housing Executive. Homes are usually two stories with small rear gardens that back up to those on parallel streets. Front gardens tend to be even smaller and concrete, with iron gates or box hedges marking the boundary between home and pavement (see fig. 4). Like any poor area, some houses look shabby while others gleam with care, with flower boxes decorating ledges and lace curtains covering front windows. Retail areas are similar. Most have seen better days, with pubs, chippies, and butcher shops interspersed between empty storefronts (see fig. 5). Even on more bustling blocks, where empty frontage is less common, retail space is often occupied by voluntary-sector organizations that contribute little to the streetscape by virtue of their limited hours. Both areas are served by black taxis, which originated during the Troubles, when it was difficult to reliably run public transportation into the city's conflict zones.

At a structural level, working-class Nationalist and Loyalist neighborhoods have more in common with one another than they do with middle- and upper-class areas of the city. A walk through the Malone Road area, one of Belfast's most tony neighborhoods, finds curving lanes and elegant housing with expansive front and back gardens. The retail strips are usually thriving, with well-stocked groceries, ethnic restaurants, and the occasional designer boutique.

Despite the similarities among working-class neighborhoods, as well as their common differences with upper-class Belfast, it is difficult to confuse a working-class Catholic neighborhood for a Protestant one, or vice versa. They are usually spatially proximate to one another, so differentiation tends to manifest itself territorially. Both sides use the same territorial

Fig. 4. Council housing, Donegal Pass, South Belfast.

Fig. 5. Empty storefronts, Sandy Row, Belfast.

markers, but the markers' content varies across the divide. Flags are the most commonly used marker, with the Irish tricolor flying in Nationalist estates and the Union Jack flying in Loyalist ones. Flag colors also appear in neat, even squares along the pavement lip on busy streets as well. Along retail areas, triangular banners festoon the street from above, in the color scheme appropriate to the estate's political affiliation. In residential areas, families fly paramilitary flags from their homes (see fig. 6).

Murals are another way working-class communities on both sides of the divide mark their space. In a seminal article "Territoriality on the Shankill–Falls Divide, Belfast" Fred Boal (1969) argues that murals are like community message boards. Those in the center of an estate usually depict "soft" images of intragroup unity, such as commemorating martyrs, celebrating shared history, or protesting shared grievances. By contrast, murals on the edge of an estate, especially those that interface with a rival neighborhood, tend to be aggressive or triumphalist, portraying menacing figures wearing balaclavas or key historic victories over the other side. Boal wrote his essay at the start of the Troubles, but the correlation between mural location and content remains true today.

The demarcation between Catholic and Protestant neighborhoods provides stark evidence that despite the obvious potential for solidarity on class grounds, religious background firmly trumps class background as a source of personal and political identification. This is not to imply that class has

Fig. 6. UVF flag hanging from a Loyalist house.

not been a vibrant source of protest in Northern Ireland. Indeed it has. However, like much else in Northern Ireland politics, class has historically been operationalized along sectarian lines. One need only review the Marxist scholarship on the conflict to see evidence of this trend. Despite using the same analytic categories, Marxists in Northern Ireland usually arrive at distinctly "green" or "red" conclusions.[1]

I begin this chapter by outlining why class remains an important variable for interpreting the conflict. I do so because some have recently suggested that it is a meaningless category of analysis (McGarry and O'Leary 1995). I then give an overview of the industrial development of Belfast and its postindustrial turn in the 1980s. The city's new development model not only contributes to the further marginalization of areas already hard hit by the Troubles, it also frames the ambivalence of many people in them to the peace process. In the third section I explain why class politics has failed to bridge the province's sectarian divide. In the fourth section I review revanchist and progressive class politics. I conclude by highlighting barriers to class solidarity across the ethnoreligious divide, focusing on the problems political Loyalists themselves have identified.

The Continued Salience of Class

Although class politics have failed to stimulate cross-community alliances and to bridge the gap between the two warring communities in Northern Ireland, class analysis continues to have relevance to the conflict. Indeed, even if class does not operate to unite the conflict's warring factions, it continues to shape the contours of the conflict, often in surprising ways.

Class is a salient variable first and foremost because the paramilitaries themselves say it is. Loyalists define themselves in opposition to Unionists by virtue of their class differences. Indeed, many are suspicious of what they see as Unionist elitism. As such, while class positioning may do little to explain relations between the two communities, it explains a lot about the fractious state of the Unionist "family."

Another reason for the salience of class is the demographic composition of the paramilitaries. The overwhelming majority of combatants on both sides of the conflict are working class. And evidence suggests that in the case of Loyalism, the average paramilitary member has become more lumpen over time (Langhammer 2003, 9). This demographic is mirrored in patterns of conflict-related deaths. In 1972, the bloodiest year of the conflict, over half of all the bombs, shootings, and arrests in the province occurred in the working-class heartland of West Belfast (Cebulla and Smyth 1996). When

---

[1] For green accounts, see Bambery (1987), Bell (1984), and Foot (1989). For red accounts, see Bew, Gibbon, and Patterson (1979), Boserup (1972), and Nairn (1981).

one looks at the death rates in Belfast specifically, a similar pattern emerges. Of the 1,541 Troubles-related deaths in the city, for example, 78 percent occurred in North and West Belfast—the two quadrants of the city with the largest concentrations of working-class and poor people (CAIN 2006l). Moreover, although many paramilitary members lost their lives during the course of the conflict, an inordinate share of civilians did as well. According to the Sutton Index of deaths, over half of those killed during the conflict were civilians: 1,857 out of a total of 3,524 deaths (CAIN 2006m).[2] And given the concentration of violence in working-class areas, it is likely that most civilian casualties were working-class or poor persons as well.[3]

Class is also an important variable because it plays a greater role in determining one's life chances—whether in educational attainment, earnings potential, life expectancy, or likelihood of becoming the victim of a terrorist attack—than does one's religious background (Coulter 1999). This is not to dismiss the systematic discrimination of Catholics by successive Unionist regimes for most of the twentieth century. However, the data suggest that working-class people in both communities have similar life chances, and their chances are considerably worse than those of the middle and upper classes of either religious affiliation (Coulter 1999). The gap in life chances between members of the working class and their middle/upper-class counterparts has only widened in the post-industrial environment. Decline in the manufacturing sector and the state's attempt to replace it with a service-based economy have resulted in marginalized, largely unemployable populations on both sides of the divide.

A fourth reason why class remains an important variable concerns the sociospatial changes associated with the growth of the service sector. Unlike their experience in the manufacturing sector, Catholic workers' experience in the service sector has been positive in that they have been able to acquire a fair share of the province's service-sector jobs. Their participation in the sector has contributed to the growth of a substantial Catholic middle class, whose members have used their newfound economic power to move out of working-class estates in the west of the city for larger houses in the city's southern quadrant—historically the home of the Protestant elite (McGovern and Shirlow 1997). Indeed, Cebulla and Smyth observe that "high-income Catholic households now proportionately outnumber well-off Protestant households" in the area (1996, 40). Revanchist activists within Loyalism increasingly use these trends as evidence that the peace process is a zero-sum

---

[2] The Sutton Index categorizes "civilian" and "civilian political activist" deaths separately. The 1,857 figure combines the two categories: civilians account for 1,799 deaths, while civilian political activists account for 58 deaths.

[3] Neither of the two major indexes of Troubles-related deaths classifies victims by socioeconomic background. The geographic area in which the killings occurred, however, can be used to make inferences about the class status of victims since most neighborhoods are segregated along class lines.

game—that Catholic gains are at Protestant expense. Although Catholic migration to South Belfast is due in large part to Protestant migration to outer-ring suburbs, zero-sum discourses hold powerful sway in Loyalist areas that have experienced relative and real decline since the mid-1980s.

The post-industrial landscape of Belfast and paramilitary manipulation of the disorder it creates also have implications for recent theoretical work on class in post-industrial economies (Kumar 2000; Gibson-Graham 1996; Gibson-Graham, Resnick, and Wolff 2000). Recent scholarship suggests that class deserves the same sort of postmodern unpacking that other categories, such as race and gender, have received. Such an unpacking is necessary because traditional Marxism is categorically limiting in its depiction of both the economy (capitalist or noncapitalist) and an individual's place within it (bourgeoisie or proletariat). Such dichotomies no longer match the reality of the multiple ways that capital is created, earned, and distributed within society (some would say they never did). Nor do rigid class categories capture the disunity of employment experiences in a post-industrial society, in which an individual may go from one category to another in a short period of time or occupy multiple categories at the same time. This is especially relevant in traditionally working-class areas of Belfast. Fewer and fewer working-class people are employed in manufacturing; most cobble together an income from a variety of sources, including government assistance, marginal employment, and illicit activity. The implication of such change is the need "to conceptualize identity more fluidly and fragmentarily in relation to class" (Gibson-Graham, Resnick, and Wolff 2000, 9).

While Marxists will undoubtedly cringe at the suggestion that class is hybrid or fluid, there is a political rationale behind such an approach. Indeed, although the postmodern celebration of hybridity can be viewed as hostile to class politics (see Harvey 1998 for a good overview), scholars like Gibson-Graham, Resnick, and Wolff posit a political goal to their work. As they explain:

> We feel an affinity with other poststructuralist theorists who are concerned with destabilizing established and restrictive identities constructed along the axes of gender, sexuality, race, ethnicity, and other forms of categorization and distinction. Like them we are interested in opening up the field of class identity. But we are also (as they may or may not be) engaged in a positive process of potentiating identities where none has previously been perceived or enacted. . . . We are interested in generating a discourse of class that offers a range of subject positions that might prompt identification. (2000, 9)

Although Gibson-Graham, Resnick, and Wolff (2000) are to be applauded for considering how to create new class-based identities that match post-industrial reality, in Northern Ireland it is just as important to identify and counter regressive class-based discourses. Indeed, in Loyalist revanchist discourse, post-industrial disorder is depicted as a plot to rob Protestants of their jobs and to give them to Catholics. These discourses resonate in Loyalist enclaves whose residents have experienced downward mobility over the last ten years. Because revanchists are dominant within Loyalism, it is often assumed that class politics is dead. A more apt depiction is that a regressive class politic is on the ascendant within Loyalism. And it is this politic that facilitates the criminality, internecine strife, and violence associated with Loyalist paramilitarism since 1998.

Class Structure in Belfast: From Industrial Giant to Service King

THE INDUSTRIAL PERIOD, 1880–1968

In the late 1800s Northern Ireland became a site of intensive industrial development. Most investment was centered in Belfast along the port area and in neighborhoods east of the Lagan River. Although it was one of the most industrial cities in the world, industrial development was narrow even by the standards of the day. Industry was concentrated in three sectors—shipbuilding, engineering, and textiles (Cebulla and Smyth 1996).

The labor markets that grew up around these industries were intensely sectarian. Protestants tended to get more and better jobs than their Catholic neighbors did (Whyte 1983). Sectarian labor markets were built, however, on earlier forms of segmentation that predated Irish independence. A full decade before partition, for example, only 5 percent of the skilled labor force in Belfast was Catholic, even though Catholics comprised 30 percent of the total population (Cebulla and Smyth 1996). Although industrialization did not create sectarian labor markets, it did rigidify and in time formalize them with the creation of the new province.

Labor segmentation during the industrial period occurred in a number of ways. In part it resulted from the natural demands of capital to hire the most skilled workers, who by virtue of earlier patterns of labor market segmentation tended to be Protestant rather than Catholic (Cebulla and Smyth 1996). Most ancillary industries were also owned by Protestant families, who unlike Catholics had enough capital to open business in the first place. The low-grade political unrest in the province after partition also kept business owners from reinvesting profits locally (Isles and Cuthbert 1957). This lack of reinvestment not only kept Catholics from accessing the dividends of the city's newfound wealth, but it helped establish strong ties between Protestant workers and Protestant owners. And because owners were represented by the Unionist Party, ties eventually developed between workers and the party of their employers.

The family structure of most businesses also allowed for the operation of "gatekeeper mechanisms," which kept Catholics out of some factories and relegated them to lower-rung jobs in others (Cebulla and Smyth 1996). The high degree of segregation in the province facilitated the use of such mechanisms. Because Catholics and Protestants tended to live in separate neighborhoods, employers could usually ascertain whether someone was Catholic by their address. Likewise, the low rate of interfaith marriage meant that it was often easy to determine someone's religious background by their last name.

Gatekeeper mechanisms were also in operation at the government level. When DuPont opened a factory in Derry in 1957, for example, it was required to guarantee that the plant manager would be in the Unionist Party and that he would hire "acceptable" numbers of Protestants (Mulholland 2002). Gateway mechanisms were equally common in the civil service. Moreover, because the province's electoral boundaries were drawn by committees derived from the civil service, Protestants were able to maintain their electoral dominance. When a committee was formed in 1966 to plan provincial development (a process with implications for electoral boundaries), for example, one observer caustically described the committee as unfit for anything except "running a Unionist garden fete" (as quoted in Mulholland 2002, 57).

By the mid-1950s the industrial core of Belfast was beginning to decline. The province's industrial base has always been heavily tied to Great Britain, and the post-war period saw Britain's share of world trade decline in real and relative terms (Cebulla and Smyth 1996). Between 1950 and 1970, the province lost 5,000 manufacturing jobs—a significant number given the size of the population.

The government's initial response to the threat of industrial decline was the 1963 Matthew Report, a government blueprint for reigniting the province's industrial base. The plan, which represented a suburbanized update to the Fordist development model, suggested creating growth poles on the periphery of Belfast and linking them to the city (and each other) with an elevated highway system. It also called for the destruction of working-class neighborhoods in the areas where the highway system was to be built (Cebulla and Smyth 1996). Although the plan was only partially enacted, it prompted the Northern Ireland Housing Trust to develop a housing scheme in line with suburban growth poles. Also, a number of working-class neighborhoods were defined as slums and subsequently destroyed, with replacement housing built in the suburbs. Both Catholic and Protestant neighborhoods were affected by the plan. Residential areas at the lower end of both the Shankill and Falls roads were, for example, bulldozed to make way for the westlink highway. The redevelopment along the Shankill was dubbed "the rape of the Shankill" by one observer as a result of the destruction of community it engendered (Wiener 1980).

Several features of Belfast's class structure on the eve of the Troubles are relevant to the topic at hand. First, although there were sizable working-class constituencies on both sides of the religious divide, on the whole the Protestant working classes tended to fare better than their Catholic counterparts. In a study of the 1970 census, for example, Aunger found that within each class rung, Protestants were clustered at the top and Catholics bunched at the bottom: "While a clerk may be a Catholic, it is more likely that the office manager will be a Protestant; while a skilled craftsman may be a Catholic, it is more likely that the supervisor will be a Protestant; and while a nurse may be a Catholic, it is more likely that the doctor will be a Protestant" (Aunger, as quoted in Whyte 1983, 15). This status did not, however, translate into substantially better living conditions for working-class Protestants. The housing stock was largely the same across the city's religious divides. Indeed, much of it would come to be regarded as substandard and torn down in rounds of redevelopment laid out by the Matthew Report. Many of the Loyalists I interviewed, for example, recall growing up in houses without indoor toilets.

Second, there was a distinct geography to the state's industrial policy. At the province level the state tended to invest a greater share of public funds in the east, in and around Belfast. When funds were invested in the west, they tended to go to Protestant strongholds like Coleraine, instead of Derry. In Belfast, capital investment was funneled to existing Protestant working-class strongholds, which meant that the eastern portion of the city fared much better than the western predominantly Catholic part of the city. Some scholars, like Osborne (1982), argue that the state's industrial policy was designed to thwart development in Nationalist areas. Others, like Hoare (1981), argue that evidence of intentional discrimination is inconclusive. Whyte (1983) states that "the government's efforts on behalf of the west improved as time went on" (23).

DURING THE TROUBLES

As the Troubles got under way during the seventies, the state changed its approach to development. Although it remained focused on manufacturing, it began to target industrial development for Nationalist areas. The change in focus was driven in large part by the belief, especially in London, that economic deprivation and lack of opportunity underpinned the conflict (McGarry and O'Leary 1995). Rowthorn and Wayne (1988) document a number of cases in which Catholic areas received a greater percentage of aid than their share of the population represented. Between 1967 and 1971, for example, 36 percent of new jobs created with the aide of the Northern Ireland government went to the western side of the Bann in Derry, an area that is predominantly Catholic and contains only 27 percent of the population. The opportunity created by most new jobs would be offset, however, by wider economic trends favoring deindustrialization.

Indeed, government attempts to redress decades of uneven development coincided with shifts in the global economy that heralded the move of production from industrial centers in the first world to boomtowns in the third. Perhaps the most infamous failed attempt to lure capital investment into West Belfast was the DeLorean plant. The company was given almost £70 million in grants to open a sports car factory in one of the city's poorest Catholic neighborhoods. The factory closed within a few years. As Cebulla and Smyth observe, the plant was designed to produce "a sports car for which there was no obvious market at a time of rising oil prices and general recession" (1996, 43).

While new efforts like the DeLorean plant failed, traditional industries slowly bled jobs throughout the seventies and eighties. Between 1971 and 1991 the percentage of people employed in the manufacturing sector declined from 45 to 27 percent of the working population (Coulter 1999). This decline represented a loss of approximately 40,000 industrial jobs in a twenty-year period.

Although Catholic and Protestant communities both suffered from the industrial pullout, Catholic unemployment figures tended to be highest (McGovern and Shirlow 1997). However, the decline had a unique impact on the Protestant working-class population. As Colin Coulter (1999) comments, working-class Protestant families prided themselves on their special place in the industrial engine of the province. They regarded their placement in the industrial pecking order as "natural"—a matter of skill and heritage. Although there was always evidence to suggest otherwise, when the job losses hit, Protestants experienced not only material loss but a sense of vertigo about their established role in Northern Ireland society—what many considered their birthright. It was and is a sentiment ripe for manipulation, by politicians and paramilitaries alike.

Post-Industrial Belfast: The 1980s and Beyond

During the mid-1980s, the government of Northern Ireland abandoned its strategy of attracting manufacturing to the province. Like other deindustrializing areas, it turned its attention to developing and attracting service-based industries and investors through a combination of tax breaks and grants (Cebulla and Smyth 1996; McGovern and Shirlow 1997). Like other deindustrializing areas with decaying urban shells, high unemployment, and mounting crime, services were "promoted as *the* way out of this economic morass" (McGovern and Shirlow 1997, 189).

Although it is difficult to measure the exact impact that state involvement had on the growth of the service sector, it is clear that the economy of the province soon became service based. Between 1950 and 1993, service-based employment increased by 22.8 percent, with most new jobs concentrated in education, security, and health and social services (McGovern and Shirlow 1997). By 1991, 80 percent of jobs were located in services, up from 68 percent in 1971 (Cebulla and Smyth 1996).

Deindustrialization and the turn to a service-based economy carried with it a particular geography. This was nowhere more true than in Belfast. While the Matthew Report had suggested that Belfast develop suburban economic cores along key transportation routes out of the city, the new focus on services called for rejuvenating the city's core. While many industrial cities witnessed declining commercial activity in city center areas during the eighties, Belfast's city center was particularly dilapidated. IRA bombs had destroyed over a quarter of the city's retail venues during the seventies, and the government's response—to lock down the city center—only reinforced its lack of appeal for business (Cebulla and Smyth 1996). Likewise, the ongoing violence associated with the Troubles encouraged working-class residents near the city center to flee for the presumed safety of the suburbs.[4] Indeed, although suburban flight began with the urban regeneration schemes of the sixties, it took off in the late seventies and eighties. By the mid-1980s the city center was, according to Cebulla and Smyth, "a twilight zone" (1996, 43). The dilapidated, vacant condition of Belfast city center meant, however, that plenty of space was available for interested businesses. And when the city added grants to the mix to encourage development in the city center, property developers found the combination of low start-up costs and potential for large returns an attractive business proposition. The 1994 cease-fires and the peace accord four years later only solidified the attractiveness of the city center for developers and property speculators.

Belfast's city center has changed significantly since the mid-1980s. In 1989, for example, the government helped establish the Lagan Side Development Corporation, a public–private partnership. The goal of the corporation was to develop 140 hectares on both sides of the river (Laganside Corporation 2005). The majority of investment has occurred on the west side of the river bordering the city center and includes a Hilton Hotel, 175,000 square meters of office space, a concert hall, and an indoor stadium called the Odyssey (see fig. 7). The development area also boasts 700 housing units, which are described on the corporation's Web site as "stylish," indicating a professional target clientele (Laganside Corporation 2005).

In the late 1980s the Castle Court Shopping Centre was also opened in the city center through a Comprehensive Development Scheme (CDS), which allows the Department for Social Development to release derelict properties for development (Department for Social Development 2005). In accordance with the design ethos of the period, the mall's entrance was

---

[4] Although many people fled the city to avoid attacks by paramilitaries on the "other" side, it is likely that just as many were fleeing the paramilitaries on "their" side. Indeed, paramilitary activity contributed to the depressed state of many working-class enclaves. As one reviewer of this book's manuscript noted, "It is a simple point but the scumbags usually victimize those nearest them. If they want a car for a job, they steal one from the next street."

Fig. 7. The Belfast Hilton.

constructed out of a combination of glass and steel, with large atriums built into the center of the two-story structure to provide internal light. The mall's anchor, Debenhams, is complemented by more than fifty smaller stores, many of them internationally recognized retailers like the Gap and Monsoon. The selection of stores also indicates a target shopper who is middle or upper income (McGovern and Shirlow 1997). Although there is nothing particularly special about Castle Court Shopping Centre, especially when compared to similarly sized malls in Great Britain or Ireland, a perusal of tourist Web sites for Belfast demonstrates that the city viewed the mall as more than just a shopping center: it was an antidote to the city's political problems. The Web site MyBelfast describes the mall as "Belfast's premier shopping experience": "Opened in the late 1980s, [the mall] was a significant statement at that time that optimism was returning to Northern Ireland despite the ongoing violence. Since then it has gone from strength to strength" (MyBelfast 2005).

In 2003 the city released land for a shopping development at Victoria Square, an area just north of Castle Court in the city center. The scheme calls for a mixed-use development of apartments, restaurants, cultural facilities, and retail space. Like Castle Court, stores cater to middle- and upper-income shoppers. The largest investment through the CDS program to date, Victoria Square, is frequently depicted as the development that will finally make Belfast's city center renewal "a reality." Indeed, government boosters argue that it will make the area "a premier regional shopping destination, well placed to compete with other European cities" (Department for Social Development 2005).

The optimism with which city officials view regeneration was also captured by the city's decision in 2002 to open an office in Washington, D.C. In 2005 the *Belfast Telegraph* published a story on the new office—the Northern Ireland Bureau—describing its location as "right in the centre of the government heartland of America" and detailing how director Tim Losty would be "making serious capital out of this week's Saint Patrick's Day celebrations" (Bell 2005). The optimistic tone of the story was noteworthy given its timing. Just two months earlier, Belfast had witnessed the largest bank robbery in its history. Widely believed to have been an IRA job, the robbery attracted intense media scrutiny and brought efforts to restore devolved government to a standstill. The murder of a Catholic man, Robert McCartney, in an IRA bar near the city center a few weeks later only added to the media frenzy, when the murdered man's sisters accused the IRA of cleaning up the crime scene and intimidating witnesses (Harding 2005b). The article, however, blithely dismissed the turmoil, remarking that "despite the stalled Peace Process, the message is 'Business As Usual' " (Bell 2005).

The city's rejuvenation, and its pride in it, is perhaps best captured by the city's new tourist slogan: Belfast, Better Believe It! In 2005 the city's tourist development board used the slogan to headline a series of sleek and sexy television commercials selling the city as a holiday spot (GoToBelfast 2005). These ads are a far cry from the gallows humor used to describe the Europa hotel, the city center's one functioning hotel during much of the Troubles—the most bombed hotel in all of Europe. For those who remember the old Belfast, there is no doubt the city has made remarkable progress: the city center has been transformed from a bombed-out shell to a bustling shopping district. And the city now draws its fair share of tourists—a rarity for most of the last thirty years. If one looks at the class structure that attends the targeted development of the service sector, however, a bleaker picture emerges. While the service sector now accounts for 80 percent of all jobs—up from 68 percent in 1971—growth in the sector is more relative than absolute. The number of new service-sector jobs created is much lower than the number of manufacturing jobs lost. As such, the growth in service-sector employment is due as much to the sharp decline in manufacturing as to significant job creation in services (Cebulla and Smyth 1996).

The new service economy has also ushered in new forms of labor segmentation (Cebulla and Smyth 1996; McGovern and Shirlow 1997; Shirlow and Shuttleworth 1999). In particular, labor has become polarized along two axes. On the first axis, jobs are clustered at the high and low ends, with little in between. High-end jobs tend to be professional and are linked to the state. Indeed, the state is the province's leading contractor of professional services, fueling the growth of the tertiary sector even as it creates a potentially dangerous condition of dependency (Cebulla and Smyth 1996).[5] Professional jobs are concentrated in education, social services, and security and normally pay well—significantly higher, in fact, than the UK average (McGovern and Shirlow 1997). Catholics have also been able to obtain an equitable number of many of these jobs, in some cases a larger share than their percentage of the population (Cebulla and Smyth 1996). On the other end of the axis are low-skill service jobs concentrated in the city's burgeoning retail sector. These jobs are part time, with low wages and limited security. Low-skill service work is also "feminized" (that is, more women than men take these jobs), and many workers are underemployed (McGovern and Shirlow 1997).

The second axis divides labor at a macrolevel, between an employed class, whose members benefit from state efforts to spur tertiary-sector growth (albeit to varying degrees), and the unemployed, whose skill set and limited education increasingly mark them as unemployable. Cebulla and Smyth (1996) label this group an emergent underclass, albeit with qualifications.[6] In Belfast the underclass can be found in Catholic and Protestant areas, and its dire circumstances have been fueled by suburbanization of the middle classes and the attendant economic isolation and social alienation it creates,[7] especially in working-class enclaves to the west and north of the city. Indeed, the Northern Ireland Statistics and Research Agency data for 2001 (NISRA 2001a) indicate that the ten wards with the worst deprivation measures in the city are for the most part clustered in these areas.[8] Moreover, when wards in the entire province are ranked, nine of the ten wards with the worst levels of deprivation are in Belfast.[9] Like many phenomena in Northern Ireland, however, the new economic isolation is filtered through sectarian lenses. For their part, the Catholic underclass tends to see

[5] Growth in the service sector began in the midseventies, when security-oriented jobs were created in response to the conflict. Growth only took off, however, in the mideighties, when the province embraced a service-based development model.

[6] The term "underclass" has been used historically in the United States to describe the inner-city black population whose economic prospects are limited by their distance from suburban growth poles and whose isolation makes their politicization difficult. Cebulla and Smyth (1996) argue that the spatial dimensions of the American model fit Belfast, but that its view of political possibility does not apply.

[7] The Catholic middle classes have tended to remain inside Belfast city limits, moving from west Belfast into southern portions of the city. Protestants have tended to move to suburbs outside of Belfast.

[8] This ranking is based on the Northern Ireland Statistics and Research Agency's Multiple Deprivation Measure score, an index of all of the agency's deprivation measures. In descending order, the ten wards in Belfast with the highest levels of deprivation are Crumlin, Falls, Whiterock, St. Anne's, Ballymacarrett, Woodvale, New Lodge, the Mount, the Shankill, and upper Springfield.

[9] The Brandywell ward in Derry has the sixth-highest multiple deprivation measure score in the province, knocking the Upper Springfield ward into eleventh place in a provincewide ranking.

"the benefits accruing from 25 years of struggle . . . [as] passing them by," while Protestants view their losses as the fault of a "Protestant middle class that has deserted them and a Catholic population who are, in socio-economic terms, in the ascendant" (McGovern and Shirlow 1997, 190).

The upshot is that the new forms of economic marginalization are seen in ethnoreligious rather than class-based terms. In many ways, this is not surprising. While labor segmentation in Northern Ireland today is markedly different from earlier forms, the province has always been divided into recognizable class constituencies that cut across sectarian divides even as they fail to produce cross-community alliances. Given the persistence of class divisions within Northern Ireland before, during, and after the conflict, it is worth considering why class has not played a central role in dampening the conflict, as circumstances would seem to dictate that it could have done.

Why Not Class?

Labor struggles have been an integral part of Loyalist resistance. When Loyalists have engaged in class politics, however, it has often been sectarian in nature. The Ulster Worker's Council strike in 1974, for example, was called after a motion denouncing power sharing failed in the Assembly on a 28 to 44 vote. The strike, which lasted for two weeks, led to fuel and commodity shortages across the province. At the end of the strike, direct rule was reinstated. For many, Loyalist labor had flexed its muscles and won (Mulholland 2002).

Colin Coulter posits two reasons for the sectarian bent of Protestant labor politics. The first is that ethno-sectarian sentiments have been encouraged by the Protestant elite. As Coulter observes, ethnic divisions "have often served handsomely the particular interests of the more elevated strata within Northern Irish Society" (1999, 96). Indeed, instrumental behavior on the part of Unionists has a long history in the province. Manipulation began as early as World War I, for example, when in 1918 the Unionist Party formed the Ulster Unionist Labour Association (UULA) to appease an increasingly radical Protestant workforce. The UULA would become a recruiting ground for lower positions in Stormont, allowing workers with no political experience or connections access to government positions and power.

Even without Unionist meddling, it is unlikely that Protestant workers would have supported an all-Ireland socialism. Although green Marxists argue that Protestant workers' ethnoreligious attachments are superficial, most scholars reject this interpretation. Mulholland argues, for example, that "Unionists did not believe that Protestant workers could be tempted into an all-Ireland settlement, socialist or otherwise. All-Ireland socialism had no appeal for Protestant workers, nor was their loyalty to the Union based upon petty bribes thrown their way by the Unionist elite. Rather, it was feared that Protestant workers, believing the constitution was secure, would vote for Labour representatives on day-to-day issues" (2002, 39). Whether one takes the green Marxist view or a view more akin to Mulholland's, it is clear that once Protestant workers became firmly planted at the top of the labor hierarchy they had little incentive to unite with Catholic workers against the Protestant bourgeoisie. Indeed, while Belfast's industrial engine was humming, the material gain accrued from Protestant workers' connections to the Protestant elite was a more powerful motive to maintain the status quo than potential (but unrealized) gains of class solidarity were an incentive to change it. Moreover, the informal and unspoken nature of gatekeeper mechanisms had the effect of normalizing the ascendancy of Protestant labor, keeping a good number of Protestant workers separated from the harsh actions that propelled them over and above their Catholic neighbors (Cebulla and Smyth 1996).

A second reason that class politics have failed to unite the two communities concerns the nature of class-based symbolism. In Northern Ireland, as in many other places, ethno-Nationalist politics tend to have a more developed symbolic repertoire than class politics have. As Coulter argues, "socioeconomic status rarely enjoys an affective power comparable to that of ethnicity or nationalism largely because it fails to produce an equally potent symbolic programme. . . . It is 'the Sash' or 'the Soldiers' Song' rather than 'the Internationale' that brings tears to the eyes of working class men as the end of licensing hours beckons" (1999, 99). As Coulter's example suggests, ethno-Nationalist notions of "us" and "them" tend to be emotively and forcefully articulated, with "others" described in scurrilous terms (for example, "taigs" or "orange bastards") meant to signify inferiority and danger. In class politics, by contrast, the other is rarely defined with such fervor. It is difficult to stir a visceral response to a faceless company or to maintain focus when the "enemy" varies from factory to factory. Furthermore, the potency of cold war discourse in the West inhibited labor from using the language of class revolution. Among members of Northern Ireland's Protestant labor force, this reticence was further buttressed by their historic connection to the state. Indeed, the Protestant tendency to define itself in terms of law and order—a frame often used to delegitimize Catholic protest and IRA violence—only served to sharpen Protestant aversion to radical variants of class struggle discourse, which tend to be anti-bourgeois *and* anti-state.

In addition to Coulter's list of reasons why Protestants have embraced sectarian or single-community versions of class struggle, I would add Protestants' religious convictions. Intellectual proponents of socialism have often vociferously decried religion and ethnicity as forms of false consciousness. And cold war discourses in the West defined both communism and socialism as "godless." For devout Protestants, such rhetoric would be more than enough to repel their participation, even in Loyalist-only forums.

In addition, even when working-class Protestants accept the Marxist proposition that ethnoreligious background is not "real," the discursive realm, where they debate which constitutional arrangement would best suit workers, is uneven. As Bruce asserts, the idea of "modern nationalism—that political units should map onto cultural ones [that is, ethnicity or religion]—has become so widely accepted, and the monocultural nation state so firmly established as the legitimate aspiration of ethnic groups, that nationalism stands in little need of further justification" (1998, 80). In short, the one religion/one territory formula inherent to nationalism means that Republican socialists do not have to reject their ethnoreligious attachments in the way that Loyalist socialists do.

This history has led many commentators on Northern Ireland to depict class as an irrelevant variable in the conflict. This portrayal may be true if class politics is defined narrowly to mean a Marxist or socialist struggle against capitalists, but if we follow Gibson-Graham, Resnick, and Wolff's (2000) argument we must look for the presence of class in new places *and* forms. In the context of Northern Ireland, this search entails an examination of class in forms that do not fit established notions of class politics as progressive. Indeed, within Loyalism, revanchists have adopted an identity politic that feeds on working-class resentment even as it creates conditions that hinder economic development.

Loyalist Class Politics

Membership in the working class is, as I mention in chapter 2, one of the primary ways that Loyalists differentiate themselves from Unionists. Every Loyalist I spoke to brought up his working-class background during the course of the interview, and often with no prompting from me. Revanchist and political Loyalists are not, however, of the same mind about what is best for the province's working-class population. Indeed, they interpret deindustrialization and city center regeneration through widely divergent frames.

REVANCHIST VARIANTS

Two tropes dominate revanchist variants of class politics. The first is given form around the notion that manufacturing is Protestant work, and that Protestants' historic dominance in the sector is a consequence of natural aptitude and familial tradition. Indeed, the issue of systematic discrimination against Catholics is not even addressed. The second trope explains the decline of the manufacturing sector as a form of punishment against Protestants. These tropes are sufficiently vague, however, to leave considerable wiggle room for specifics, such as who is levying the punishment and whether it is deserved. Combined, these tropes allow revanchists to depict Protestants as oppressed.

When I interviewed Frankie Gallagher in 2004,[10] for example, he began our discussion by describing Protestants as oppressed. Indeed, he likened their oppression to that faced by Ulster Protestants who sailed to America in the seventeenth century. As he explained:

> There's nowhere here [in Northern Ireland] for us. We're being oppressed again, the same as the American people were oppressed who filled the Appalachians, who went to Virginia. Who went to all the rest of the places, and the problem we have now is that the world's a much smaller place. There's nowhere to go. So, we're trapped. We're still suffering in exactly the same conditions, propaganda and everything else, that the founders of America suffered. We're still the same, except we've no where to fucking go. We can't sail west no more. Because you can't go there. We can't do it. And, that's real important if you're going to do anything. Somebody needs to get that point across that we're still oppressed the same as the Protestants were in the 1600s.

When I asked Frankie to explain how Protestants were oppressed today, he suggested that Protestants were the victims of a propaganda war:

> CAROLYN: Tell me how you're oppressed. I mean, I know what you mean, but just to tease it out a bit. Like, you know, where's the oppression coming from?
> FRANKIE: It's coming from a psychological perspective. There's a PR campaign, propaganda war, being fought for thirty years, to highlight every person who is Protestant as a bigot, as a sectarian bigot. There's this demonization of people who fought the IRA. If you notice, if you notice anybody that defended Ulster, that as soon as the paper's got their name, they put a precursor on their name. Like, say, with Johnny Adair. It was "Mad Dog." Say Billy Wright. It was "King Rat." . . . Anybody that [fights for] Ulster will be a Mad Dog, a King Rat or a Doris Day,[11] or fucking, you know, all these connotations. So, there's this propaganda war.

Frankie also described Protestant oppression in terms of deindustrialization. He pointed to East Belfast, where he grew up, as an example:

> East Belfast has lost something like 4,000 jobs last year. . . . But the problem is that not only are we losing jobs and investors, our infrastructure, our physical infrastructure is derelict. And there's a brain drain. Anybody that can, follow the jobs wherever they go, leaving the lot worse for the people left behind. . . .

[10] Although Gallagher's view of class relations in Belfast is revanchist, on other issues he has adopted a progressive stance (see chapter 7). He is a good example of how the divide between revanchist and progressive Loyalism can play out at the level of the individual.

[11] Jim Gray, a former UDA brigadier in East Belfast, earned the nickname Doris Day for his bleached hair, fake tan, and fondness for garish track suits (Murray 2005b). Gray was stood down from the UDA in March 2005 and was murdered the following October.

We're right in the middle of a deep trough, and its getting deeper and longer over a period of time because the people have went and left these areas, have moved on. They're not here no more. It's a sad sad indictment. But nobody seems to be doing anything about it.

The old Harland and Wolff steel cranes were visible in the skyline just a few blocks north of the converted storefront on the Newtonards Road where we held our interview. The cranes dominate the skyline in much of East Belfast, providing a stark reminder of the city's old economy and Protestants' place within it. In our interview Gallagher reminisced about that period. His recollections depicted Protestant dominance in the sector as organic—a matter of family tradition:

Anywhere manufacturing was, Protestants were in. And, if you remember at the turn of the twentieth century, it was huge, with the industrial revolution. But, in Belfast, there was only something like 10 percent of the population [that was] Roman Catholic. There was no Roman Catholics here. It wasn't until the industrial revolution came that they came . . . [so] Protestant people would have been traditionally in the manufacturing jobs because there were all Protestants here at the beginning [of industrialization]. . . . It isn't unlike any country in the world where if your father was a coppersmith or your father was a welder, you would want your son [to do the same]. I mean, look at the steel industry and all the rest of it. Or the motor industry. You know, you have six, seven generations of kids there. We were no different.

Gallagher also depicted deindustrialization as a form of punishment against the Protestant population. Indeed, although he acknowledged that globalization underpinned industrial decline, he maintained that it began as an organized plot to demonize Protestant workers. As he continued:

But all of a sudden that [industrialization] went. Investors went out because of PR and the demonization of *our* people. The bad imagery on television about "it's a bad place to invest." So manufacturing got hit worst. Then you had globalization and the downturn, putting cheap labor into third world countries. That had a massive impact on us. So, therefore, all of the traditional employment that Protestants would have been in are gone. And the only thing that is left now is the service industry. And we're now creating a Europe, and an America, of shopkeepers. We're not manufacturers no more.

In another part of our interview Gallagher was even more direct in his assertion that job loss was a form of punishment: "We're also now being blamed for eight hundred years of the oppression of Catholics. So, therefore, *our* jobs that we were traditionally in have been taken away from us."

The perception that "Protestant jobs" are being taken away out of retribution is echoed in Protestant views about the changing religious balance of

Belfast, which has shifted from 34.1 percent Catholic in 1971 to 47.19 percent in 2001 (CAIN 2006c). Catholics and Protestants alike refer to this trend as the greening of Belfast, although Loyalists prefer the term "greening strategy" because it implies that political maneuvering lies behind the changing demographic balance (Casciani 2001; Totten 2002). These shifts are presented as further evidence that Protestants are losing not only "their" jobs, but "their" city as a result. An excerpt from my conversation with Frankie illustrates this view:

> FRANKIE: If you go into a restaurant or you go out for a night and if you were openly having a debate about being a Protestant, or [saying] I'm a Protestant, you would be conscious of not being able to talk too loud in case someone heard you. We won't let anyone know we're Protestants in here. That's in *our own* city, *our own* town.
> CAROLYN: Aren't Protestants dominant [demographically] in Belfast?
> FRANKIE: Yeah, there's a majority of Protestants [here].
> CAROLYN: So, you
> FRANKIE: But, they're not in the city centers. In the city centers. They're not in the service industries. It's a majority of Catholic people. Plus, most people that get the jobs now are Catholic people so they are more prone to go out and have meals than anybody else.

Beverly Davidson-Stitt, a Loyalist community worker in East Belfast, expressed a similar view of the city center. And, like Gallagher, she linked the changes to the loss of traditionally Protestant jobs, describing the impact as one of pushing Protestant out of "their" city. As Beverly explained:

> So Belfast city center isn't inclusive to Protestant people. It's just not. But all we ever hear of is that they [Nationalists] feel excluded. I don't understand. And I do not understand why people are only listening to that one side. Why they aren't looking at what's happening to us. We've got no jobs. We're losing all *our* jobs. We're losing *our* homes. We're being pushed further out of *our own* city.

Catholics and the province's new minorities would likely find offense at the statements posited by Frankie and Beverly. And their offense would be understandable given that the city belongs to all of its inhabitants rather than just some of them. It is important, however, not to dismiss out of hand the anxiety that Gallagher and Davidson-Stitt give voice to. In my interview with Beverly, for example, she recounted two experiences of intimidation she had faced in the city center—one of which she felt occurred because of her religious background. Indeed, although overall violence is down since the 1998 accord, in many neighborhoods intercommunity violence is a daily event. And it often spills over into the city center when residents from interface areas meet one another in town. It is also easy to see why Protestants in working-class neighborhoods feel a sense of cognitive dissonance regarding the city center. Although both working-class neighborhoods and the city center suffered damaged infrastructure and decaying services during the Troubles, their paths have diverged dramatically since the cease-fires. While working-class areas have remained stagnant or gotten worse, the city center bustles with development and a crane-laden skyline.

The significant problem with the revanchist reading of post-industrial Belfast is found not in the anxiety it gives voice to. These feelings are to be expected in the post-industrial context. Rather, the problem is twofold: revanchists feel entitled to possess the best jobs, and they see post-industrial decline as a plot to take these jobs away and give them to Catholics. The negative changes associated with Belfast's move to a service-based economy, however, have not affected only Protestants. Indeed, the effects have left sizable pockets of impoverished neighborhoods in both communities.

Unfortunately, Loyalists who acknowledge that post-industrial disorder affects both communities and seek to address it in cross-community forums often come under attack. They are often branded Fenian lovers or Lundies. The use of tags like these—which imply an intimate connection with the other—is a typical feature of antagonistic identity politics. Militants with criminal motives benefit when dissent is taken out of civil society, where debate is permitted, and placed on a war footing, where a "with us or against us" ethos rules. Such tags force "dissidents" to keep quiet or risk being shunned. Indeed, even educated Loyalists who reject sectarianism would likely cringe to be called these names by another Protestant. The residue of thirty years of conflict is not easily washed from the psyche, even in the face of logic. It can be wrenching to have one's loyalty to one's community called into question. In a recent article in the *Blanket*, Billy Mitchell describes the feeling.

> I have lost count of the times when party colleagues and myself have had to deal with such insults. It is quite an experience to return from a function where you have been vociferously heckled by young militant socialists only to be further heckled by militant loyalists for daring to fraternize with the "other side." Yes, and some of my colleagues have been expelled from their communities and some have lost their lives. (2002b)

As Mitchell's comments indicate, the revanchist response to cross-community work on class grounds can sometimes degenerate into violence. The 2000 feud between the mid-Shankill UVF and the lower Shankill UDA C Company, which I detail in chapter 6, led to the expulsion of people affiliated with the PUP from their homes in the lower Shankill. Members of the PUP were targeted in part because their advocacy of socialist positions were posited as traitorous to "real" (that is, revanchist) Loyalism.

Revanchist criticism of cross-community work has also been labeled communist, although the term is usually applied to work specifically undertaken or sponsored by the PUP, which has a socialist platform. UVF ex-prisoner and community worker Michael Atcheson observed, for example, that PUP critics commonly conflate the party's socialist platform with communism:

> It's essential that the working class who want to use that term [working class] get involved in politics. And, yes, if you do start trying to fight the case over social or economic deprivation, you know, [there is] the connection that to be a socialist and a communist are the same.

Tom Roberts also noted that PUP critics label the group as communist in an effort to undermine it.

> The PUP advocate broadly socialist policies, and that is used against them by middle Unionism. You see constant references to communists, to the UVF and PUP being communists. That is used as scare tactics to the electorate not to touch these people, because they are communists.

As Roberts's comments indicate, revanchist discourse is as much a product of Unionism as Loyalism. However cynical these discourses may be, they resonate in the conservative culture of working-class Protestantism. And that resonance makes it difficult for progressive voices in Loyalism to engage in building class consciousness or doing cross-community work. As Tom continued:

> It [the communist label] has a pretty damning consequence with regard to being able to build a political base here because the people here are very conservative, and Unionism is ultra-conservative. And although the working class here, traditionally as I said before, allowed their politics be left in the hands of their betters . . . they still listen to that sort of diatribe that comes from middle Unionism. They are very susceptible to listening to that, and they vote for the safe option if you like. It would never dawn on a lot of working-class Protestants that communism's dead anyway, so why try to say that the PUP is going to pose a communist threat?

While Tom is pessimistic about the prospects of class politics uniting workers across the ethnoreligious divide, he and many of his peers remain committed to keeping the option on the table. It is to their politic that I now turn.

PROGRESSIVE VARIANTS (AKA POLITICAL LOYALISM)

Political Loyalists are often socialists. However, their political efforts are not confined to, or even concentrated in, standard working-class activism. Indeed, most political Loyalists argue that traditional socialism is no longer applicable in Northern Ireland. Political Loyalists are fond of remarking that most Loyalists are no longer working class. As Plum Smith observed:

It's not working class here anymore. Now we see ourselves as an underclass. Because there are no jobs here. There are no factories here. And, the ethos of Protestant working class, the ethos of working from seven in the morning, that's all away because there's no jobs like that anymore.

Billy Mitchell also described the Loyalist constituency as an "underclass" and made comparisons to groups in the United States. As he noted:

> In the twenty-first century, class is the wrong term. Today it's about powerlessness, about inequality, or structural injustice. . . . The old breakdown doesn't work—the old labor adage, "work done by hand or brain." . . . But you could use class in terms of an underclass. They'd be like the "poor white trash," the blacks and Latinos, and Mexican immigrants [in the United States].

Mitchell also argued that the violence in Loyalist enclaves increasingly mirrors inner-city rather than political violence. As he explained:

> If we didn't have a constitutional crisis [here in Northern Ireland], we'd still have a class crisis in terms of the underclass.

When I asked him if he thought underclass Catholics and Protestants would still fight one another if the constitutional issue were solved amenably, he continued:

> Perhaps. What's happened in the ghettos [here], as in any inner-city ghetto, it's people fighting each other because of territory. It's like gang territory, but the conflict is with the police and with civil society.

Political Loyalism's use of the term "underclass" is more than a pedantic matter. As Billy's comments about Loyalists fighting civil society indicate, many in the paramilitary structure are opposed to the normalization (that is, demilitarization) of society. In this context, old-style worker politics—strikes, work stoppages, rallies—are largely meaningless. Political Loyalists believe normalization requires discursive and material change.

At a discursive level, political Loyalists hope to change the frames through which Loyalists understand the peace process. One frame political Loyalists reject is the term "conflict resolution." Plum Smith, for example, avoids the term because he believes it creates unrealistic expectations.

> Naïve people thought—we signed the Good Friday Agreement on a Friday night, and on Saturday you have perfect peace. It doesn't work like that. It's not like a water tap, [where] you [can] turn the water tap on, and you just go and turn it off. Whereas with conflict transformation, it will be maybe twenty or thirty years yet. It's how you get there, right. It matters what you do, but, it's a long haul.

Billy Mitchell also eschews the terminology, noting that trying to resolve Northern Ireland's conflict means answering the constitutional question, and in a fragile peace environment that would only entrench sectarian hatreds. As he put it:

> In Northern Ireland it's a constitutional problem. So when you resolve the constitutional issue Republicans will have to become Unionists or Unionists will have to become Republicans. Conflict transformation is about transforming the nature of the conflict. From violence through dialogue to politics. But also more important you transform the nature of the relationships between people in the conflict. So when you hold the ultimate goal as conflict resolution, and obviously if you believe in conflict resolution as the goal, you want it resolved in your favor. So your whole mind-set, your whole mind-set in terms of dialogue, activity, strategy will be to have a resolution in your favor.

Although changing terminology is discursive, it has, as Billy notes, ramifications for cross-community work. It determines how one carries on a dialogue with one's enemies. Resolution begins with a utopian goal of changing minds; transformation begins on the pragmatic ground of trying to understand one another after thirty years of conflict. It is, in essence, a strategy of purposefully putting the horse before the cart.

Political Loyalists are also trying to challenge what they see as the hegemony of Nationalist interpretations of socialism. Although community workers like Mitchell are routinely labeled communists by revanchists, their reception in socialist circles is equally inhospitable. In the fall of 2002, Billy Mitchell discussed this problem at length in an article in the *Blanket* titled "Can the Course of Labour Afford to Wait?" (Mitchell 2002b). The article was in response to an essay in the previous issue by Queen's University historian Brian Kelly (2002), who had argued that there were compelling parallels between the politics of poor whites in Alabama during the Jim Crow period and working-class Loyalists today.[12] Kelly wrote,

> In the American South, as in the north of Ireland, the fundamental division was not between white and black (Protestant and Catholic), but between the rich and the poor of both races. But their attachment to a historical tradition that—like Orangeism—has been very deliberately cobbled together by local elites to guard against the possibility of a challenge from below meant that the "poor white trash" too often saw in the Civil Rights movement a threat to their own precarious status. And, although . . . history makes it clear that it was the white ruling class of the South that oversaw the planning of "massive resistance" to black demands, the truth is that very many poor whites, deluded by the trappings of white "cultural heritage" . . . enlisted as cannon fodder in the campaign to put blacks back in their place. (2002)

[12] Kelly's argument was based in part on his book *Race, Class and Power in the Alabama Coalfields, 1908–1921* (2001).

Loyalists, Kelly concluded, must bury their "dogmas" once and for all.

Mitchell began his response by noting that "there is little in Brian Kelly's article with which I would disagree." Mitchell noted, however, that Kelly's article provoked "some thoughts that I feel need to be expressed in the light of Brian's desire to see the 'dead dogmas of the past' well and truly buried." In particular, Mitchell chided Kelly for assuming that dead dogmas were the sole province of Loyalists. As he argued:

> Contrary to the popular belief it was not always the bigoted redneck prods who refused to pursue a "joint struggle alongside their fellow workers from the Falls or the Short Strand." The Catholic hierarchy, Gombeen Nationalists and various Republican leaders were just as anxious as any unionist to divert the working classes away from the real issues that affected their every day living. (2002b)

Mitchell also took umbrage at what he deemed Republican triumphalism:

> But in these days of chronic nationalist self-righteousness the politically correct version of history exonerates the nationalist-republican community and lays the blame squarely on the unionist family—especially the "poor Orange trash" of the unionist working class communities. If, as Brian Kelly wishes, we are to see through the tissue of lies that have been fed to us and if we are to bury "the dead dogmas of the past," socialists need to acknowledge that the unionist community does not have a monopoly on those old time-worn dogmas. If there is to be a funeral service for the past it will have to be attended by both communities. (2002b).

In post-conflict societies it can be a risky endeavor to try to apportion blame. It is equally dangerous, however, to paint an entire community with one broad brush, essentially depicting it as the victimizing community and laying the onus for reconciliation at its feet. Indeed, a true cross-community class alliance can only succeed if both groups acknowledge their faults as well as their grievances. Bringing Protestant workers to discursive heel while giving Republican workers a complete pass will only prevent an alliance from forming.

It is equally vital that Nationalist socialists acknowledge the hard work undertaken by progressive elements within Loyalism, who often work in an extremely hostile environment. As Billy observed,

> It is ironic that those working-class Unionists whom pro-nationalist socialists criticize most are not the groupings within Loyalism that are still wedded to sectarianism or violence, but those of us who are striving to rekindle the spirit of independent thought and break free from the shackles which held us captive for so long to the Unionist establishment. Both *Fourthwrite* and the *Blanket* have been criticized by socialists for allowing people like myself space to air

our views, and at one of the Voice of the Lark debates it was a self-proclaimed socialist who objected to Tommy Forman reading a paper on my behalf. We have been picketed and heckled by socialists demanding working-class unity but rejecting our right to be part of that unity. (2002)

These problems give rise to questions about the very nature of socialism in Northern Ireland. As Billy continued,

Rather than genuinely seek to develop working-class unity on crucial social and economic issues, many socialists seem committed to a policy of maintaining a single-identity socialism that is rooted squarely within the nationalist community and tradition—a socialism that accepts non-nationalists into the fold only insofar as they are prepared to turn their backs on their cultural identity and their legitimate desire to maintain their citizenship within the United Kingdom. (2002b)

In the post–cold war period, most socialists have abandoned the more grandiose elements of the Marxist project. In Northern Ireland, however, many socialists continue to subscribe to the notion that the worker's struggle is the Republican's struggle. Although socialists of a Nationalist bent are certainly entitled to support the concept of a united Ireland, it is clear they will never gain allies in the Protestant population by requiring a doctrinaire reading of socialism. Indeed, working-class unity will remain an abstract concept unless and until Republicans and Loyalists agree to disentangle the constitutional issue from the worker issue.

In addition to their discursive work, political Loyalists also engage in community work. Their work does not, however, focus on traditional class-based activities such as organizing drives, awareness campaigns, and the like. Given the general state of decline in Loyalist enclaves, most of their work is grassroots social work, designed to help communities develop the capacity to solve their own problems.

The projects that Loyalist community workers manage are varied. Plum Smith, for example, has obtained grant funding for several years to take Protestant and Catholic youths to Los Angeles to participate in soccer camps with disadvantaged Latino and African American youths. The goal behind the program is to help poor children develop relationships with their peers on the "other" side of the religious divide. The LINC Resource Centre, which Billy Mitchell helped cofound, has received funding (in coordination with a Republican group) for a series of cross-community dialogues. Dialogues are held between Republicans and Loyalists on contentious issues in which some common ground has been identified. The goal of these dialogues, the LINC Web page (2005) explains, "is not to change each others beliefs but to help us change our misconceptions about each others beliefs.

The process is about understanding and respect, not about conversion or recrimination. Hence no one is asked to compromise their beliefs or their values. The search is for mutual understanding, trust and respect."

Perhaps one of the most important effects of such projects is that they have created employment options for Loyalists coming out of prison. As I note in chapter 2, although many Loyalists earned college degrees while in prison, most have had trouble finding professional employment since release. In response, many ex-prisoners have formed their own organizations to apply for grant funding. The effect has been a flowering of storefront NGOs willing and able to employ ex-prisoners. In Loyalist communities these opportunities have been especially important for developing a sense that Loyalists can advocate on their own behalf rather than waiting for Unionists to do it for them.

Although all these efforts have been important, there is much work still to be done by political Loyalists. In the next section I look at some of the obstacles to their work. Some of these barriers are related to the grant-driven nature of much community work, and I discuss these in detail in chapter 6. Other barriers relate to the actions of the Republican community workers with whom Loyalists must work. I discuss these problems here.

Republican Bad Faith

A Breach of Trust

Although many political Loyalists support cross-community initiatives, such projects were put in serious jeopardy in late 2002. The reason was the so-called Stormont spy ring, an imbroglio in which Sinn Fein administrative staff members were accused of collecting information on Unionists and Loyalists (Murray 2002). Unionist politicians cried foul, alleging the IRA was using Sinn Fein employees to engage in a massive intelligence-gathering operation (BBC 2002). Loyalists were also angry. The Police Services of Northern Ireland (PSNI) contacted several of the persons I interviewed for this book, for example, to alert them that their personal information had been found in files on Sinn Fein computers in the Stormont building. Tom Roberts told me: "The police raid[ed] their [Sinn Fein] Stormont offices and [did] subsequent raids on houses. And it [personal details] was recorded on computer. So the police came to us with things that had been held on file." In Northern Ireland, when the police determine that personal details are being collected on someone, they usually issue a warning to the person. Indeed, the collection of personal details about someone can signal that he or she has been targeted for assassination. As I discovered, however, Loyalist community workers were largely unconcerned about such threats: most have been under some form of warning for much of their adult lives. Rather, they were angry at the breach of trust the spying represented. Plum stated, for example:

> If I'm sitting having a meeting with Nationalists, sometimes I'll talk about very sensitive issues. And finding a year down the lane that somebody was going away from there and recording information. I mean, you don't do those things. So that trust has broken down. They need to retrieve that.

Political Loyalists were also angry because the spying appeared to validate the revanchist viewpoint that cross-community work was traitorous. Tom explained:

> We went into many projects with these people on good faith, and this is what's been discovered, what was happening. And the other consequence of that there was the people within our own constituency who weren't very happy with us engaging with them in the first place were able to turn around and say "what did you expect, we told you not to do these things anyway." So they [the spys] were actually helping the more extreme elements of Loyalism, giving them a stick with which to beat us.

The fact that Tom and other Loyalist community workers were contacted by the PSNI also indicates that the spying was about more than political machinations between Sinn Fein and Unionist Party competitors but reached instead into the field of community work in which Unionist politicians are rarely involved. Indeed, when I asked Tom what sort of data had been collected on him and his peers, he explained that most files contained not only personal information, such as home address and pubs frequented, but political information, such as individual political views, internal political debates, and strategies employed in community work. In the end, seeing the files that had been collected on them helped Tom and his peers narrow down the potential offenders. And, as the following excerpt of our conversation indicates, it was not difficult for Tom to connect the spying to the IRA:

> TOM: I don't class all Republicans in this. This was elements within the Republican movement.
> CAROLYN: What elements were they?
> TOM: Well, we can clearly define meetings where we said certain things [that appeared in the files], so we have it narrowed down to a few organizations that were dealt with, but I don't want to go into naming them.
> CAROLYN: Yeah.
> TOM: But we can clearly identify where the majority of the information was gathered.
> CAROLYN: So, would these be actual community groups on the Nationalist side?
> TOM: Yeah. Yeah.
> CAROLYN: So we're *not* talking about Sinn Fein or the IRA specifically, we're talking about feeders?

Том: Well, at the end of the day Carolyn, the IRA must have directed people to do this.

Tom then offered to show me the files. Before doing so, however, he stipulated, "I wouldn't want you to quote any person's name on this, because it's pretty sensitive." He then asked me to turn off my tape recorder.

Republican commentators argued that the charges against Sinn Fein were trumped up. Some suggested that the PSNI investigation of Sinn Fein computers at Stormont was a psychological operation (Friel 2002). Others depicted the investigation as a diversionary tactic, allowing the PSNI to avoid investigating a spate of UDA-led murders in the wake of the organization's internal 2002 feud (Crean 2002).

In December 2005 the Stormont spy ring story took a strange twist when the government dropped charges against its primary suspect, Dennis Donaldson, Sinn Fein's administrator at Stormont. The government claimed it was no longer in "the public interest" to continue with the case (Hookham 2006). Commentators suggested that the sudden dismissal of the case was evidence a police informer had been involved in the spying. A few days later, Donaldson came forward with the very revelation, admitting he had been a British spy since the mideighties.[13] Gerry Adams hastily issued a statement that read, in part: "this operation was a blatant example of political policing aimed at collapsing the political institutions" (Adams 2005).

Much remains unknown about the spy ring, including who ordered the spying—Donaldson on behalf of his handlers, or others within Sinn Fein— but it is clear that spying did occur. As Tom's comments demonstrate, sensitive information about Loyalists had been gathered to which only a handful of Republicans were privy. Whatever the genesis of the spying—a topic beyond the scope of this book—the most important ramification for the purposes at hand is the difficulty the spying created for political Loyalists vis-à-vis their revanchist competitors. It gave revanchists in Loyalism an opportunity to discredit cross-community work, and in so doing gave the revanchist viewpoint a hearing it did not deserve.

DEAD DOGMAS ALIVE AND WELL

One of the most trenchant complaints that Loyalists make about the post-accord era is that Republicans put little effort into working with Loyalists. Indeed, Loyalists argue that in some cases Republicans appear to go out of their way to make cross-community alliances impossible. One way they do so, Loyalists complain, is by framing class-based issues that affect

[13] Donaldson was found murdered the following April in County Donegal, in the Republic of Ireland. He had retired to a rundown cottage in the county after his double life was exposed. Although many observers suspect the IRA was behind the murder, the group denied any involvement in his death. Donaldson's murder has yet to be solved (Moore 2006).

both communities in partisan, Republican terms. In so doing, Republicans essentially limit the attractiveness of class struggles for Loyalists. As an example, Billy Mitchell discussed the way Republicans framed the issue of water privatization in Belfast:

> Most working-class Protestants would be opposed to the privatization of water. But once Republicans got [involved], they didn't say "We're opposed to privatization." It was "The British government is putting the boot to the Irish people." You know, once you start using that language, then working-class Protestants aren't going there, won't engage.

Republicans may legitimately feel that water privatization is part and parcel of a colonial project. However, it is also clear that in order to develop cross-community alliances based on class, new discourses that are not explicitly linked to either community have to be developed. As Michael Atcheson remarked,

> That [discourse] makes it difficult for the work we're trying to do, because what we're trying to do is look at collective ways that we can link together that affect both communities.

Billy Mitchell also noted the difficulty many Loyalists had participating in the anti-war marches that preceded the U.S. and British invasion of Iraq. Many saw the war as a war for oil that would largely benefit the capitalist classes. However, the marches became, Mitchell explained, a pretext to bash the British, and in the process Loyalists were alienated from them.

> You know, I was, as I said, very anti-war. I don't believe in this war. . . . I was totally opposed to it, but at the same time, once Republicans began to attack British soldiers. You know, it's not a soldier's fault. Soldiers go where they're sent. [They should be] without blame. I know a number of PUP people went to Glasgow to join in the anti-war marches there, after the war had started, because they had no intention of identifying with Eamonn McCann and other Republicans, who just turned it into an anti-British [thing].

Using radical or progressive discourses with cross-community appeal should not require a worker to abandon his or her attachment to nationalism or Loyalism. For struggles like water privatization, workers are better served by discourses that can mobilize cross-community support. It is important to note, here, however, that I am not suggesting that class politics can evolve outside of ethno-Nationalist locations. Such a politic would be a socialist form of cosmopolitanism, and a utopian one at that. It may indeed be possible, at some point in the future, for a plural class-based identity to take root cross-community. But for that to happen, both sides must first be able to come together, and to establish trust and a working relationship around issues that do not require invoking the constitutional question.

In this regard, I disagree with the province's premier socialist, Eamonn McCann, who has been a consistent critic of sectarian socialism. McCann has argued, for example, that the PUP's working-class rhetoric "is not a modern phenomenon." It is, he argues, simply the most recent articulation of long-standing tensions between Protestant workers and their Protestant bosses (2000). McCann suggests these spats are less about protecting workers than they are about protecting Protestant workers. Furthermore, he asserts that until Protestant socialists break from Loyalism, their socialism is unworthy of support. However, by holding the PUP to a standard it can never meet, given its social location, McCann is only helping revanchists, the very Loyalists whose class politic is the most detrimental to workers of all religious backgrounds. This is not to suggest that the PUP does not have room for improvement. It clearly does, but its efforts are distinguishable from their revanchist peers and deserve support, not a doctrinaire dismissal.

In the next chapter I examine Loyalist cultural repertoires. As I demonstrate, there are also significant differences between political and revanchist versions of Loyalist culture. It is to the culture industry that I now turn.

4 Fighting with History instead of Guns

Although paramilitaries on both sides of Northern Ireland's ethnoreligious divide agreed to put their arms down in 1998, commentators and scholars alike agree that the constitutional question remains unanswered and that the battle to answer it conclusively, once and for all, continues. It is merely the weapons that have changed. Of course some Loyalists and Republicans continued to use their guns after 1998, a state of affairs I cover on the Loyalist side in chapters 6 and 7, but increasingly, Loyalists and Republicans use culture—language, history, art—as a weapon.

In the years since the 1994 cease-fires, both sides have busied themselves with building cultural repertoires that include linguistic, historical, and artistic elements. In many ways, these projects are clear proxies for the contrasting geopolitical visions that gave rise to the conflict in the first place. Indeed, by building these repertoires, Republicans and Loyalists hope to demonstrate the ineffable imprint of Irish or British culture, respectively, on the province and, in so doing, justify a geopolitical connection to it.

These cultural projects are not without their critics, as debates surrounding the linguistic projects of both Republicans and Loyalists demonstrate.[1] Some criticisms are petty and largely sectarian in nature. Sammy Wilson, the former lord mayor of Belfast, once dismissed the Irish language as a "leprechaun language" (Friel 1999), while a common Republican refrain describes Ullans as a "DIY (do it yourself) language for Orangemen" (Wikipedia 2005c). Other criticisms, however, are serious and many originate from internal critics. The ULTACH Trust, which is designed to promote the Irish language in Northern Ireland, argues for example that "not

---

[1] English is the official language of Northern Ireland, but in the last twenty years Irish and Ulster Scots have witnessed a revival of sorts.

all Irish-language activists are well-meaning"—many have a political agenda designed to foster "Unionist alienation from the language, and to identify Irish ever more closely with the nationalist community" (ULTACH, as quoted in O'Reilly 1997, 112). Likewise, Unionist academic and some-time commentator John Coulter has argued that Ullans is nothing more than a "broad rural Ballymena accent, washed down with a healthy support for Glasgow Rangers Soccer club!" (2004).

The gist of these criticisms is that such projects are inauthentic, that they represent attempts to revive long-since-expired cultural artifacts for political purposes while pretending they have always been present in the culture. Of course culture is by its very nature fluid and thus subject to manipulation. Indeed, cultural reproduction almost always occurs within a political context, with all of the power dynamics this implies, meaning that some actors necessarily have greater ability than others to select which cultural traits are accorded legitimacy. In short, no culture can claim an uninterrupted chain to an authentic, foundational moment, but the political nature of cultural reproduction means that elites will make just these sorts of claims about the cultural traits of their choosing.[2] This axiom has been especially relevant to the construction of national myths, which are built, as Benedict Anderson (1991) famously argued, around "imagined communities."

The goal in analyzing such cultural repertoires, therefore, must include more than establishing the authenticity of their elements. Although estab-lishing authenticity, or the lack thereof, is an important part of historical analysis, it is less relevant to a cultural study, where the focus is on the mo-tives behind the promotion or suppression of cultural elements—an issue that bears analysis whether an element is newly invented or thousands of years old. Indeed, most cultural elements can be shown to have changed or been manipulated over time. The more salient question for cultural analysis is how cultural myths are deployed and to what ends by different groups in society. The question of motives is a particularly important one in post-agreement Northern Ireland. As I demonstrate in chapter 5, millions of dol-lars have flowed into the province in the wake of the Belfast Agreement, and a good deal of this funding has gone to cultural groups affiliated with para-militaries.[3] This funding provided paramilitaries with new avenues of expo-sure and influence. It has also, according to some commentators, exacerbated sectarian tensions at just the time they should be decreasing (Langhammer 2004).

The seismic shifts within the world of Loyalist paramilitaries, between re-vanchist and political Loyalism, can also be mapped in Loyalist cultural

---

[2] See Nic Craith (2001) and Shirlow and McGovern (1997) for the application of this argu-ment in Northern Ireland.

[3] Some cultural groups employ former paramilitary members and ex-prisoners. Others have contact by virtue of their location in neighborhoods controlled by paramilitaries.

work. The ability to delineate between the two has important ramifications for the post-peace environment. One of the key findings in the scholarship on the criminalization of war is that criminally motivated militants legitimate and frame their fighting through identity politics. The creation of Loyalist cultural repertories is integrally related to identity politics because these repertoires are used to redefine Loyalism in the post-agreement era. Which notion of Loyalism—revanchist or political—becomes dominant will tell us much about the province's prospects for lasting peace.

The difference between these two politics is also relevant to the discussion of particularism and cosmopolitanism in the first chapter. Although critics of particularism argue that particularist identity politics can give rise to renewed fighting, it is clear that political Loyalism, while particularist, posits a peaceful path forward for Loyalism. The more relevant issue for consideration should therefore be whether the Loyalist identities proffered by Loyalist cultural work are constructed antagonistically, where others are seen as inferior and the boundaries between them are deemed impassable. I take this approach because the idea that cosmopolitanism can take root in Northern Ireland is naïve. In both Catholic and Protestant working-class neighborhoods there is often deep antagonism not only toward the "other" community but to the very idea that the two communities share anything whatsoever. The working-class background of most Republicans and Loyalists also means that their access to professional avenues (where "tribal" attachments tend to decline) is limited. A more pragmatic goal, therefore, is to identify and support notions of Loyalism and Republicanism that are not built on antagonism. As Calhoun (2003) argues in more general terms, most people gain "a sense of belonging" through the very particularist categories that cosmopolitans reject or define as secondary. Cosmopolitanism is therefore more an expression of privilege than a workable alternative (Mittelman 2005).

I begin this chapter with an overview of Loyalist culture. As I demonstrate, a prevailing theme within Loyalism is the assertion that Loyalists do not know who they are. This mantra provides the backdrop against which current Loyalist cultural work occurs and is legitimated. In the next section I overview two elements of an emerging Loyalist cultural repertoire—Ullans and the concept of the Cruthin—and introduce the reader to debates around them. In the third section I analyze how these elements are used to bolster a revanchist view of Loyalist identity in the post-peace era. Although these elements are seemingly unrelated—one linguistic, the other historical—they are considered a joint endeavor by their boosters. In the fourth section, I detail the largely negative response of political (paramilitary) Loyalism to this cultural work. I conclude the chapter with some thoughts about what progressive Loyalism is doing, and can do better, to blunt revanchist cultural work.

A Sound or an Echo?

Arthur Aughey has argued that Unionism "has an inadequate understanding of its own 'inner experience' "(1989, viii) and, as a result, has been and continues to be politically inarticulate. Although Aughey was writing for an academic audience, his argument affirms a common refrain among the population at large: simply put, Protestants don't know who they are; they suffer from a crisis of identity.

ACADEMICS ON THE PROTESTANT CRISIS OF IDENTITY

Academics have probably written more about the Protestant identity crisis than any other group. Not surprisingly, their explanations for the crisis vary. Most agree, however, that progress comes as a result, rather than at the expense, of particularist identities.

Some scholars think that the Protestant identity crisis stems from the Protestant population's inability to develop a Nationalist ideology (Miller 1978; Nairn 1977). Nairn argues, for example, that Protestants in Northern Ireland are not a people in a Nationalist sense. They are better categorized as a " 'white settler' or colonialist minority" (1977, 231) and, like other settler groups, cannot clearly identify with either colonial or native. This ambiguity explains the Protestant community's attachment to outdated icons, such as King Billy, as well as its militant nature. Other scholars argue that the root of the Protestant identity crisis is found in the religious sphere. Bruce (1986) argues, for example, that evangelical Protestantism is the only thing that unites an otherwise fractious people. The central place of religion in Loyalism, however, prevents it from developing a Nationalist ethos. Indeed, the enduring strain of anti-Catholicism within Presbyterianism in particular leads Protestants to reject plural and even Protestant notions of nationalism because the concept is firmly equated with the Catholic population.

Geographers contend that unstable boundaries lie at the heart of the Protestant identity crisis (Graham 1998; Graham and Shirlow 2002). Graham (1998) argues, for example, that Unionist discourses attempt to answer the political question of who should control Ulster rather than the cultural one of what defines the people who live in Ulster. This state of affairs leaves Protestant identity vulnerable to political shifts that a culturally grounded identity could withstand, and reactive because of it.

Other scholars maintain that Protestant identity is governed by a siege mentality (Anderson and Shuttleworth 1994; Lee 1985). This mind-set is characterized as pathological in that it reads Catholic gain as Protestant loss and uses this interpretation to justify Loyalist violence. The peace process has only buttressed the siege mentality, adding self-pity and defeatism to the mix (McKay 2000). Other scholars reject the portrait of Protestants as defeatist by nature. Finlay argues, for example, that until the Anglo-Irish Agreement in 1985, Protestants "identified themselves in terms of modernity, triumph, and rationalism." It is only after 1985 that Protestants embraced defeatism, and it had as much to do with the decline of industry as with ingrained fatalism. Indeed, Protestant defeatism is better read as an attempt to find an identity "in a context where identity politics have, themselves become hegemonic" (Finlay 2001, 16).

There are often sharp debates among the academics who write on Protestant identity, as Finlay's (2001) critique of the defeatist discourse indicates. Nonetheless, most scholars agree that Protestants lack a secure identity and that they need a more stable sense of who they are before they can successfully engage the peace process. Indeed, even Finlay, who sees most identity politics as "pathetic" and questions their efficacy, champions Protestant attempts "to engage positively both with Protestant fatalism and the need for change" (2001, 4).

In this regard, academics accept that particularist identities will be part of the post-accord era; they encourage affirmative notions of Protestantism rather than new categories to takes its place.[4] The Belfast Agreement takes a similar approach. Indeed, the accord recognizes "parity of esteem" between the two "traditions" and goes so far as to guarantee the right of all citizens to define themselves as British or Irish in perpetuity, despite any future changes to the province's geopolitical status.

Although the accord has been criticized for institutionalizing sectarianism (Langhammer 2004; Wilson 2005), these critiques do not detract from the academic argument that Protestants must understand who they are before they can fully embrace universal identities (or peace). Indeed, the problem is not in the agreement's recognition of particularist identities but in the fact that its structure favors revanchist versions over political ones.

Loyalists on the Crisis of Identity

Like academics, Loyalists also worry that Protestants have an unclear, even incomplete notion of themselves. Loyalist perspectives on the Protestant identity crisis are generally articulated by Loyalist cultural organizations that have sprung up in the province, most notably in Belfast, since the 1994 cease-fires. Although many of these groups were founded by persons outside of Loyalist circles, most are headquartered in Loyalist areas. Two of the most prominent groups, the Ulster-Scots Heritage Council and the Ulster-Scots Language Society, share an office on York Street in a Protestant enclave in North Belfast. The Heritage Council also runs a library in the staunchly Loyalist neighborhood of Sandy Row. Another group, the Bally-

---

[4] Some scholars define "affirmative" as civic (Porter 1996). Others define it as being more than "not Catholic" (Graham 1998).

macarrett Arts and Cultural Society, is located on the Albertbridge Road in the shadows of the old Harland and Wolff cranes, iconic symbols on the landscape of Protestant dominance in East Belfast. Although there is a clear geographic disconnect between the Unionist roots of Protestant cultural groups and their location in Loyalist strongholds, the groups' view of the Protestant identity crisis bears analysis because some parts of the Loyalist paramilitary structure have adopted their work, as paramilitary statements, public art, and writings indicate (McAuley 1991).

One of the most active cultural organizations within Loyalism, the Ulster-Scots Heritage Council, was founded in 1995 to promote all things Ulster Scots. The group's director, Nelson McCausland, a member of the Legislative Assembly for North Belfast (DUP) and a Belfast city councillor for the Oldpark area, described to me the need for the council by noting the Protestant identity crisis: "People in the Ulster Scots community are often told 'you have an identity crisis. You don't know what you are.'" One of the problems, McCausland explained, is that Protestants are told to look in the "wrong" direction for their culture. As he put it:

> Everything is being pushed in that north–south direction, whereas our natural cultural connections are not north–south, they are east–west. The pipe bands are meeting with the pipe bands in Scotland. They're the largest branch in the world, the Scottish organization. The language society here is linked to the one in Scotland. So is the country dance society. The Burns clubs are members of a federation in Scotland. Our linkages are all east–west. Not north–south. But they are not treated equally and equitably in terms of resourcing. I noticed even yesterday, the universities in Northern Ireland and the universities in the Republic have formed Universities Ireland.[5] Well, if you're going to have a north–south connection, I have no problem with that. What about an east–west one as well?

Another group doing cultural work on the Loyalist side is the Ulster-Scots Agency (or, in Ullans, the Boord o Ulstèr-Scotch). The organization is a part of the North/South Language Body, a cross-border organization developed out of the Belfast Agreement.[6] The group, which promotes the Ulster Scots language, or Ullans, also situates its work in the context of the Protestant identity crisis. A section of its Web page is devoted to "awareness":

> The Agency recognises the need to communicate with all audiences—i.e. Ulster-Scots and non-Ulster-Scots, as to why the movement has a value. It needs to explain what the culture is about, why the language has survived and

---

[5] In 2003 Universities of Ireland was created "to promote co-operation and collaboration among universities in Northern Ireland and the Republic of Ireland, and to enhance their reputations internationally" (Universities Ireland 2005).

[6] The North/South Language Body is an umbrella organization for both the Ulster-Scots Agency and the Foise na Gaeilge, which is charged with promoting the Irish language.

why it should continue to survive in a way that adds positively to life within the island of Ireland. Ulster-Scots today has a voice and identity thanks to recent initiatives from the Agency. (Ulster-Scots Agency 2005)

Loyalist paramilitaries also acknowledge the Protestant identity crisis. Most put it down to an education system that failed to educate Protestant youth on the province's history. Tom Roberts, the director of EPIC, recalled that

> we had quite a reasonable education, but had virtually no sense of Irish history. Protestant history in Northern Ireland is, well, we were taught British history. And that's the British mainland. They taught you about all the queens and kings of England back to god knows when. You know, Oliver Cromwell, all the revolutions, all those things. But I knew not a single thing, I knew absolutely nothing, about Irish history. I was born in 1951, thirty years after the partition of the state of Northern Ireland, and to me in my younger life Northern Ireland had been around since biblical times. That's how naïve I was about it. I didn't know how it came about. Didn't know nothing about the 1916 rising. Basically, all I knew about was the 1690 Battle of the Boyne.

Michael Atcheson agreed, noting that most Protestants are only taught about a few historical events. As he explained:

> I mean, every young working-class Protestant is brought up with the Battle of the Boyne and the siege of Derry, but at the same time they couldn't tell you much more about [our history than] that.

David Ervine recalled that his education was similarly limited:

> From where we sit, we're about a mile from the place where Henry Joe McCracken was hung. Now Henry Joe McCracken was a prime mover in the Presbyterian rebellion against the British. I was about sixteen before I knew that Henry Joe McCracken existed and that he was hung about a mile and a half from where I was born and reared. I didn't know anything about Henry Joe McCracken or that there was a Presbyterian rebellion. . . . But I learned all about the kings and queens of Europe.

Frankie Gallagher had a comparable recollection. He explained to me, for example, that it was only after his stint in the Royal Air Force that he learned Protestant history:

> So when I came back I realized that the world was bigger than Northern Ireland. The world was bigger actually than East Belfast, because that's all I knew, East Belfast. I was in the Mediterranean, western Europe mostly. Maldives, Cyprus, all that type of thing. And, it wasn't until after that that I started learning about Unionism and Protestantism and my local history. That I started

realizing that hey, I'm from a family of twelve kids. I have an elder brother and an elder sister dead. There's ten of us surviving. There was high infancy death rate whenever we were kids. So, you know, I started realizing just how we were excluded. We weren't accepted. We were looked down upon. People in the Orange Order or the Unionist establishment would've looked down on us. We were from the poorer classes. And I realized as well that we were educated to a degree. We were educated to do certain work and that was it.

As Gallagher's comments suggest, he views the Protestant identity crisis as a matter of not only poor education but oppression as well. Indeed, in a speech he gave to the Glencree Summer School in the summer of 2003,[7] he likened Protestants in Ireland to immigrants and refugees whose low social status makes them unable to articulate or disseminate their history and culture. The *Irish Independent* reported on the speech.

> Northern Protestants suffer the same social and historical exclusion as refugees and asylum seekers in the Republic, Glencree Summer School in Wicklow heard over the weekend. Shockingly, Protestants have been "air brushed" from the Republic's culture as though they never existed—and a visit to any museum here will underline the point graphically, Frankie Gallagher of Ulster Political Research Group told the school. Rarely, if ever, will an exhibit show [that] over 1 million Protestants live on this island, with little to illustrate the common if parallel histories of the peoples living on it, said Mr. Gallagher. (Whelan 2003)

Gallagher told the summer school group that not only do such absences contribute to the now infamous Protestant siege mentality but that "there will be no solutions until these barriers are broken down" (Whelan 2003).

As these comments indicate, Loyalist cultural groups and paramilitaries generally agree that Protestants lack a firm sense of their history and that these absences leave Protestants unsure of who they are and how to define themselves in the post-agreement era. What these divergent Loyalist voices do not agree on, however, is the form that a revived Protestant identity and culture should take.

Cultural Weapons

In this section I look at two elements of a newly emerging Loyalist cultural repertoire: the Ullans language, and the Cruthin and the legend of Cuchulainn. The legitimacy of these linguistic and historical elements is

[7] The school is sponsored by the Glencree Centre for Reconciliation in the Republic of Ireland. The Glencree Centre was established in 1974 to address violence in Northern Ireland by providing a space for reconciliation. Conflict actors from across the globe have since used it (Glencree Centre for Reconciliation 2005).

hotly contested. I review them here not to make a definitive judgment on their authenticity but to provide readers with enough background to understand my analysis of their place in Loyalist identity politics.

ULLANS—DIALECT OR LANGUAGE?

To its boosters, Ulster Scots is a distinct language. It developed during the seventeenth century when Scottish planters were given large plantations, mostly in Northern Ireland, by King James I. Planters brought their peasants, who spoke Scots, with them to work the land.[8] Over time, boosters argue, their Scots developed into a distinct and separate language known as Ulster Scots. Since many readers may not be familiar with Ulster Scots, I include a few phrases in English and Ulster Scots below:

	English	Ulster Scots
Introduction from an Ulster Scots group's Web page (Reynolds 2006)	This web page has been set up to promote poetry, songs and stories in the Ulster Scots Language that is still spoken in parts of Counties, Antrim, Down, Londonderry/Derry and Donegal. It is simple to read, just scroll down the page and enjoy this forgotten part of the Heritage of Northern Ireland.	Thes wab page hes bain pit thagither tae pit forrit tha Ulster Scots leid thaut es spake in pairts o' tha coonties o' Entrim, Doon, Derry an' Donegal. Jest scroll doon tha page tae luk aut tha oul tung thaut es pairt o' tha very hairt o' Ulster's Heritage.
Twenty-third Psalm, verses 1–3 (Ulster-Scots Language Society 1994)	The Lord is my Shepherd; I shall not want.	The Lord bees ma herd for aye, A winnae hae want o ocht.
	He maketh me to lie down in green pastures:	He gard me lay doon in green pasture-laun,
	He leadeth me beside the still waters.	an airts me fornent the lown waters.

Ulster Scots is also known as Ullans or Lallans. Although these terms are often used interchangeably, they have distinct meanings. The term Ulster Scots is the English phrase for the language (or dialect) spoken by the descendents of Scottish planters and peasants. The term Lallans refers to the Scots language and the dialect spoken by people living in the lowlands of Scotland. The poet Robert Burns described the Scots tongue as Lallans in

---

[8] Scottish landlords brought peasants with them because the domestic labor force was in demographic collapse after fifty years of an English razed-earth policy on the island, a policy that began with Henry the VIII's 1542 declaration to bring Ireland under Tudor control. It was also reasoned that settlers would "guard against native resistance and build a society based on Protestantism, English law, and (in contrast to Gaelic pastoralism) settled agriculture" (Mulholland 2002, 3).

his poetry and peppered his poetry with its speech. Before the recent revival of interest in languages in Northern Ireland, Lallans was also used to refer to the language spoken by the descendents of Scottish planters and peasants in Ulster. Today Ullans is used to describe the Scots variant spoken in Ulster. It is a new word, indigenous to neither Scots nor its Ulster variant. According to Nelson McCausland it was created by the Ulster-Scots Language Society in an effort to distinguish between Scots in Scotland and the variant spoken in Ulster: "They [the Ulster-Scots Language Society] were looking for a word to represent Ulster Scots and the magazine that was produced by the language society. They called it Ullans. I think it was an acronym for Ulster language, literature, and native speech. But it was based on the word *lallans*. So it's just a recent word that was created." Other sources credit the Language Society's founder, Ian Adamson, with developing the term (Wikipedia 2005d). The term Ullans was meant to end the confusion over terminology, but it continues today because different boosters use different terms. Nelson McCausland, for example, told me that he prefers to use the term Ulster Scots because Ullans is not native to the language itself.

The 1998 Good Friday Agreement officially recognized Ullans. In the third plank of the subsection titled "Economic and Cultural Issues," found under "Rights, Safeguards, and Equality of Opportunity," the agreement states that "all participants recognise the importance of respect, understanding and tolerance in relation to linguistic diversity, including in Northern Ireland, the Irish language, Ulster-Scots and the languages of the various ethnic communities, all of which are part of the cultural wealth of the island of Ireland" (Multi-party Negotiations 1998). Although the agreement goes on in the next paragraph to specify a detailed program for protecting and encouraging the Irish language, a move not undertaken on behalf of Ulster Scots,[9] proponents of Ulster Scots were pleased with the wording. Indeed, while critics point to this discrepancy as evidence that the agreement does not define Ullans as a language, Ullans boosters claim that the wording does just that (the term "linguistic diversity" can imply a language or a dialect, they argue). They were also pleased because they reckoned (correctly) that official recognition for Ullans would open the heretofore closed doors of granting agencies.

The official recognition the agreement afforded Ullans has given it a healthy institutional base. The Ulster-Scots Agency, organized under the auspices of the North/South Language Body, funds the promotion of Ullans, and the government of Northern Ireland now accepts correspondence

---

[9] The next paragraph of the agreement reads: "In the context of active consideration currently being given to the UK signing the Council of Europe Charter for Regional or Minority Languages, the British Government will in particular in relation to the Irish language, where appropriate and where people so desire it: take resolute action to promote the language" (Multi-party Negotiations 1998). The plank goes on to list six other recommendations for promoting Irish. No recommendations are made for the promotion of Ullans.

in Ulster Scots; it even hired an official Ulster Scots translator (BBC 1999). A search of the Web using either "Ullans" or "Ulster-Scots" as a search term returns hundreds of sites devoted to the language, including encyclopedic entries, discussion boards, and the like. These institutional efforts are complemented by orthographic work on Ullans completed just before the agreement, including James Fenton's Ullans dictionary (1995) and Philip Robinson's book on Ullans grammar and syntax (1997).

The institutional buttress for Ullans has not, however, translated into widespread use of Ullans. The relative obscurity of Ullans, even among Protestant people in the province, has led many commentators to suggest that Ullans is not a language. For their part, linguists generally classify Ullans as a dialect of Scots rather than a distinct language (Kirk 2000; Macafee 1996; Mac Poilin 1999). Mac Poilin argues, for example, that although sixteenth-century Scots and English were distinct languages, the 1603 merger of Scotland and England, and the greater power held by England afterward, eroded the Scots language. The same process occurred regarding the Scots spoken in Ulster. In essence, the Scots language of the sixteenth century is no longer spoken. In light of this history, Mac Poilin sees politics behind recent efforts to codify modern Ulster Scots as a distinct language. As he argues,

> The case for Ulster-Scots being a distinct language, made at a time when the status of Scots itself was insecure, is so bizarre that it is unlikely to have been a linguistic argument. It may reflect, in emblematic cultural terms, an ideological division within unionism between a British political identity (within the UK) and an "Ulster" political identity, the latter finding its most extreme form in a movement for an independent Northern Ireland,[10] or, as its advocates put it, an independent Ulster. (1999, 1)

Michael Billig (1995) rejects the language claims made for Ulster Scots on similar grounds. He remarks that the Scottish themselves tend to view Scots as a dialect. As evidence, he points to a thesis written in Ulster Scots at Glasgow University in the early nineties. The university's administration, he notes, allowed the thesis to be written in Ulster Scots on the grounds that it was a dialect of the official language, English, and thus permissible.

Some linguists, like Robinson (1997), reject this view, arguing that Ullans is a specific language. Robinson has called the dominant linguistic paradigm into question, observing that most of its scholars are outsiders. As he explains: "Linguistic studies making mention of Ulster-Scots have been conducted almost exclusively by academics with an English language specialism and from an English language perspective. Indeed, with very few excep-

---

[10] According to John Coulter (2004), Nelson McCausland, one of Ulster Scots' most prominent boosters, was involved in the Ulster Independence Movement before he joined the UUP. McCausland later switched his party affiliation to the DUP.

tions, these scholars have not been themselves speakers of Ulster-Scots and their consequent 'dialectal' approach to Ulster-Scots may have increased, rather than decreased, its marginalization" (1997, x). A few social scientists and historians have also participated in this debate. The historian Michael Montgomery argues, for example, that Ullans is classified as a dialect not for linguistic reasons but because it has no written history: "In Western Europe spoken languages are routinely disparaged because they lack a standard written form and therefore prestige, and are unjustly dismissed as 'dialects' if not worse on this basis alone" (2002). Nic Craith agrees, noting that "in contemporary times it appears that the status of a language or dialect is largely dependent on the political status of its speakers" (2001, 27).

Although the academic boosters of Ullans hold sound credentials, their work is sometimes disregarded because of their close connections with lay Ulster Scots groups. Michael Montgomery, for example, is president of the Ulster-Scots Language Society, and both he and Philip Robinson figure prominently on the Web page of the Ulster-Scots Agency.

ULSTER'S FIRST INHABITANTS — GAELIC OR CRUTHIN?

Although much about ancient Ireland remains unknown, conventional Irish history holds that the majority of Irish people are descendents of a Gaelic or Celtic peoples who brought agriculture to Ireland during the Iron Age (Howe 2000). In the seventeenth century, Scottish planters and their peasants arrived on the island. Although most scholars believe the Irish and the Scots share a common Celtic origin, the political dynamics of the plantation period lead most historians to categorize Protestants as settlers or colonists (Nairn 1977).

After Irish independence, most Irish historians developed an interpretation of the island's history that was anti-imperialist. Ellis calls this a "nationalist interpretation of history" because it was premised on the idea that "the Irish people had a moral right to fight for their political, economic, social and cultural independence against the imperial ethics of their big neighbor" (1989, 2). In Northern Ireland, Republicans have embraced this view of history. Unionists and Loyalists, by contrast, have struggled to come to terms with their place as settlers (outsiders) within it.

In the 1970s, a few historians began to publish work that rejected the conventional, Nationalist view of Irish history. The most prominent of these scholars were Garrett Fitzgerald (1972) and Connor Cruise O'Brien (1974). Both argued that on the eve of Irish independence, most of the population did not support separation from England. Each in his own way also posited a view of Ulster as distinct from the rest of Ireland. Both scholars have been branded revisionists, and on a few occasions as traitors. Fitzgerald came under particular assault: his father had participated in the 1916 Easter Rising and later became an active member of Sinn Fein, and his mother, although an Ulster Protestant, was both a committed Republican and an Irish-language supporter. Ellis (1989) remarks with some satisfaction that commentators have derided Fitzgerald for "spitting on his mother's grave."

Although this approach failed to gain much traction in the early seventies,[11] Ellis (1989) argues that it prompted Unionist historians to reconsider the history that defined them as settlers and outsiders. Most notable in this regard is Ian Adamson's *Cruthin: The Ancient Kindred* (1974), in which he contends that the Celtic or Gaelic people were not the first inhabitants of Ireland.[12] While traditional Irish history holds that the Celts were the island's first permanent population (neolithic peoples in Ireland are thought to have died out), arriving around 300 BC, Adamson argues that the island was actually settled much earlier by the Cruthin people (also known as the Pretani or Picts), who came from Scotland around 7000 BC. The Cruthin settled on the northern parts of the island and eventually developed a rudimentary monarchy run by a warrior elite. According to Adamson, the Gaels and the Cruthin battled for centuries. One of their most notorious battles was the Cattle Raid of Cooley, which is mythologized in the Ulster Cycle, a collection of poetry and prose. In the grueling battle, the Cruthin warrior Cuchulainn manages to ward off the advancing army of Queen Maeve of Connacht through a combination of strength and cunning. Eventually, however, the Celts succeeded in overtaking the Cruthin people in a series of battles in the sixth century AD, driving many to flee to Scotland and the remainder to submit to Celtic rule. Eleven hundred years later, their descendents returned to Ulster during the plantation.

It is an understatement, at the least, to say that Ian Adamson's depiction of Irish history goes against the grain. Archeologists have widely rejected his theory. Mallory and McNeill argue, for example, that "the Cruthin as a distinct ethnic group are archeologically invisible, that is, there is not a single object or site that an archeologist can declare to be distinctly Cruthin" (1991, 177). Even archeologists who claim the Celtic people never gained a strong foothold in Ireland dismiss Adamson's theory of the Cruthin as fiction (Warner 1999). Historians are equally suspicious, arguing that Cuchulainn is a mythological, not historical figure, and a Celtic one at that. They have derided Adamson's work as "invented history" (Higgins 1999), "reactionary" (Hadden 1995), and "frankly outrageous" (Sluka 1999). Ellis sees sectarian motives behind the *Cruthin* volume. He describes Adamson's theory as "rather like the philosophy of Zionism," remarking that in his account

---

[11] According to Ellis (1989), this approach, which he labels the new anti-Nationalist school, is now gaining popularity and credence.

[12] The terms Celtic and Gaelic are often used interchangeably to refer to the people who arrived in Ireland during the Iron Age. These people are generally though to be a part of a race or group of people, originally from central Europe, who shared cultural traits and spoke Indo-European languages of a common root.

Protestants are "no longer newcomers settling on the lands of the dispossessed natives but a 'chosen people' who had returned to their 'Promised Land' " (1989, 4).

Adamson forcefully rejects the suggestion that his work is sectarian and decries those who use his work to suggest that Protestants have a stronger claim to the island than Catholics because they were "here first." He suggests that most people in Ulster can trace their heritage back to the Cruthin rather than Celtic people, meaning that the province's history offers "the hope of uniting the Ulster people at last" (1991, 104). Adamson does not, however, entirely disassociate himself from the political ramifications of his work. Indeed, he acknowledges that his work represents an attempt to "recover" history from Republicanism. As he explained in *Cruthin*:

> So total has become the Gaelic domination in language and culture that even in these modern times Gaelic Ireland is synonymous with Irish Nationalism, and the Gaelic tongue is unequivocally known as Irish. That the Irish Gaelic suffered under late English domination is but one side of the coin which carries on its reverse the long cruel extermination of the population and culture of the ancient kindred of the Ulster people. (as quoted in Higgins 1999, 189)

A Revanchist Take on Culture

Ullans may indeed be a distinct language rather than a dialect, and there may well have been an ancient people in Ulster called the Cruthin. As a geographer cum international studies scholar, I leave the professional assessment of these theories to the linguists and archeologists, respectively. It is clear, however, that both Ullans and the Cruthin concept are used to bolster a revanchist view of Loyalist identity. This identity is revanchist because it seeks to establish Ulster as a definitively Protestant place in a way that voids, negates, and otherwise delegitimizes an Irish/Catholic place in the province.

Although Ullans and the Cruthin are disparate topics, they are discursively a joint endeavor. Indeed, the connection between them mirrors the structural connections between the Ulster Scots language and history boosters. Ian Adamson, the author of *Cruthin*, was also the founding chair of the Ulster-Scots Language Society, and he currently serves on the board of the Ulster-Scots Agency, which promotes both linguistic and historical elements of Ulster Scots culture. Indeed, it is often difficult to distinguish between the organizations devoted to the promotion of Ulster Scots culture. They share members, board directors, and even office space.

Not surprisingly, given the interconnections of these organizations and thus their mandates, Ullans and the Cruthin thesis are linked in the minds of many Loyalists. When I interviewed Kenny McClinton, for example,

I asked him what he thought about the books that had been written about Loyalist paramilitaries. I began by asking if he'd read one of the oldest and most widely read books, Steve Bruce's *The Red Hand* (1992). Kenny responded by telling me about Ian Adamson's book.

> I'll be quite honest and tell you I haven't read it. But I know of it, *The Red Hand*. But I am more familiar with the works of Ian Adamson, and the Ulster identity, and the Cruthin, which means the ancient ones, the indigenous people of this island. And we were invaded by the Gaels about 700 BC, driven up to the north part of the island. And [the Cruthin] had a great relationship with the Scottish people in what they called the kingdom of Dalaradia. And they treated the Irish Sea in those days as a great pond rather than a sea, and they went back and forward. And archeologists agree that the graves, and the dolmites, and the cultures, and much of the Ulster Scots, or what you guys [Americans] would call the Ulster Scots Irish language and things like that are all commensurate with this theory.

The focus on Ullans and the Cruthin is central to Loyalist cultural work because it provides a geographic basis for continued union with Great Britain. This geographic basis—legitimized academically—plays out in different and sometimes contradictory ways. Ullans boosters, for example, tend to emphasize Ulster's links with Scotland. In my interview with Nelson McCausland, he prefaced our discussion of Ullans by recalling the primacy of this connection:

> There is an Ulster Scots tradition here that goes back to the plantation, and beyond, because the connections between Ulster and Scotland have been a constant factor throughout history. It's been observed that there's more of a connection between Ulster and Scotland than is between Ulster and the rest of Ireland, in fact. Geographically, historically, the sea was never a barrier. The sea between Ulster and Scotland was a bridge. It took days to get from Belfast to Dublin. You could get across to Scotland and back in a day. And they'd go backward and forward during the day.

The durability of Ulster's east–west connection to Scotland, McCausland concluded, frames the current revival of Ullans today.

> So it's a tradition [the east–west connection] and has expressed itself in many ways. In more recent times, it was in 1992 that the Ulster-Scots Language Society was established. The founding members were a small group of native speakers and also people who had been members of the Scots Language Society.

McCausland also argues that Ulster's relatively stronger east–west linkages are mirrored in the greater influence of Scots (rather than Irish) on the English spoken in the province. As McCausland explained in an interview he gave to writer Sean Fleming:

We have three language traditions—Ulster Scots, Gaelic and Ulster English. . . . Both Gaelic and Scots have influenced Ulster English. In fact if you look at the *Concise Ulster Dictionary* it is clear for obvious reasons that the influence of Ulster Scots on Ulster English was greater than Gaelic because they are sister languages. (Fleming 2004)

Boosters of the Cruthin concept tend to emphasize Protestant connections to Ulster rather than Scotland. Indeed, although the Cruthin of Adamson's theory first came from Scotland, their arrival in Ireland, and Ulster in particular, is emphasized because it occurred before that of the Celts. It is this history that allows Loyalists today to redefine Cuchulainn as *not* Irish. A UDA mural in East Belfast, for example, commemorates Cuchulainn as "an ancient defender of Ulster from *Irish* attacks over *2000* years ago" (see fig. 8) and depicts him rising from a British flag with a Loyalist paramilitary man standing at the ready in the foreground. McAuley (1991) argues that advocates for Ulster independence within the UDA embraced Cuchulainn to legitimate their claims historically. Although Cuchulainn has failed, as McAuley (1991) notes, to take hold as a symbolic figure for independence, he has become a symbol of Loyalist roots in Ulster, especially in the wake of the 1994 cease-fires (Hadden 1995).

Fig. 8. UDA mural commemorating Cuchulainn.

The geographic underpinning of both of these arguments is problematic: each represents an attempt to define Ulster as more authentically Protestant than Catholic, albeit in different ways. In the case of McCausland's comments on Ullans, for example, Ulster's connections to Scotland are given primacy over its links to the rest of Ireland. Although Ullans boosters are well within their rights to identify and even celebrate the connections between Scotland and Ireland, they often do so in ways that suggest almost no formative role for the rest of the island. In McCausland's account, for example, the sea between Ulster and Ireland is no barrier, while the low hills between Ulster and the rest of the island are all but insurmountable. His depiction may hold true for parts of coastal Ulster, where the divide is only nine miles, but it is hardly applicable for interior and western portions of the province. Likewise, he depicts Irish as having negligible impact on the English spoken in Ulster, even though most linguists disagree. These omissions are glaring but not surprising, given that revanchist identity politics are characterized by attempts to erase the presence of others.

In the case of the Cruthin theory, Ulster is proffered not only as a homeland for the Protestant people but as a place invaded by Irish (read Catholic) intruders. In effect, the Cruthin story represents a flip on the traditional Nationalist view of Ulster history, which depicts Protestants as invaders and glosses over the powerlessness of Scottish peasants in the plantation system. Whereas Loyalists have been correct to criticize the narrowness of Republican discourses that skim over the oppression meted out to portions of the Protestant population during and after the plantation period,[13] the Cruthin and Cuchulainn discourses represent little more than a crude switch on the invader discourse (Howe 2000). In my interview with Kenny McClinton, he was blunt in describing what he saw as the political implications of the Cruthin theory: "We see ourselves as the indigenous people of this island. And every argument that Sinn Fein and IRA would give to the British government—give us back our land—we would say that same thing to them: give us back our land." This sort of discourse is a problem, especially in the hands of paramilitaries, because it has been used to justify a continuation of the fighting.

Ironically, even though the notions of space that underpin Loyalist deployments of Ullans and the Cruthin concept are particularist *and* essentialist, their boosters often go to great pains to present their work as pluralist. In my interview with Nelson McCausland, for example, he described Ulster as a mix of cultures:

Ulster Scots culture is one element in what Ulster is. Cultural diversity here is Scottish, English, and Irish all mixed together. And the illustration I used on

---

[13] Loyalists often point out, for example, that the British applied its penal laws to Presbyterians as well.

the day when we launched this organization, and I've used it a thousand times since then is, if you look at traffic, below the Cathedral Hill. At the traffic lights, when you are sitting there, you look up and there are three streets that meet at one point—Scots Street, English Street, and Irish Street. They are the only three streets that there are no traffic lights. And that's a perfect picture. There's Ulster sitting at the traffic lights, and three streets all leading here.

Cultural boosters even adopt a postmodernist script on identity, emphasizing the hybridity and fluidity of identity. As McCausland told me:

> We're all mongrels. We're a thousand and one different things. . . . Identity is multiple and multilayered. I have a full range of identities. And they're not coterminous.

Despite McCausland's claims to mixing and multiplicity, a conversation he recounted for me about his response to being labeled Irish indicates that his claims to pluralism are, at least on a personal level, largely for show. As the following excerpts from our interview demonstrate, McCausland denies any connections between the British/Protestant and Irish/Celtic cultures, even going to great lengths to expunge any Celtic presence from his personal genealogy:

> These folks, last week at the Community Arts Centre, they were telling me I was Irish, and I was saying I'm not. And, they say, "but everybody who's in Scotland, Wales and Ireland is Celtic. You just are, that's it." I said, "I'm not. How am I Celtic? Do I speak a Celtic language? No, I don't. Do I identify with Celtic culture? No, I don't."

Later in our interview McCausland recalled a similar conversation he had on the matter with a member of the Ulster Project, who had also told McCausland he was Irish:

> He always makes a point when we're up speaking [at conferences and public gatherings] to say, "there's Nelson, and Nelson's background is the O'Calons, who are Celts." . . . Well, I got up and said, "I didn't know until very recently—a professor at the University of Dublin told me—that the O'Calons were actually Anglo-Normans. They're not Celts at all!" . . . You could see the blood draining from his face. . . . Why do people get hung up on this thing that we're ethnically Celtic? I just find that terribly old-fashioned, sad, and racist.

McCausland is well within his rights to define his identity in any way he sees fit. And he is equally justified in rejecting outsiders' attempts to set that identity for him. However, his response—to verify (in genealogical terms) that he has no Celtic or Irish heritage—completely contradicts the hybrid approach to identity he claims to embrace.

It is not difficult to imagine that McCausland's personal aversion to Irishness could color his work at the Heritage Council or, more importantly, on the city council. Indeed, McCausland has often been accused of being anti-Irish for his efforts (on and off the council) to deny city funds for Irishthemed events. In 2000, before he became a member of the city council, for example, McCausland was accused of successfully blocking council funding for a parade organized by the Nationalist St. Patrick's Day Carnival Committee. That year, McCausland and Lee Reynolds applied for funding under the name of the St. Patrick's Day Heritage Association. Given the competing claims for funding, the council voted to forgo giving funds to either group. Shortly after the council's announcement, however, McCausland and Reynolds abruptly canceled their plans to hold a parade. The Republican newspaper *An Phoblacht* was harsh in its assessment of the move. As an editorial stated at the time:

> At the time of December's vote, applications for funding had been received from the St Patrick's Day Carnival Committee, organizers of the previous year's events, and the unionist St Patrick's Day Heritage Association, which was fronted by Nelson McCausland and Lee Reynolds. This group was seen as a red herring whose only aim was to block the Carnival Committee from getting funding . . . the Unionist St. Patrick's Day Heritage Association are saying that they will not now be holding a parade. This announcement highlights what nationalist have known all along, that the whole strategy of the Heritage Association has been to stop any St Patrick's Day Parade from taking place at all. (*An Phoblacht* 2000)

In 2002, McCausland also ran afoul of Nationalists when he, along with fellow Unionists on the city council, refused to fund the Celtic Film Festival, which had applied to the council's arts funding body. The move inspired derision in the local Nationalist/Republican press:

> This time he has forced the City Council's Arts committee to refuse funding for the Celtic Film Festival on the grounds that . . . well, no-one knows for sure. He admitted that the application to stage this prestigious, international film festival fulfilled all the proper criteria and that it would attract over six hundred visitors to the city at a time when tourism is at an all-time low, but still he insisted that it be denied any kind of civic support because, well nobody knows for sure because Councillor McCausland was unable to explain his objections . . . maybe it is because he is, dare I say it again—anti-Irish. (Ó Caireal-láin 2002)

When the festival applied for funding in 2005, it was also rejected. According to one angry letter writer, McCausland is purported to have argued at the hearings on the matter that the festival should not be funded because Northern Ireland is "not a Celtic country." As the writer stated:

When an application was made to Belfast City Council to fund the Prestigious Celtic Film Festival, DUP Councillor McCausland turned the request down because "this is not a Celtic country." What a wit! The mono-cultural Nelson is well named after the one-eyed British Admiral and his bigoted incoherence reminds us of another British general who, on being called "Irish," retorted: "Being born in a stable does not make one a horse." (Marksman 2005)

Although these criticisms are easy to write off because they come from Republicans, some Loyalists have also ascribed sectarian motives to those doing revanchist cultural work.

Political Loyalists on the Revanchist Cultural Repertoire

While some Loyalists in the paramilitary structure, especially elements within the UDA, actively agree with and support the revanchist cultural work I've described, some Loyalists are adamantly opposed to it or uncomfortable with it. Most of these critics are in the UVF/PUP structure. Many of the paramilitaries I spoke with, however, wished to remain anonymous on this issue. To protect those requesting anonymity, I do not quote anyone in this section by name.

Most progressive Loyalists focused their criticism of Loyalist cultural work around Ullans rather than the Cruthin theory. This is not surprising since the Cruthin theory has received less public attention than Ullans. In their comments, however, most referred to the larger body of cultural work going on in conjunction with Ullans.

Most of the Loyalists I interviewed do not believe that Ullans is a language. Indeed, the notion was a common refrain. As one ex-prisoner bluntly told me:

Well, when I was in prison, I learned the Irish language. There is no such a thing as Ulster Scots.

Another ex-prisoner concurred:

I don't regard it as another language. . . . Really, Ulster Scots is only a dialect. I probably speak it a bit because I use some words that wouldn't commonly be used in the standard English.

Another prominent person in Loyalist paramilitary circles told me:

I don't believe it's a language, it's a dialect . . . you know, [to] most of us, when Ulster Scots is reduced to writing, it looks ridiculous.

When I asked these Loyalists paramilitaries what they thought of recent efforts to boost Ullans, most were suspicious, albeit to varying degrees. One Loyalist paramilitary told me, "Ulster Scots is a sectarian thing." When I asked him to explain why, he replied that its proponents were mostly anti-agreement Loyalists. As he put it:

> In the Good Friday Agreement, there was a section on cultural memory and all this here. And obviously, Republicans had their agenda for the Irish language. To a counter to that there, anti-agreement forces seen that as a means for [supporting] Ulster Scots. But there is no Ulster Scots language. There is an Ulster Scots dialect. There's no Ulster Scots culture.

Another paramilitary also saw politics behind the revival of Ullans.

> I think its one of those cases where "they've got Gaelic so we'll have to manufacture a language so we'll have one of our own."

Some paramilitaries were less harsh in their assessment of Ullans, although they worried that it could divide rather than unite Loyalists. As one explained:

> I think it has to be explored, I think it has to get brought in, but at the same time I'm concerned that they are isolating other Protestants, you know, if you want to play on this, you must be Ulster Scots. They're forgetting about the Huguenots, they're forgetting about the Church of Ireland, they're forgetting about the Anglo Protestants. You know, it's all based around Ulster Scots.

Another ex-prisoner suggested that efforts to boost Ullans were legitimate but largely irrelevant:

> I think there's some people [who are] very genuine about the sense that there has been this loss of the Ulster Scots culture, song, dance, language, or phrase. And that's legitimate . . . [but] it's confusion, it's a side show. It's not the cause of the problem nor the solution.

While these paramilitaries were largely critical of the Ullans movement, many argued that the overt Republicanism of the Irish-language movement created the space for it to emerge in the first place. As one paramilitary explained to me:

> It started in '69 when the Troubles started again. Republicans used the Irish language as a tool, a political tool. They want their cultural rights. And Protestants seen that Irish Gaelic became a Republican thing. Irish games became a Republican thing. Which means that Protestants shied away. I often say that the Republicans hijacked the Irish language. They've hijacked the Irish culture.

As a political tool. Which is why there is such an animosity by Protestants toward the Irish language.

This particular paramilitary member argued that the best response for Protestants and Loyalists would be to reclaim the Irish language and Irish identity for Protestants.

> So, what people have done is create a language. Try to create a culture to equalize the Republicans. I don't believe in that. I believe I'm Irish. I learn Irish Gaelic, Irish dancing, and whatever.

This viewpoint is in line with unionist commentator John Coulter, who has made a similar argument. Coulter, who has, as I mentioned in the beginning of this chapter, derided Ulster Scots as nothing more than a Ballymena accent, argues that Protestants need to reclaim aspects of Irish culture because they belong to Protestants as much as Catholics:

> But what Protestants need to do practically is to form their own version of the Gaelic League and reclaim the Irish language back from republicans. They should forget about making fools of themselves by trying to repackage the Ulster Scots Ballymena accent. Instead, Protestantism should concentrate on retaking those elements of culture, such as the Irish language and St Patricks Day, which republicanism has paraded as part of Irish nationalism's supposedly unique ethnic identity. (2004)

Progressive Loyalists' critiques of Ullans are noteworthy and their self-definition nothing short of remarkable, but their reticence to be quoted on the matter indicates a troubling trend—the growing prominence of revanchism within Loyalist circles. Indeed, it is ironic that paramilitary members are uneasy speaking their mind about Ullans and doing so on the record. However, the following is exactly how one of my interview subjects prefaced his desire for anonymity: "Well, that's one thing I wouldn't like to be quoted on, because you know, I could bring a lot of grief on myself for saying it, but I'm quite content to live with English, Carolyn. You know, I don't see the need to talk in Ulster Scots." This particular paramilitary, who would speak to me on record about issues I considered far more delicate, was expressing a real concern. Indeed, revanchist discourse is increasingly attractive to Loyalists who believe the Belfast Agreement has delivered more to Republicans than to Loyalists. This perception may be unfair, but until it is addressed, revanchism will be at a distinct advantage within the Loyalist fold.

Developing Progressive Loyalist Culture

While progressive Loyalists are generally focused on economic issues, they are acutely aware that Loyalists need cultural referents for the post-peace era. Their work to date has, however, been minimal, especially when compared with their economic record. Still, they are beginning to make important strides in this regard. Graham and Shirlow (2002) point, for example, to the UVF's appropriation of the battle of the Somme in their efforts to build a Protestant identity.

Traditionally, Unionist governments have taken a muted approach to the commemoration of the Somme. As Graham and Shirlow note, successive Stormont governments used the symbol sparingly: "like much else in Protestant history, it was largely buried by the Stormont state" (2002, 889). By contrast, the UVF's commemoration of the battle of the Somme, in new murals across the province, has been "highly visible."

In many ways the Loyalist connection to the Somme was accidental. In 1913 Sir Edward Carson organized a private militia called the Ulster Volunteer Force. The group, as many as 100,000 strong, had signed Carson's Ulster Covenant and promised to fight home rule.[14] Mounting tensions in Ulster were interrupted, however, by British involvement in World War I. The British war minister, Lord Herbert Kitchener, issued a call for volunteers, purportedly making a special plea for "Ulster Volunteers" (Taylor 1999b). Thousands of Protestants, many in Carson's UVF, heeded the call and were organized into the Thirty-sixth Ulster Division. On 1 July 1916, the division was deployed to the front lines in northern France, along the River Somme. The battle that ensued was one of the war's bloodiest. The British army lost almost 20,000 soldiers during the first day of fighting. Although the Thirty-sixth Ulster Division was one of few divisions to make progress in the early days of the battle, it incurred heavy losses as the fighting wore on: over 5,000 of its men were killed. The number was astronomical for a place as small as Northern Ireland. Taylor (1999b) notes that only 70 men from the 700-strong West Belfast Battalion of the division made it home alive.

Graham and Shirlow (2002) argue that the UVF's commemoration of the Somme plays two roles that can at times be difficult to reconcile. First, embracing the Somme affords the UVF legitimacy: by connecting itself to the Thirty-sixth Ulster Division, the modern-day UVF avails itself of a wealth of historical symbols.[15] That these symbols are from the recent past, rather

---

[14] The Ulster Covenant was written in response to a home rule bill introduced in the British Parliament in April 1912. The document, which was widely publicized across the province, asserted the necessity of direct rule. Carson and fellow Unionist James Craig were able to collect the signatures of over 230,000 men in support of the document. A "sister" declaration was signed by a roughly equal number of women.

[15] Graham and Shirlow (2002) state that the modern UVF, formed in 1966, has no direct linkage with the Thirty-sixth Ulster Division that fought at the Somme in 1916.

than the distant past of the Battle of the Boyne or the Siege of Derry, makes them a more effective counterweight to the IRA's historical repertoire, which embraces the period's other key event, the Easter Rising.

Second, appropriating the Somme is used to establish the centrality of a working-class ethos to Loyalist identity. Indeed, the UVF murals commemorate the mostly working-class men who died by the thousands on the battlefields of northern France, not the British or Stormont governments that sent these soldiers to certain death. This focus on the war dead, Graham and Shirlow argue, allows the UVF to represent the betrayal of Loyalists by the Unionist elite:

> Photographs of the dead are still to be found on mantelpieces and in family albums. The Somme is remembered by the protestant working classes who can grasp it to say "it is ours" ("it is making protestant history just like the republicans do"). It symbolizes sacrifice and loyalty but also the questioning of loyalty and unionism, a renegotiation forced upon the working-class protestant people through their palpable sense of betrayal. (2002, 898)

In this sense, the Somme is not a proxy for anti-nationalism or anti-Republicanism but for anti-Unionism. As Graham and Shirlow succinctly state, "after decades of use and abuse by their own politicians, working class Protestants see themselves as 'puppets no more' " (2002, 886).

The UVF has also commissioned other murals that have historical themes, although these murals do not usually fit into a theme package in the way that the Somme murals do. One mural, on the upper Shankill, for example, depicts the Ulster heritage of U.S. president James Buchanan (see fig. 9). The mural quotes Buchanan as saying "my Ulster blood is my most priceless heritage." The mural is significant because it allows Ulster's Protestants to lay claim to America in the way that Republicans routinely do. While Buchanan is a relatively little known U.S. president (in the United States or Northern Ireland), the mural is also noteworthy because it bears no mention of Buchanan's religious background.

It is tempting to see these sorts of murals as places where Catholics and Protestants can come together. Yet all of these murals are, by virtue of their location or message, distinctly Protestant. The commemoration of the Ulster roots of James Buchanan, who was president from 1857 to 1861, is a clear reference to the largely Protestant Ulster-Scots migrants of the eighteenth century. (Most Irish Catholics migrated to America in the mid-nineteenth century, contemporaneous with Buchanan's presidency.) Although it is natural to hope that Protestants and Catholics can find a body of symbols that will eventually bring them together, it cannot happen until each group develops notions of their "side" that allow people to feel confident in their own sense of self and community, and in ways that do not rest on an antagonistic view of the other. Only then can new symbols aimed at

Fig. 9. UVF mural celebrating links between Ulster and the United States.

crossing the religious divide be regarded as nonthreatening. In this regard, the UVF's murals represent an attempt to fill in the gaps of Protestant identity, and to do so in ways that are neither sectarian nor otherwise regressive in nature.

Unfortunately, the UVF's cultural repertoire is not as developed as that of their revanchist competitors. Thus, while progressive Loyalists are to be lauded for their critiques of revanchist cultural work and for their own attempts to provide alternatives, their efforts do not yet offer a cohesive or effective alternative to the revanchist project. As I show in the next chapter, much of the money that has flowed into Northern Ireland in the post-peace environment has inadvertently helped the revanchist cultural project, and in so doing exacerbated sectarian tensions.

5   Loyalism and the Voluntary Sector

For many people, peace agreements are about endings. Combatants put down their guns, the fighting stops, and things go back to the way they used to be. After a protracted conflict, however, things rarely return to the way they were. In Northern Ireland the city center was rebuilt, but with glitzy shops and high-end pubs instead of family businesses and low-cost eateries. Investment was enticed back to the province, but it concentrated around services instead of manufacturing. Combatants agreed to put down their guns, but those they had murdered did not return from the grave. More often than not, peace agreements are about beginnings, about creating a new normal out of what often feels like very thin air.

One of the new dynamics that emerges in societies coming out of war is the growth and influence of nongovernmental organizations (NGOs). In Northern Ireland, NGOs are usually described as belonging to the voluntary sector (Cochrane and Dunn 1999). The term "voluntary" is used because NGOs usually perform work that benefits the public and is not for profit (National Council for Voluntary Organizations 2005). In peaceful societies, voluntary-sector organizations engage in a wide range of activities, including charity work, advocacy, and issue-based education. In conflict zones, the voluntary sector usually focuses on establishing or maintaining peace. Voluntary work in post-conflict zones includes counseling victims, helping ex-combatants reintegrate into society, and encouraging dialogue between divided communities.

In this chapter I review the rise of the voluntary sector in Northern Ireland, with a particular focus on how it affects Loyalism. I begin by detailing the structure of the voluntary sector in Northern Ireland and tracking the funding that supports it. I then examine two problems that have emerged as a result of the sector's growth in Northern Ireland.

The first problem is the entrenchment of the voluntary sector in Loyalist enclaves.[1] As I note in chapter 3, Loyalist estates have been in a state of decline since the mid-1980s. The emergence of the voluntary sector has been a welcome addition in these areas, providing training, skills, and even employment for enterprising Loyalists. The voluntary sector was never designed to be permanent, however. Granting agencies provide funding for specific, time-limited projects intended to develop local social/economic capacities. As a need is met, granting agencies shift their funding elsewhere, and service providers close up shop or move. In Belfast, however, the voluntary sector has not gradually faded away but rather has morphed into a full-fledged peace industry. Yet it is highly dependent on grants for survival and so is not a viable source of stable employment (for ex-prisoners) or urban renewal (for Loyalist neighborhoods).

The second problem I examine is the potential for peace funding to contribute to sectarianism. Criticism of this sort usually falls into two categories. Some critics contend that grant money has made its way into the hands of paramilitaries, who have used it not only for personal enrichment but for paramilitary operations, which are sectarian in nature. Others focus on the nature of projects funded by the European Union. These critics argue that single-identity projects in particular do little more than create "better bigots" (Langhammer 2003).[2] Groups with sectarian motives use EU money to articulate their own views and to promote them widely. Although the charge that peace work contributes to sectarianism is difficult to prove, the argument is gaining traction (McCandless 2003; Langhammer 2003, 2004; Kelly 2005).

Funding Peace Work

The biggest single source of funding for peace work in Northern Ireland is the European Union. To date there have been two distinct funding lines from the EU. The first was the Special Support Programme for Peace and Reconciliation in Northern Ireland and the Border Counties of Ireland, more commonly known as PEACE I (European Communities 1998). The initiative received 72 percent of its funding from EU bodies. The remainder came from the British and Irish governments and the private sector. This

---

[1] Although I do not discuss it here, the voluntary sector has also become entrenched in nationalist communities. Thus many of the dynamics in this chapter apply to nationalist communities, albeit only broadly, because community work functions quite differently in the two communities.

[2] Single-identity projects are usually schemes designed to help a community develop its identity. Such projects may include organizing cultural festivals, producing educational booklets, and fostering language awareness. Some single-identity projects contain cross-community components, including provisions for sharing information with partner groups from the other community.

funding track, which coincided with the 1994 cease-fires, covered a five-year period, from 1995 to 1999. Approximately €500 million were distributed through the program (BBC 2005e).

The second funding line was the EU Programme for Peace and Reconciliation in Northern Ireland and the Border Region of Ireland (Directorate-General of Regional Policy 2005). This program, known as PEACE II, was initiated in 2000 for a five-year period. In June 2005 the commissioner for regional policy at the EU, Danuta Hubner, announced a two-year extension of the program and £97 million more in funding (BBC 2005e; RTE News 2005). Like PEACE I, the majority of its funds (75 percent) are public, coming from different EU bodies.

PEACE I and II monies have been distributed through one of three bodies: government agencies, intermediary funding bodies (IFBs), and local partnerships (Directorate-General of Regional Policy 2000). In Northern Ireland, local partnerships are known as district partnerships; in the Republic they are called county council task forces (Directorate-General of Regional Policy 2000, 38). For PEACE II, the Special EU Programmes Body was also chosen to distribute a limited amount of funds.

Although PEACE I and PEACE II have the same overall goal—to foster a lasting peace in Northern Ireland—the programs were designed with different emphases and structures. PEACE I focused on social inclusion, with 60 percent of its funding targeted to the issue alone (Directorate-General of Regional Policy 1999). The program was also designed with a bottom-up approach. IFBs and local partnerships (rather than the two governments) were targeted to distribute as much of the funds as possible.[3] These groups, in turn, distributed their funds to even smaller groups to implement and deliver actual services. Proteus and the Northern Ireland Voluntary Trust are examples of IFBs,[4] while organizations such as EPIC and LINC are typical of the groups that receive grants from them.

In contrast to its predecessor, PEACE II has funded economic development programs, such as training and job creation. PEACE II has also tended to fund IFBs that are large in size and scope or that support programs that are (Henry 2003). Successful applicants for PEACE II funds must demonstrate how their work will specifically contribute to peace, a requirement that was not a part of PEACE I protocols. The two programs are quite different, as Shaun Henry, the director of PEACE II in Northern Ireland, notes: "PEACE II is not a continuation of PEACE I. In many ways the flamboyant, avant-garde PEACE I parent has, much to its surprise, spawned a rather more sensible and pedestrian off-spring—PEACE II. In retrospect perhaps

---

[3] Records indicate that approximately 60 percent of the program's funds were distributed in this way (Directorate-General of Regional Policy 1999, 18).

[4] In 2002 the Northern Ireland Voluntary Trust changed its name to the Community Foundation for Northern Ireland (Community Foundation for Northern Ireland 2005).

more attention could have been given at the naming ceremony, to help prevent confusion in the public's mind between parent and child. This is definitely not the case of 'like father, like son' " (2003, 10).

In 2006 the EU announced it would launch a PEACE III funding track beginning in 2007 and running through 2013. In the run-up to the announcement there was extensive lobbying to secure more funding. Those lobbying for a new tranche included political parties, labor groups, and voluntary-sector organizations. When Danuta Hubner announced a two-year extension for PEACE II, for example, Sinn Fein responded by asking for a PEACE III track and even suggesting a timeline—from 2007 through 2013 (Sinn Fein 2005a). The UUP offered a similar response, welcoming the extension but indicating that it was already in negotiations to procure a third line of funding (Ulster Unionist Party 2005). The Community Workers Cooperative (CWC) and the Northern Ireland Council for Voluntary Action (NICVA) also called for a PEACE III line. In a joint report they argued that without a third line of funding, "much good work developed since 1994 will be lost" (2004, 10).

Other groups extended their support, albeit with qualification. At a press conference after Hubner's announcement, for example, DUP member Jim Allister (an MEP, or member of European Parliament) complained that Nationalists had received more PEACE I and II monies than Unionists had. And he promised to withhold support for a PEACE III funding line unless the disparity was redressed during the extension period. Without change, he warned, "I will have no interest in seeking a PEACE III because I would have no interest in perpetuating inequality." He challenged Protestants, however, to apply for funding, stating that "it's important that unionist do not lose out by default" (Democratic Unionist Party 2005).

As Allister's comments indicate, the infusion of peace monies into Northern Ireland has had it share of controversies. It is impossible to cover all of them here, let alone proffer any comprehensive analysis of the overall success of the PEACE I and PEACE II programs. Even if the peace process were complete, which it is not, such an analysis would not easily fit into the space afforded a single chapter of a book. My analysis is therefore confined to criticisms relevant to the topic of this book—Loyalist paramilitaries. I begin by examining the economic role that peace work has come to fill in Loyalist neighborhoods.

The Business of Peace Work

DEPENDENCY

While both PEACE I and PEACE II were designed to spur economic development (albeit to different degrees), they were never intended to turn peace-related NGOs into permanent businesses. Some of the criticism leveled at both programs indicates, however, that this is exactly what has happened. Indeed, a variety of critics have taken both programs to task for their failure to offer core funding for applicant groups. Core funding usually covers expenses such as salaries and operating costs (for example, rent and office supplies). Although international NGOs and national charities are large enough that they can pay these costs without the help of PEACE I or II, local grassroots groups are not. That locally based NGOs are requesting core funding suggests that they are becoming established service providers rather than temporary peace outfits and are lobbying for structural changes to make it happen.

Groups on both sides of the divide have launched such complaints. The Loyalist group Families Acting for Innocent Relatives (FAIR), for example, argues on its Web page that the PEACE II guidelines, in particular, favor outsiders and larger groups:

> Core funding is vital to the sector if we are to attract and retain profession educated and able staff. . . . The greatest problem facing the area of funding is the encroachment of service providers, professional businesses and consultants. Their ability to develop a business type plan for the work due to the deployment of a particular model or programme devised not by but imposed on victims gives them a natural advantage in the area of applying for funding. (Frazer 2005)

Sinn Fein has also complained that PEACE II does not adequately address the issues of core funding. Although the party does not receive funds from the PEACE I and II programs (political parties are ineligible for peace funds), the voluntary sector is strong in the working-class communities that comprise its electoral base:

> The support for core organisational costs, and not just the project costs, should be provided for initiatives which do not receive core funding from elsewhere. This is to ensure that the activities of the projects are placed within a context of development and not isolated as single unsustainable projects. (Sinn Fein 2005b)

The director of PEACE II, Shaun Henry, acknowledged such critiques in an article he wrote for *Scope*, a magazine that covers the voluntary sector:

> There has been much comment on how the Peace Programme has failed to support the core costs of community and voluntary sector. Peace II was never intended to provide core funding, important as it is. The debate on core funding, which should and must take place, is essentially a debate for another arena. The issues of sustainability of the sector require a more complex response than that which the Peace II Programme alone can provide. (Henry 2003, 10)

Although Henry is correct that neither PEACE I nor PEACE II was designed to be a core-funding source for community groups, both the structure of the peace agreement and the broad funding guidelines issued by the PEACE I program in particular have encouraged the participation of groups that cannot easily raise their own funding.

As I mention in the first chapter, low-intensity conflicts often end in a draw, with no clear winner. The peace accords that are struck during such conflicts tend, therefore, to contain broad concessions to armed parties. This was certainly the case in Northern Ireland, where paramilitaries were able to win the release of most of their political prisoners as well as important flexibilities on the issue of decommissioning. In short, the mechanics of the agreement means that paramilitaries have been active participants in the peace process rather than bystanders watching events unfold from the sidelines, or in prison.

The most obvious example can be found in the fact that many voluntary-sector groups formed since 1994 are headed by ex-prisoners. Whatever one thinks of the Belfast Agreement, and there are many in Northern Ireland who think it was an undeserved bonanza for the paramilitaries, it is clear that the most important challenge today is to ensure that combatants have something to turn to besides continued paramilitarism or criminality. Membership in a paramilitary often combines equal parts job, neighborhood watch, and status symbol. If members are to leave this life behind, they must have other options for obtaining livelihood and status (see Gomes Porto and Parsons 2003; Herbert 1996). Indeed, after the 1998 agreement, the EU identified ex-prisoners as a specific target group for social inclusion programs, putting them on par with victims. In a midterm report on the program, issued a few months after the agreement was signed, it observed:

> The attainment of a peaceful and stable society depends, in part, on helping victims cope with bereavement and trauma as well as on addressing the exclusion and alienation which is suffered by former politically motivated prisoners and their families. (European Communities 1998, 16)

The report also quoted Billy Mitchell, in his capacity as manager of LINC, on the need to work with the paramilitaries in the transformation to peace:

> If we're going to salvage anything out of this Peace Process it's the paramilitaries we have to work with . . . and we have to stick at it to keep building confidence, building trust. (As quoted in European Communities 1998, 16)

The IFBs and local partnerships for PEACE I heeded the signals. Proteus, an IFB, allocated 7 percent of its PEACE I funding to prisoner groups. The percentage was larger than the funds reserved for youth-related projects (4 percent) and roughly equivalent to its allocation (8 percent) for women's projects (Proteus 2001).

The preponderance of ex-prisoners employed in the voluntary sector is also related to the fact that they face significant barriers when attempting to move into good jobs in the private sector. As I show in chapter 2, many ex-prisoners on the Loyalist side of the conflict obtained college degrees while in prison, and often in marketable subjects like computer science and math, which have little to do with the nature of their work in the voluntary sector. Martin Snodden, for example, whom I describe in chapter 1, received a dual degree in math and computer science. His voluntary-sector work, however, is psychological in nature. Should Martin choose to apply for work outside of the sector, he is likely to face substantial barriers. Applicants for most jobs have to respond to questions about previous felonies, and answering these questions honestly is usually enough to ruin a person's job chances. The options are even bleaker for ex-prisoners in the voluntary sector who do not have college degrees. Indeed, although ex-prisoners cum community workers obtain a plethora of marketable skills, including grant writing, budget assessment, and conflict mediation, their chances are even slimmer than Martin's because their criminal backgrounds are compounded by a lack of "proper" qualifications.

The local roots of most voluntary-sector groups working in Northern Ireland also explain the sector's propensity for self-entrenchment. Both PEACE I and II were designed to funnel substantial funds through locally based IFBs and local partnerships. These groups, in turn, made it a point to fund even smaller local groups for the delivery of services. The logic behind this emphasis was that the peace process would have a greater chance of success if local people and groups were involved in the process (European Communities 1998). Indeed, the literature abounds with critiques of international NGOs as service delivery agents in post-peace environments (Hulme and Edwards 1997; Mertus 2000). Local NGOs, however, do not have the same incentives as international NGOs to close up shop once a particular service has been delivered or is no longer necessary. Whereas international NGOs are run by boards of directors who can make decisions about the distribution of resources and people from afar, local NGOs are run by people in and of the neighborhoods they serve. Any decision to close up shop is intensely personal and can feel counterintuitive after years spent building an organization. In short, local NGOs are more likely to reorient services to new funding priorities than to close down. Their efforts at lobbying for more core-funding provisions from grant providers are a testament to its reality.

The structural constraints I've outlined help explain why many ex-prisoners remain in the voluntary sector. They also help explain why many Loyalist organizations formed to help in the transformation to peace are still around almost a decade after formal peace arrived. The transformation of Loyalist ex-prisoner groups provides a case in point.

THE TRANSFORMATION OF EX-PRISONER GROUPS

Although Northern Ireland's paramilitaries have always had organizations to advocate on behalf of their prisoners, these organizations took on heightened significance in the run-up to peace. As I note in chapter 2, the 1994 cease-fires hinged, especially for Loyalists, on the issue of prisoner releases (McEvoy 2001; Taylor 1999b). And the Belfast Agreement, which allowed for the release of most prisoners, put ex-prisoner groups at the forefront of both Loyalist and Nationalist aid organizations. Not surprisingly, when EU monies became available, prisoner groups associated with all of the province's major paramilitaries applied for funding.

Ex-prisoner groups have been successful at receiving funding from both PEACE I and early rounds of PEACE II. In 2004, when Lord Glentoran asked her majesty's government for an accounting of the public monies given to ex-prisoners' welfare organizations in Northern Ireland, the government indicated that £17.3 million had been distributed to organizations working on behalf of ex-prisoners. The written response also broke the figure down by receiving organization, indicating that ninety-one separate ex-prisoner groups had received funding during the period (*Hansard Parliamentary Debates* 2004a). Most funded projects focused on issues of reintegration, such as helping prisoners find homes and stable employment.

The province's political prisoners were released during a truncated time period (between 1998 and 2000), so, not surprisingly, interest in reintegration as a funding priority has waned with time. In the 1999–2000 fiscal year, for example, £5.1 million went to ex-prisoner groups, but the following two years saw a marked decline, with £1.1 million and £1.8 million allocated, respectively. The 2002–3 fiscal year saw a slight uptick, with funding at £3.2 million, but the following year saw another drop (*Hansard Parliamentary Debates* 2004b). Such a decline is to be expected given the truncated release period: the agreement stipulated that all eligible prisoners would be released by October 2000. But the decline does not imply, of course, that ex-prisoners cease to have problems; the nature of their problems is usually long term and falls outside the purview of granting organizations.

Ex-prisoner groups have responded to the decline in funding opportunities in a number of ways. In some cases, ex-prisoner groups simply close up shop. The Loyalist Prisoner's Aid group (LPA), which is affiliated with the UDA, appears to be on this track, although its loss of funding began with dodgy behavior on its part rather than a decline in demand for its services. In the summer of 2000—a peak year for prisoner releases—bomb-making materials were discovered in the group's Shankill offices (Department of Finance and Personnel 2000). The Northern Ireland Voluntary Trust, the IFB in charge of distributing peace monies to the group, froze its funding in response (BBC 2000b). The organization has continued to operate with a volunteer staff, but by the summer of 2004 it had few active ex-prisoner cases on its books anyway. In the following excerpt from my interview with Del Williams, one of LPA's voluntary workers, Williams put the LPA's funding problems down to its decision to hire Johnny Adair. Williams neglected to mention the 2000 imbroglio when I asked him about the group's funding problems. Adair, whom I discuss in the next chapter, was the UDA's flamboyant and controversial brigadier for West Belfast, and he is widely credited with starting the 2000 internecine feud between the UDA and UVF. Despite LPA's problems—with Adair or clandestine bomb factories—Williams acknowledged that demand for the group's services had shrunk considerably:

> DEL: We resettle prisoners coming out of prison. We lead them on the good path. We take them to get jobs, and try and find work for them if they want it. Johnny Adair came out of prison as an ex-prisoner. So we brought him onto a community thing here, gave him a job, where he got a weekly wage. And, they said, because of his profile, they took the money away from us. And we've never had it back.
> CAROLYN: So, how are you funded today?
> DEL: We're not. This is a voluntary-run office. This office is run through the money, the extra money we have now through donations toward prisoners. Because, we haven't got many prisoners in now. We've got three.

In other cases, ex-prisoner groups have expanded or changed their focus. EPIC Mid Ulster, for example, recently changed its name to REACT, an acronym for reconciliation, education, and community training, to account for its new, more expansive focus. Marian Jamison, a community worker with REACT, described the group's trajectory in a videotaped interview she gave to *Slí na mBan*:

> It [EPIC] was established, originally in Belfast, up at the Woodvale, at the top of the Shankill, to work with ex-prisoners in Red Hand Commando in UVF on reintegration. Then we started EPIC here—EPIC Mid Ulster—to work with ex-prisoners. But because our work changed and developed, the management committee here felt we needed to reflect that more in the name—that we're not just working with ex-prisoners anymore. So hence the name changed to REACT, to reflect the wider work that we do. (*Slí na mBan* 2002)

With their expanded focus, the group's funding sources have also diversified. As Jamieson explained:

> Now we have a youth worker who's funded by BBC Children in Need. As of next week we'll have a training coordinator and a community development officer; they will be funded under the European PEACE II measures. My post is funded through the Community Foundation, through the core funding for ex-prisoners. (*Slí na mBan* 2002)

For its part, the EPIC office on the upper Shankill Road in Woodvale has also expanded the focus of its work, although the group has not changed its name. When I interviewed members of its staff in 2003, they were busy working on grant applications for a number of non-prisoner-related projects. Plum Smith, for example, was trying to secure funding for a joint project with a muralist in Philadelphia. As he explained to me:

> We're trying to get money for murals. Because a lot of murals in our communities are hard, in your face, paramilitary-style murals. I'm in touch with Jane Golden [a muralist] from Philadelphia, who was over here.[5] And she works for Philadelphia Mural Arts Program. And they do a lot of murals within Philadelphia. . . . You know, simplistic people, or the middle class and upper class, who don't know our communities well, turn around and say, "oh, well just take the murals off the walls." That's not going to happen. So you de-paramilitarize the murals by softening the image. . . . So I am working with different people in the states, hoping that we can get the funding for them to do murals here. . . . Jane's actually got two artists ready to come over here. What we're looking for now is funding.

The LINC Resource Centre, managed by Billy Mitchell, has also expanded its focus. Its funding sources have shifted away from EU money as well. Between the 1995–96 and 1999–2000 fiscal years, for example, the LINC Resource Centre received yearly grants from the Northern Ireland Voluntary Trust (an IFB) for work related to ex-prisoners (Northern Ireland Assembly 2000). By 2005, however, the Resource Centre's five funded programs included none that were specifically targeted toward ex-prisoners, and only one program was funded through EU monies. Its other donors include the Atlantic Charities, the International Fund for Ireland, and the Community Relations Council (LINC Resource Centre 2005). A scan of the group's Web site also indicates that the group does not define itself as an ex-prisoner organization.[6] Furthermore, its services, although appropriate to the needs of ex-combatants, are not exclusive to them.

---

[5] Golden received an Eisenhower travel fellowship to study Northern Ireland's murals (Carbin 2003). After she came back from her trip in March 2003, she began looking for funding opportunities that would allow her to return. She described her impressions of post-peace Belfast to the *Philadelphia City Paper*: "There's an identity crisis. There's a strange combination of being relieved that violence is over and trying to hold onto their identity. Even though the themes are relevant, they need a vision of the future."

[6] On its Web site, LINC defines itself as a "Nazarene Compassionate Ministry working for Peace, Reconciliation and Social Justice in Northern Ireland" (LINC Resource Centre 2005). The UK Parliament, however, classifies LINC as an ex-prisoners' group (*Hansard Parliamentary Debates* 2004a). Although the Parliament's classification criteria—doing funded work on ex-prisoners—can lead to the occasional anomalous categorization (for example, the Committee for the Administration of Justice is labeled an ex-prisoners' group), defining LINC as an ex-prisoners' group is not a stretch. Its manager is an ex-prisoner, and it has ex-prisoners among its development officer staff.

This review of ex-prisoner groups is far from exhaustive, but it does indicate that many groups have shifted their focus rather than close their doors in the face of changing grant norms. These shifts suggest that voluntary-sector groups are becoming consolidated and taking on the characteristics of established service providers. There are pros and cons to such consolidation. On the one hand, the entrenchment of organizations like LINC is a positive turn of events. It indicates that local peace groups are flexible, that they are able to deliver a wide range of services and in such a way that keeps pace with the changing needs of their target population. It also demonstrates that such groups have developed roots in the community, and thus they are trusted to handle new problems and needs. When a group such as LINC survives, and even thrives, it represents the development of social capacity on the ground.

At an economic level, however, the entrenchment of the voluntary sector in Northern Ireland is worrisome. The sector is not sustainable because it depends on grants not only for its programming expenses but its core costs as well. Moreover, EU peace money is time limited—as peace in Northern Ireland consolidates, the monies will be diverted to other places and priorities. Dependency on these funds creates problems for individual workers in the sector as well as for the neighborhoods in which the sector is concentrated. At a personal level, the community workers in voluntary-sector organizations often live with chronic job uncertainty. When I interviewed Plum Smith in July 2003, for example, he described the precarious nature of his position:

> PLUM: You know, we got funding [after the agreement]. Got the doors opened to us, but as the time went on, those doors became closed.
> CAROLYN: What kind of funding do you need?
> PLUM: Well, for my job. My funding is only through May.
> CAROLYN: This May coming up?
> PLUM: No, May there, May passed. Right? And the government has refused to fund it for me.
> CAROLYN: What are you going to do?
> PLUM: Well, luckily enough we have another source where we were able to tap into. But, if we hadn't that source? See, what we want is the mainstream government funding.

Job uncertainty is characteristic of post-industrial work, but it has potentially disastrous ramifications in a place where peace is fragile and otherwise imperfect. Many voluntary-sector workers, like Plum, are ex-prisoners. Others are at risk of joining a paramilitary (or criminal remnants thereof) by virtue of their gender (male) and neighborhood (Loyalist enclaves). If community-sector work, which is intellectually engaging and affords status, is eliminated, many may choose to return or move into the paramilitary/criminal world, with its lucrative if illegal "business" opportunities. Moreover, if these job opportunities are not replaced with meaningful alternatives, the EU's invest-ment in ex-prisoners will have been for naught.

The entrenchment of the voluntary sector also has implications for the neighborhoods in which it is concentrated. As I detail in chapter 3, Loyalist neighborhoods have witnessed a steady decline over the last twenty years as work in the manufacturing sector declined and middle- and upper-income families moved to the suburbs. The recent economic boom has also largely passed these neighborhoods by. In some of them, the only new development to arrive in the last ten years is the voluntary sector. The economic boost af-forded by the voluntary sector is relatively meager—Loyalist enclaves in Belfast are still remarkably deprived—but it has allowed the city to put off enacting more substantial development schemes for these areas.

None of this is to imply, of course, that the EU's job is to subsidize an en-tire industry because there is nothing else to take its place. Peace is a process rather than a discrete moment in time, but the march *to* peace is not meant to stretch on indefinitely. The entrenchment of ex-prisoner groups demon-strates, however, that there are still significant barriers to reintegration. In-deed, the EU's and the governments' goals for reintegration remain unmet. And it is time for Northern Ireland to consider other means for meeting the challenge.

If society can trust paramilitaries and ex-prisoners with the delicate job of peace, perhaps it can trust them to work in the public sphere as well. In-deed, the civil service would be an ideal point of entry for such public ser-vice. Ex-prisoners cum community workers have developed a skill set appropriate to such jobs: negotiating the peace-funding bureaucracy is no small task, and those who do it learn how to write grants, design and im-plement projects, and oversee budgets. By hiring ex-prisoners, the govern-ment also ensures that members of Loyalist communities are actually integrated into the fabric of Northern Irish society in a sustainable way.

I approach this idea in more detail in the conclusion of this book. In-deed, there are a variety of proposals for absorbing paramilitaries into normal civilian life, including warden-level policing and officer training corps (Langhammer 2003). Suffice it to say here that the peaceful elimina-tion of Northern Ireland's paramilitaries and the absorption of their mem-bers into mainstream society remains the peace process's greatest unmet challenge.

Public-Funded Sectarianism?

Most people looked positively on the EU's decision to support the bur-geoning peace process in 1995, but some commentators have since con-cluded that the peace industry is fueling the very sectarianism it was meant to reduce. One of the great ironies of the process, critics argue, is an unintended consequence with dire consequences. Criticisms in this vein usually fall into two broad categories.

SKIMMING OFF THE TOP?

Some critics argue that EU money has found its way into the hands of paramilitaries, who have used it for personal enrichment as well as workaday paramilitary "business." In April 2005, for example, the *Economist* reported on the arrest of Jim Gray, the UDA brigadier who had just been ousted from the organization that March for unspecified offenses.[7] The magazine stated that when Gray was arrested he was carrying "a banker's draft for euro 10,000." It further suggested that Gray, who was later charged with money laundering, had gotten the money by pilfering public monies earmarked for Loyalist community groups:

> The misuse of state cash that helped festoon some of the provinces' thickest necks and wrists with heavy gold necklaces and bracelets has also been checked. Genuine community activists (i.e. those not fronting for paramilitary gangs) have been telling the government for years that money pumped into regeneration schemes invariably ends up being trousered by gangsters. (*Economist* 2005)

The Independent Monitoring Commission has also highlighted the potential for funding to end up in paramilitary hands, although it puts the problem in a wider context of charitable organizations (which includes privately funded groups as well as those receiving public monies). In its third report, for example, the commission noted that the charitable sector is largely unregulated in Northern Ireland and thus prone to manipulation by paramilitaries:

> We have been struck by the limited controls over charities in Northern Ireland. We have heard frequent allegations that this has facilitated the activities of paramilitary groups by making possible illicit use of money and the diversion of funds obtained from crime. (Independent Monitoring Commission 2004, 33)

The IMC did not cite any specific examples, but it did go on to observe that a high proportion of organizations registering as charities had never made any official charitable donations:

[7] The UDA's terse statement to the press did little to explain why Gray was stood down, but the media suggested a number of reasons, from speculation that his flamboyance embarrassed the organization to claims that Gray was too "pacifist" in his approach to LVF encroachment in East Belfast (Murray 2005b). Johnny Adair even commented on the standing down from Bolton, telling the *Belfast Telegraph*: "It's no big surprise to me. . . . He's nothing but a Scarlet Pimpernel who shed bad light on the UDA for many years" (Gordon 2005a). In October 2005, Gray was assassinated on the street in front of his father's house.

It is difficult to know whether and to what extent such a problem exists, either generally or in relation to paramilitary groups. However, reasonable suspicion is aroused by the fact that about two years ago of over 3,500 charities which had approached the Inland Revenue from the Belfast area, only 40% had sub-sequently made gift aid or other tax claims. We are anxious not to draw specific conclusion from these figures, especially because we know that the charitable sector in Northern Ireland is not identical to that elsewhere. Never-theless, the low follow-up rate means that 60% had a response from the Inland Revenue in the form of a letter bearing a reference number and accompanying material and had then done no other charitable business involving tax. In some cases this letter could be used for the purposes of passing off an organization as a new charity, for example in opening a bank account. There is no doubt a nat-ural rate of attrition, when people hope to start new charitable work but fail to do so, or they do so without wanting to claim tax relief. The figure of 60% is nevertheless high. It tends to lend credence to the view a number hold that charitable status is abused by some, and that it may be a channel for the misuse of paramilitary funds. (33)

A number of individuals and organizations have suggested that the para-militaries are pocketing a share of EU grant monies, but it is an assertion that is, as the IMC's report makes clear, difficult to prove. During my re-search in Northern Ireland I heard the same assertion made, although no one I spoke with was able or willing to give specifics. It is clear, however, that the dynamics of paramilitary structure make such an arrangement a distinct possibility. Foremost is the fact that paramilitaries did not stop charging protection fees in their neighborhoods after 1998. And there is no reason to think that community groups would be immune from such fees. Even community groups that are directly affiliated with paramilitaries would likely pay such fees, although they would probably class these fees as dues rather than protection money.[8] It is also worth noting that few com-munity groups are in a position to complain publicly about such arrange-ments. Indeed, because paramilitaries have historically served as de facto policemen in the estates they control, community groups would have needed (and in some cases would still need) the consent of paramilitaries to run operations in them.

The more diffuse power structure of Loyalist paramilitaries also makes the "seepage" of EU funding a distinct possibility, especially among voluntary-sector groups working in areas controlled by the UDA. Although the UDA has an inner council, the group is effectively run as a confederacy. Brigade leaders have a great deal of autonomy, and it is rare for the central leadership to get involved in the internal affairs of brigade staff. Unham-pered by central dictates, brigade leaders are free to extort money from

---

[8] Even if a community group uses private funds to pay its protection fees, this money is made possible by the EU because most such groups would not exist without its support.

whomever they please. And there is nothing in the UDA's history to suggest that they are choosy about where they get their money. Even the UVF, which had a more centralized command structure than the UDA, was not immune to racketeering post 1998. As I discuss in chapter 7, a UVF commander in South Belfast ran amok of UVF policy when he launched an intimidation campaign against immigrants in 2003. Some argue that the genesis of these attacks was a racketeering arrangement turned sour.

SINGLE-IDENTITY WORK AND "BETTER BIGOTS"?

While some commentators have focused on the paramilitary manipulation of EU funds, others focus on the nature of the funded programs themselves. Critics point to single-identity projects in particular. Of course, at a technical level, virtually all organizations that receive grant funding in Northern Ireland do single-identity work. Indeed, Northern Irish society is too segregated, socially and spatially, for many cross-community groups to even exist, let alone apply for funding. When critics point to single-identity work, they usually mean programs that involve cultural work—that is, programs designed to identify and promote a particular community's history and traditions. These sorts of programs are analogous to the cultural work I analyze in chapter 4. Councillor Mark Langhammer argues, for example, that single-identity programs tend to produce a professional class of agitators who spend the majority of their time trying to promote their side at the expense of the other side. In a paper he circulated to the Northern Ireland Office team in 2003, Langhammer used colorful language to make his point: " 'capacity building' schemes such as those routinely funded under the EU Peace programmes . . . have a propensity to turn into 'better bigot schemes.' " In a speech he gave the following year, Langhammer extended his criticisms to indict the Northern Ireland Assembly for funding sectarianism as well. He cited the generous funding packages for members of the Legislative Assembly (MLAs) as particularly mettlesome:

With their £70,000 plus MLA packages, through party office grants and party "research" grants, there is direct financial interest to subsidize an array of people paid to represent "their side." . . . How this works on the ground is instructive. A few years ago, when Stormont was going, I had to attend two tenants association meetings in my constituency in the same evening, one in a largely Protestant estate, the other in a largely Catholic estate. In the first, the issue was "Why are the Taigs getting an option of Gas Fired Heating and we're only getting an Oil Fired option." In the second meeting, the issue was the reverse. "Why are them Snouts (Protestants) getting three foot board fencing when we're only getting two foot picket fencing." You couldn't make it up. A sense of grievance is manufactured from nothing, and stoked up by representatives keen to "lead" their people. . . . I am immovably of the view that, with regard to local sectarian politics, the old adage holds true, that "less is more." (Langhammer 2004)

Frances McCandless, the director of policy at NICVA, has also suggested that community development may be fostering sectarianism. In a presentation at NICVA's annual conference in 2003 she addressed the issue by asking her colleagues to consider if their work was making sectarianism "more articulate":

> At one of a series of roundtables which NICVA held across Northern Ireland recently on Peace II, someone made the comment about some forms of community development—"Sure all we're doing is developing people to be better bigots." How many of us recognise a truth in that? Are we as organisations working in communities making sectarianism more articulate, giving it legitimacy and credibility for its demands and its structures? Is this a perverse offshoot of community development? (McCandless 2003, 5)

Although McCandless's goal, as she stated at the beginning of her speech, was to play devil's advocate, and she admitted that "I don't know if there are answers to all of my questions," the setting of her remarks—an annual conference for people working in the voluntary sector—suggests she thought the problem was real (2003, 1).

A report commissioned by Groundwork Northern Ireland to assess the state of community-based work in Northern Ireland also notes that "single identity work can lead to better-informed bigots" (Jarman et al. 2004, 34). While the report cautioned that single-identity work was important for developing confidence, and was thus a necessary precursor to cross-community work, it offered the following observation:

> By itself it [single-identity work] is not enough. A shared society can never be secured if "otherness" is continually held to be a threat or cause suspicion. An interdependent and sustainable society can never be secured if people only look "to their own tradition" and are unwilling to meet people from different traditions and more recent newcomers as equal and valued citizens. (2004, 46)

As a social scientist I am not comfortable diagnosing my research subjects as bigots. The duration of an interview—one to two hours—is not long enough to make such an assessment. Indeed, few individuals will make such pronouncements to someone they have just met and are even less likely to do so to an American researcher. However, in my interviews with community workers in Belfast, I did encounter single-identity projects that exhibit some of the problems discussed in this report.

One of those groups was Power to the People. According to John Wilson,[9] a development officer with the group, Power to the People was

---

[9] John Wilson is a pseudonym. I choose not to reveal the real name of the caseworker because criticism against Power to the People should be directed at the consortium of groups that devised it rather than the workers who implemented it.

founded in 1999 from a consortium of twelve Protestant/Unionist groups, the largest two of which were the Ulster Society and the Ulster-Scots Heritage Council. The group's mission is, he explained, to provide Loyalists with "cultural education." Shortly after its founding, Power to the People applied for and obtained a grant under PEACE II. The Special EU Programs Body, which catalogues the program's successful applications, lists the following description of the group's project:

> Power to the People seeks to assist in the creation of a confident and articulate Protestant community by raising its capacity and cultural awareness. The consortium also seeks to achieve a positive and equitable working relationship with Nationalist communities throughout Northern Ireland. PTTP proposes to achieve the above aim through the further development and delivery of its dynamic cultural and community training programme, and to provide this training on a rolling schedule to local communities. (Special EU Programmes Body 2005, project number 007982)

When I interviewed Wilson about his work at Power to the People, he prefaced his account by telling me why such work was important in the first place.

> The infrastructure in the Protestant community is weak. There's no sort of history, no depth of experience in community work or doing things within the community, unlike the Catholic community, which has had a long-term sort of ethos of community self help. The Protestant community, it doesn't exist here. We're very individual. You know, you do what you need to do for yourself and you don't worry about the community.

To counterbalance that tradition, Wilson told me, Power to the People offers "a four-phase education project" to members of the Protestant community. The "course" is offered free of charge.

> And the first phase is that we do what's called capacity building . . . [we] teach Prods about how to do things. We teach them about how to set up a residents' group. How to take part in a committee meeting. How to do, you know, this, that, and the other. It's all about, you teach them lobbying skills. Very general stuff. To try and encourage them to get involved in the community. . . . And we move on from that there and we teach them historical things. So we're looking at things like, you know, the Plantation, the founding of Northern Ireland. . . . Then, the third phase, we get them to engage in debate in the Unionist community. So we have people from the different political wings of Unionism come and talk about different issues that are of concern to them. You know, in the last series, we brought in a speaker to talk about Ulster Scots cultural issues. And just getting them all in to talk. To debate things. To force them to engage in debate. . . . At the end of the project, cross-community work is part of it.

The cross-community element of Power to the People's project figures prominently on the Special EU Programmes Body Web page, but when I asked Wilson to explain how he engaged with Nationalists, it became clear that the cross-community element was a minimal part of the program and an optional one at that.

> We take them on to engage in debate with Nationalists. [But] we say to people at the outset, "we're taking you to these things [debates] so that you feel confident enough to engage in debate." We don't expect, uh, we say to people, if they aren't happy about it [going to the debates] we won't make them do it. But the goal should be that they will have achieved a certain level of competency.

During our conversation, Wilson was also upfront that his organization was political. Indeed, in the following excerpt, he implies that other funders had steered clear of the group because of his group's overt politicism:

> JOHN: There's an attitude within some of the funders that they don't particularly like giving money to us because we can be seen as overtly political.
> CAROLYN: How are you seen as overtly political?
> JOHN: Well, because we actually say that we want to do things for the Protestant community. That we want to encourage people from within the Protestant/Unionist/Loyalist community to get involved in politics, to learn about their politics, about their culture, and to get involved and to do things for the benefit of that community. And we say that, we say that openly. What we're about is advancing the Protestant community.

As I discuss in chapter 4, scholars, politicians, and practitioners alike agree that Protestants need to develop a sense of history and identity. The work of Power to the People is filling such a void. The description of the group's work as "advancing the Protestant community" is, however, problematic. Indeed, it posits Loyalist community work as a competition of sorts whereby Loyalists need to learn to better compete with their counterparts in Nationalist communities. Such a configuration borders on antagonism, even if it avoids it in a technical sense. The "other" is a competitor, not a partner or fellow traveler.

The institutional affiliations of Power to the People are also disturbing. As Wilson explained in our interview, Power to the People emerged from a consortium of Protestant advocacy groups. One of those groups, the Ulster-Scots Heritage Council, is a purveyor of a revanchist identity politic. Indeed, Power to the People's office, where I conducted my interview with Wilson, was a veritable library of publications, pamphlets, and booklets produced by Ulster Scots groups such as the Heritage Council. It is not difficult to imagine that if someone were to take the four-phase course offered by Power to the People, he or she would become conversant in theories about the Cruthin and generally espouse a viewpoint that was consistent with a revanchist politic.

Loyalist groups are well within their rights to offer cultural education for the Protestant community. And it is not surprising that Loyalists view their cultural work as a competition of sorts. Indeed, although this book is focused on Loyalism, there are numerous Nationalist cultural organizations that denigrate Loyalism and view the culture business as a contest. The infusion of grant monies into this already fraught environment is, in some cases, simply adding fuel to the fire. Granting agencies must be vigilant in how they distribute their funds. And in the context of Loyalism, they must be vigilant in ensuring that their funds do not go to groups that are espousing a revanchist identity built on notions such as the Cruthin. This constraint would narrow the number of groups eligible for funding, but it would also help break the monopoly that revanchists within Loyalism currently hold in the cultural arena.

6   *Loyalist Feuds*

Two years after the signing of the Belfast Agreement, the British army returned to Belfast to bring order to its streets (S. Breen 2000; Reuters 2000). Its presence, however, was not precipitated by renewed violence between the IRA and Loyalist paramilitaries. Rather, soldiers were brought in to patrol the Shankill Road after a week of internecine Loyalist feuding between the UDA's C Company, based on the lower Shankill Road, and the UVF leadership, based at the top of the road. The feud, which lasted for several weeks, resulted in seven deaths and the displacement of between 500 and 1,300 Protestants within one of the most recognizably Protestant places in the province.[1] It also split the Shankill Road in two for a time, with Tennent Street serving as a de facto border between the two paramilitary-dominated areas (see fig. 10). Residents on both sides treated the border as impassable for weeks, and those on the northwest side had to find an alternative route into the city center. Fallout from the 2000 feud triggered an internal feud within the UDA two years later when its inner council expelled Johnny Adair, C Company's charismatic leader, and effectively stood down the majority of the company (Lister and Jordan 2003).

In this chapter I review the mechanics and meaning of the 2000 feud. My goal in doing so is twofold. First I examine the balance of criminal and political motivations that led to the feud. Much of the literature on low-intensity conflict assumes that guerilla and paramilitary violence is inherently criminal or becomes so over time (Kaldor 1999; Kaplan 1994; Mueller 2004; van Creveld 1991). This viewpoint is echoed in popular assumptions about Loyalism today. Indeed, the 2000 feud inspired harangues from all manner of quarters about the criminals presumed to be behind it. Jonathan

---

[1] The Northern Ireland Housing Executive estimated the numbers of displaced at 547, but community workers put the numbers much higher, at more than 1,300 (McCabe 2001).

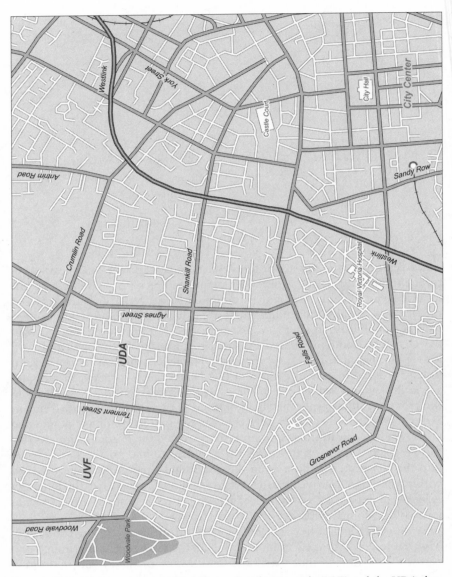

Fig. 10. Tennent Street, the unofficial boundary between the UVF and the UDA during the 2000 feud. By Nuala M. Cowan, Department of Geography, George Washington University.

Freedland's (2000) snarky observation in the *Guardian* captures the flavor of such commentary. "In true Monty Python style," he intoned, "no one can name a doctrinal difference that separates Adair's UFF from the Ulster Volunteer Force which it hates so bloodily." As I demonstrate here, however, examining the 2000 feud in light of the divide between revanchist and political Loyalism suggests a more nuanced interpretation.

To be clear, one side of the feud *was* criminal, or at least motivated by largely personal rather than political urges. The feud's key protagonist, C Company's leader Johnny Adair, is a case in point. Some writers suggest that Adair's motivations were economic. McDowell (2001) argues, for example, that Adair started the 2000 feud to gain control over the upper Shankill so that he could extend his drug and racketeering operations. Others argue that Adair's primary motivation was feeding his outsized ego. As Bruce argues, "the most plausible explanation of Adair's actions is megalomania."

> Like [Billy] Wright, Adair believed his own publicity. Basking in the approval of his small band of devoted followers and buoyed up by his success in driving senior UVF men out of the lower Shankill area, he came to believe that he was "Simply the Best" and once Wright was dead he saw himself as the man who would lead a new united Loyalist terror organization. Whether he led it into peace talks or back to violence did not seem to matter much to him; what mattered was that he led it. (2004, 517)

Whether Adair was motivated by crime or ego, or some combination thereof, there is little evidence to suggest his motivations were political. Indeed, Adair's eventual embrace of an anti-agreement message was largely expedient (and thus cynical). Adair knew many Loyalists were suspicions of the agreement. He chose anti-agreement rhetoric to legitimate his criminal endeavors because it resonated with everyday Loyalists.

The other side of the feud was not, however, apolitical or motivated by criminality. At the time, the UVF leadership fully supported the peace accord and the endeavors of its political wing, the Progressive Unionist Party, to develop a progressive agenda built around socialist principles. The UVF's participation in the feud was largely reactive: the organization responded to an attack at a UVF bar and the expulsion of at least two hundred civilians from their homes in the lower Shankill Road area. And although UVF violence was no less bloody (a bullet does the same damage whether the shooter's motivations are criminal or political), it was not driven by criminal motivation. Indeed, the UVF leadership saw Adair's attack as revenge for its support of the peace agreement, and it couched its response as a matter of defending peace.

What, then, do we make of such a feud? In this chapter I argue that the feud was political. Indeed, a conflagration can be political (even when one side is criminal) if its actions occur in a wider political context and have a direct impact therein. As I noted earlier, the political context in the autumn of 2000 was the simmering divide within Loyalism over the legitimacy of the peace process. And although Johnny Adair vacillated between pro- and anti-peace positions, he chose specifically political targets, leaving criminal competitors alone during the feud. His choice of targets may have been based on the logic that political Loyalism was bad for business (political Loyalists had publicly complained about his drug dealing), but his actions had the effect of dampening political discourse nonetheless. Any dissent from Adair's revanchist line could result in harassment, intimidation, and expulsion, if not death. To that end, it did not matter if Adair was adopting his anti-peace line cynically. The effect was to narrow the political discourse substantially, to cast dissent from a revanchist line as traitorous and worthy of assault.

The mechanics of the feud also demonstrate that it is not only civil society groups that may provide progressive alternatives to criminal elements. Progressive voices emerged most strongly from elements *within* the UVF. Indeed, most Unionist politicians had little to say about the feud, and those who did often made latently sectarian appeals, beseeching Protestants not to embarrass themselves in front of Republicans. UUP councillor Jim Rodgers, for example, chastised the feud participants with his statement that "Republicans must be laughing to see Protestant killing Protestant. This has to stop" (S. Breen 2000). Some religious leaders even used the feuding to bash the peace process. William McCrea, a Presbyterian minister and DUP member, argued that pro–Belfast Agreement Unionists were responsible for the infighting (Pat Finucane Centre 2005). However unpleasant, even paradoxical, the idea of progressive voices within paramilitarism may be, the absence of progressive voices in mainstream Unionism means that political Loyalists have an important role to play in the post-accord era. Unfortunately, as I demonstrate at the end of this chapter, political Loyalists can only do so much from within the confines of a paramilitary structure. Indeed, the UVF's decision to stand down in May 2007 was likely premised at least in part on political Loyalists' recognition that their good work was continually overshadowed not only by their location within a paramilitary structure but also their inability to control the criminal elements who shared the space with them (Edwards and Bloomer 2005).

My second goal in reviewing the 2000 feud is to highlight the geographic patterns that emerged from it. Although a variety of scholarship on the post-conflict period indicates that segregation between Catholics and Protestants has increased since the peace accord was signed in 1998 (Jarman 2002; Shirlow 2002, 2003), the 2000 feud demonstrates that segregation has also occurred within Loyalist areas along paramilitary lines. Segregation by paramilitary affiliation has not, however, been the result of congregation. Coercion was a fundamental part of the process. In some cases, Loyalists were forced to align with the paramilitary in charge of the neighborhood or move to another neighborhood. In other cases, unaffiliated Loyalists found themselves marked by virtue of where they lived. While such marking was external rather than by choice, those so marked were still vulnerable to the consequences of their presumed affiliation, including discrimination, likelihood of attack, and the like.

Unfortunately, Loyalist segregation by paramilitary affiliation has functioned in much the same way that segregation between Catholic and Protestant neighborhoods has. It has created social space interspersed with no-go areas and traversed only by circuitous routes. After 1998 a young person growing up in a UDA-controlled area of Belfast, for example, would be likely to avoid Nationalist areas and quite possibly UVF ones as well. This added layer of segregation—internal to Loyalism—has had a negative impact on vulnerable populations whose access to education, jobs, and better life chances is already hampered by the effects of ethnoreligious segregation.

The degree to which internecine segregation will continue as Loyalist paramilitaries close up shop is an open question. It will depend on volunteers' compliance with stand-down orders as well as the PSNI's willingness to aggressively police those that do not. However, if patterns of ethnogreligious segregation are any indicator, desegregation is an unlikely outcome at least in the short term.

History of Loyalist Feuding

In his now seminal book *The Red Hand*, Steve Bruce (1992) details the rivalry that marks the relationship between the province's two largest Protestant paramilitaries. Until the 2000 feud, however, the UDA and UVF had only engaged in one large-scale feud, during the winter of 1974–75, when both organizations were new. Bruce's rendition of that feud, pulled from interviews and newspaper clippings of the time, gives the impression of a barroom brawl gone awry.

The feud began during the Ulster Workers Council strike in 1974. At the time, Loyalist women were pressuring the leadership of both the UDA and the UVF to close the groups' social clubs and pubs for the duration of the strike. Many of the striking husbands had taken to spending their days in the pub, and Loyalist women were understandably upset by the drain on family income it produced. After consultation, both paramilitaries complied with the women's demands and ordered all pubs and social clubs shut for the duration of the strike. A lone UVF-affiliated pub on the Shankill Road remained open.

On a November night in 1974, a UVF man named Joe Shaw visited the pub for a drink. While there, he was "ribbed by the regulars about having allowed his 'local' to be closed" (Bruce 1992, 124). A few pints later, Shaw and some friends decided to return to their local, on North Queen Street, and open it up. UDA men patrolling the area saw the pub's lights on and ordered Shaw and his friends to close the place down and go home. Shaw refused, and the UDA men left, but they returned a short while later with a shotgun, determined to close the pub down. In the brawl that developed, Shaw was fatally shot (Bruce 1992).

The next day, Andy Tyrie, then leader of the UDA, met with the UVF's chief of staff, Tommy West, to negotiate an outcome. They agreed that the shooting had not been intentional and issued a joint statement prohibiting any of their men from retaliating with weapons. Their order did, however, make an exception for those members whose "ill-feelings [might result] in violence," noting that "fisticuffs would be permitted on a man to man basis" (as quoted in Bruce 1992, 125).

Despite the leaderships' attempt to avoid a feud, one ensued in short order. Two nights later two UDA men, Stephen Goatley and John Fulton, were murdered by the UVF. Their shooters justified their actions by calling Goatley and Fulton, who had allegedly fired the shots that killed Shaw, "UFF assassins" (Bruce 1992, 125).

As a follow-up a few days later, the UVF issued a press release from its political wing condemning the UDA for engaging in sectarian (that is, nonpolitical) murder. The statement cited two bombs as evidence—one in a pub in Greencastle, the other in a pub in Bangor—and implied that the UDA was behind both. The Greencastle and Bangor bombs were, however, perpetuated by members of the UVF. The first, in Conway's Bar, was the bombing that Martin Snodden and Eddie Kinner were involved in as a part of a UVF youth brigade. The second was a bombing for which a UVF man was ultimately held responsible (Bruce 1992).

The UDA retaliated by attacking a UVF bar in East Belfast and wounding two members. The UVF responded a few days later by nabbing a man out of a UDA bar and shooting him. The attacks then moved to individual houses, with the UDA organizing a spate of attacks on UVF homes on 30 March and the UVF responding with their own attacks. The feud continued into early May 1975, even extending beyond Belfast before it finally petered out.

Bruce posits a number of explanations for the feud. One of his informants suggested that neither organization had the experience to handle the unruly hard men attracted to paramilitarism. They would develop that skill only with time. As the informant explained to Bruce: "The hostility, a lot of it was just bumming and blowing—our team's better than your team. I don't want to use the word but I would say that we didn't have the breeding. We didn't have the experience of handling men that could have sorted out those kinds of problems. We were just brickies and plumbers" (1992, 127). Bruce also notes that the structure of Loyalist paramilitaries does little to inhibit the occurrence of feuding. Unlike the PIRA, which has a strong, centralized leadership, neither Loyalist paramilitary had (or has) such a high degree of centrally organized leadership. Although the UVF's command structure was always more centralized than the UDA's, neither had the tight, hierarchical chain of command found in the IRA. And while the IRA had competition from the OIRA and the INLA among other groups, its dominance was never seriously in question. There was no such imbalance between the UDA and the UVF, which were in constant competition to be *the* paramilitary of the Loyalist people. Bruce also argues that it should surprise no one that a feud might erupt in the paramilitary world. As he bluntly concludes, "paramilitary organizations are in the violence business. Their members regularly kill. They have guns. When they fall out, they use them against each other" (1992, 127).

There are several points about the 1974–75 Loyalist feud that bear highlighting. First, despite the weak check on feuding that Loyalist paramilitary structure provides, Loyalism experienced no significant internecine feuding for the remainder of the Troubles. Moreover, while the UVF claimed a political mantle by branding the UDA as sectarian, the feud was, as Bruce illustrates, essentially a barroom brawl gotten out of hand. Indeed, the UVF's alleged concern over the UDA's sectarianism was a ploy meant to divert attention from its own sectarianism (Bruce 1992). In short, the feud was not about a difference of political opinion.

Finally, although the feud disrupted some estates more than others, it was not territorial in nature. Neither side was attempting to seize turf from the other or to "cleanse" members of the other group from its turf. The focus on bombing paramilitary bars, for example, was most likely the result of tactical thinking. If an assailant wanted to get a UDA man, a good place to find one would have been in a bar frequented by UDA men. Indeed, although most Loyalist estates were controlled by one or the other paramilitary, it was common for estates to include members and affiliates of both groups, as well as those unaffiliated with either paramilitary. Paramilitary territory existed, of course, but it was mainly for two purposes: establishing and protecting a perimeter from PIRA attacks, and creating an agreeable division of territory for racketeering purposes. These boundaries were not used to regulate the movement of everyday Loyalist people based on their paramilitary affiliation. As I explain in the next section, this geography is fundamentally different from that of the 2000 feud.

The 2000 Feud

The key protagonists in the 2000 feud were the UDA and the UVF. In functional terms, however, the geographic concentration of the feud on the Shankill Road meant that the feud was, at least initially, a battle between specific segments within the two organizations. On the UDA side, the feud was largely the work of C Company, which was based on the lower Shankill Road and headed by Johnny Adair, the UDA's brigadier for West Belfast.[2] For most of the feud, the UDA's other brigadiers remained on the sidelines, declining to get involved because the organization's confederate system dictates such a hands-off approach (Connolly 2000). C Company's opponent in the feud was described in news reports as simply the UVF, with no mention of a specific brigade or battalion. This does not mean that the entire UVF was intimately involved in the feud, however. Journalists and commentators used the term UVF because it was the group's leadership that was, by virtue of its location on the mid-Shankill, primarily involved in the feud. A third protagonist was the Loyalist Volunteer Force (LVF), a splinter group established in 1997 by Billy Wright, who was expelled from the UVF the previous year for breaking the group's cease-fire when he ordered a sectarian murder near Lurgan (Taylor 1999b). Although Billy Wright was murdered in the Maze prison three years before the start of the 2000 feud, his presence often seemed to hover in the background—his ideological split with the UVF helping to explain the feud's political backdrop and the initial rationale for the tit-for-tat murder spree that gripped Loyalism for half of 2000.

The feud is generally regarded as beginning in August 2000, but several events in the months preceding set the stage for its occurrence. The first was the particularly contentious marching season in the spring of 2000. Johnny Adair's C Company was involved in contesting a number of marches cancelled or rerouted by the then new Parades Commission. Adair had also been particularly active in the contentious Drumcree march that year (BBC 2000c). A series of tit-for-tat murders within Loyalism at the start of the year also suggested the early makings of an internecine feud, albeit one between the UVF and the LVF. The first murder, of a well-liked UVF commander in Portadown, Richard Jameson, was believed to have been conducted by the LVF. It was followed shortly by the double murder of two teenagers, Andrew Robb and David McIlwaine. The press reported that Robb had a connection to the LVF although his family and others insist otherwise.[3] The presence of Johnny Adair at Robb's funeral was regarded as an ominous sign by some observers that the LVF and the UDA were making common cause.

During the spring of 2000, C Company had also commissioned a number of new murals in the lower Shankill. As Gallaher and Shirlow document

[2] The West Belfast brigade territory that Adair controlled was much larger than the area at the bottom of the Shankill Road. The lower Shankill was, however, Adair's power base. He not only lived in the area, but it was the home turf of the brigade's most active and loyal (to Adair) unit—C Company.

[3] The CAIN Web site lists Robb as a civilian. McIlwaine appears to have been at the wrong place at the wrong time.

(2006), these murals were incendiary not only to Catholics but, of importance to the topic at hand, to the UVF as well. One of the murals commemorated Oliver Cromwell's bloody march through Ireland in which thousands of Catholics were massacred (see fig. 11). Another depicted a bulldog (Adair's nickname was Mad Dog) chasing a frightened, simian-looking Gerry Adams out of the Shankill (see fig. 12). Interspersed among the sectarian images was a relatively staid mural honoring Billy Wright (see fig. 13). Although the UVF was no fan of Wright on the best of days, his commemoration was regarded as especially provocative given that the LVF had (presumably) murdered Richard Jameson earlier that year (Gallaher and Shirlow 2006).

To celebrate their new murals, C Company organized a cultural festival for 19 August on the Shankill Road and hinted that a number of key LVF members might attend. In response, the UVF issued a stark warning that the LVF was not welcome. Four days before the planned festival, Johnny Adair survived a pipe bomb explosion in the Oldpark district of the city. Although he blamed Republicans, the RUC soon concluded that the bomb fragments were consistent with the type of bomb commonly used by Loyalist paramilitaries. For many observers, the news portended trouble within the Loyalist paramilitary subculture.

Four days later, when the C Company festival and parade got under way, things turned violent. As the parade made its way up the Shankill Road, it

Fig. 11. C Company mural commemorating Oliver Cromwell.

Fig. 12. C Company mural of Johnny "Mad Dog" Adair chasing a simian-looking Gerry Adams out of the lower Shankill.

Fig. 13. C Company mural honoring Billy Wright.

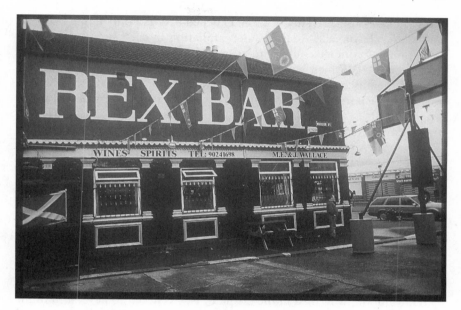

Fig. 14. The Rex Bar, a well-known UVF watering hole.

stopped at the Rex Bar, a well-known UVF pub (see fig. 14). Outside the pub, members of C Company hoisted an LVF banner, while a raucous band played. Several men poured out of the UVF bar, and a fracas ensued. In the melee, several shots were fired into the bar. It is difficult to identify the source of the shots or to ascertain whether the bullets hit intended targets. By most accounts, however, the guns were fired by members of either the LVF or C Company, given that shots were fired *into* the bar (McDowell 2001). Three people were injured before the brawl dissipated.

Later that night, festival participants returned to the bar and firebombed it. At a rally afterward, Johnny Adair read out a list of names of those he intended to drive out of the neighborhood. "The lower Shankill will," he promised at the end of the reading, "be UFF by Christmas" (Pat Finucane Centre 2005). The words were no doubt chilling to those on the list, who included well-known UVF and PUP members as well as ordinary citizens. Adair commenced to making good on his threat that same night by having UVF patriarch Gusty Spence dragged from his home and his house promptly firebombed. Spence's son-in-law, Winston "Winkie" Rea, was also put out of his house. The house next to PUP politician Billy Hutchinson was also fired at—likely by someone intending to get Hutchinson. Over the next few weeks, dozens of other families were expelled from the area. Journalist Anton McCabe (2001) estimates that "at least one in five families was forced out of the Lower Shankill, a one square mile area of about 1,000 houses." Many of those expelled had had only limited contact with the UVF. Indeed, Adair defined affiliation in such broad terms that even minimal contact could lead to expulsion.[4] Thus, people who lived next door to UVF men were expelled, as were those who dated them or had had friendly contact with them. The internecine divide on the Shankill was, McCabe noted, "unprecedented" because it targeted civilians and entire families.

Two days later the feud escalated when a gunman fired shots from a passing car at UDA commander Jackie Coulter and his companion Bobby Mahood as they sat in a parked car in front of a bookmaker's shop on the Crumlin Road at noon (S. Breen 2000; CAIN 2006e). Coulter died at the scene, and Mahood was rushed to the hospital. Johnny Adair and John White, then spokesperson for the Ulster Democractic Party (UDP), the UDA's political wing, visited the scene of the shooting and gave an impromptu press conference. White decried Coulter's murder, protesting that Coulter was only a Loyalist community worker (BBC 2000g), and blamed it on the UVF. Most commentators, however, described Coulter as a UDA man and an associate of Johnny Adair (BBC 2000a; Pat Finucane Centre 2005). Mahood, who died in the hospital, was believed to have been in the UVF but, according to CAIN (2006e), "opposed the Belfast Agreement and the policies of the Progressive Unionist Party." In Belfast, the shooting was widely viewed as UVF retribution for the chaos of the August 19 expulsions. Indeed, speaking to the *Irish Times* in the wake of the killings, Billy Hutchinson told journalist Suzanne Breen (2000) that the killings were a tragedy, but they were not unexpected: "Did they actually think when they carried out gun attacks against people [in the Rex Bar], that people were going to sit back and not do something about it?"

The day after the shootings of Coulter and Mahood, Peter Mandelson, then secretary of state of Northern Ireland, revoked Johnny Adair's license—he had been released from prison under the provisions of the Belfast Agreement—on the grounds that he was participating in terrorist activity. Mandelson told the press, "My priority is public safety and I cannot give freedom to an individual intent on abusing it. I am satisfied that this particular individual [Adair] has breached the terms of his licence" (as quoted in Watt and Wilson 2000). While many people were undoubtedly happy to see Adair locked up, spokesmen for both paramilitaries' political wings expressed fear that his arrest would lead to more violence. The UDP's

---

[4] Political violence scholars note that in low-intensity conflicts, the absence of uniforms and other ready identifiers often leads to such distortions. In her work on the Colombian civil war, Robin Kirk describes this phenomenon as contamination by contact. "All of Colombia's armies seemed to assume, barring clear proof to the contrary, that everyone in their path was suspect, a potential 'military target.' Contact was contamination and contamination was death. Had a store owner bought from or sold to a guerilla? Death. Had a telephone exchange operator placed a call for a paramilitary? Death" (2003, 182).

John White, for example, told the press, "I think the police have made a mistake in rearresting Mr. Adair. If they are accusing him of orchestrating the recent troubles he will be able to do that from inside prison as well as out. They have taken a big risk" (as quoted in Watt and Wilson 2000). Billy Hutchinson also expressed reservations: "I think the feud will now intensify and I'd expect attacks against our party and the UVF" (as cited in Watt and Wilson 2000). White and Hutchinson would prove to be correct. The next night a young UVF man, Samuel Rockett, was shot and killed in the home of his girlfriend in North Belfast (CAIN 2006e). The UFF claimed responsibility for the murder.

A short peace followed as funerals were planned and held for Coulter, Mahood, and Rockett. From the paramilitary regalia and long funeral processions, an observer transported from 1985 might easily have mistaken any of these as funerals for victims of the IRA. Indeed, during the height of the Troubles, the most elaborate funerals were usually held for those killed by the IRA.

Mahood's funeral was held first, on 24 August. Although he was a member of the UVF, the Apprentice Boys gave a "guard of honor mount" for his coffin, and a UFF contingent followed behind his casket (Pat Finucane Centre 2005). More than a thousand people attended Coulter's funeral the next day. Many of them were young men in full paramilitary dress, with shaved heads and sunglasses (Pat Finucane Centre 2005). Rockett's funeral, the day after, is also estimated to have attracted more than a thousand mourners as his coffin was carried through the UVF-controlled streets of the Shankill.

The quiet was disrupted a few days later, 28 August, when the home of Samuel Rockett was destroyed in a fire deemed to be arson (Pat Finucane Centre 2005). The next day troubling news also indicated the feud had moved beyond the confines of the Shankill Road area when police reported over thirty attacks on homes in the predominantly Protestant Carrickfergus and Greenisland. The police alleged that the attacks had been orchestrated by the UDA and UVF battalions in the area.

On 29 August, a day after Rockett's house was firebombed, the PUP issued a statement blaming C Company for starting the feud and revealing that the festival organizers had broken a promise, given before the event, to keep LVF members away from the parade. Ten days later, a pipe bomb was again launched at the house of prominent PUP politician Billy Hutchinson. He moved his wife and father-in-law, who lived in the house with him, to a safe location. Houses on either side of Hutchinson were also evacuated.

The feud was reignited in October when another round of tit-for-tat killings occurred. The spate began on 28 October, when UDA member David Greer was shot and killed during a barroom brawl with members of the UVF (CAIN 2006e). Three days later two men were executed. The first victim, Bertie Rice, worked for the PUP as an election officer and was shot at his home. The UDA took responsibility for his death (CAIN2006e). The second, believed to be in retaliation for the first, came later that same day, when UDP politician Tommy English was shot and killed, also in his home. His death was blamed on the UVF. The next day, 1 November, the UDA shot UVF member Mark Quail in retaliation. It was the seventh feud-related murder to occur since the feud had begun in mid-August.

The feud continued, albeit at a slower pace, through November and into December. Representatives from both sides were meeting secretly with each other and third-party negotiators to bring the feud to a close, but it did not officially end until 15 December, when the Inner Council of the UDA, the Brigade Command of the UVF, and the Brigade Staff of Red Hand Commandos issued a joint statement to the press. The statement began my declaring an "open-ended and all encompassing cessation of hostilities." It also noted that a protocol had been established for dealing with future disputes: "A series of mechanisms have been created at both leadership and local level throughout each organisation to ensure that any disputes that may arise are resolved in a peaceful manner to the benefit of all our members and communities in which they live." The statement also included an apology of sorts, albeit a likely insufficient one for many: "We fully recognise the pain and suffering that has been inflicted on our community and we resolve that under no circumstances will such events be repeated." The concluding paragraph of the joint statement indicated, however, that Loyalism's internecine differences had not been fully resolved: "Neither the LVF nor any activity carried out under its name or any flag of convenience such as the Red Hand Defenders, Orange Volunteers, or Loyalist Freedom Fighters has the support of any organisations bound by this agreement" (BBC 2000e).

While the UVF and the UDA signaled their distance from, and lack of support for the LVF, its absence in the negotiations was regarded with trepidation. Among the province's three leading paramilitary organizations, the LVF has been the only group to consistently oppose the Belfast Accord. In the run-up to the agreement, the LVF issued a statement explicitly threatening Protestants who supported the "peace surrender process designed to break the Union and establish the dynamic for Irish unity, within an all-Ireland Roman Catholic, Gaelic Celtic state" (BBC 2005b). When it signed on to the agreement, it did so only to encourage a no vote. Indeed, even though the statement promised to accept the vote of the people, it simultaneously described the agreement as a "sell out," leading David Ervine to describe the statement as "good news" but "difficult to understand" (BBC 1998):

> The LVF are now calling an unequivocal ceasefire to create the proper climate in people's minds, so when they do go to vote they will make the proper decision for Ulster and that is to vote no. But as we have stated the final decision lies

with the people, whatever decision is made, we have to accept it. The LVF wish to go on record that they were never part of the sell out. We think it is wrong and we hope people will see it as well, or Northern Ireland is lost forever. (Loyalist Volunteer Force 1998)

The absence of the LVF in the negotiated cessation of the feud was also troubling given the key role it had played in the 2000 feud. From the UVF's perspective, the feud started because the LVF was allowed to participate in the 19 August festival and to march through its territory. That it did so soon after the murder of Richard Jameson was regarded as insulting, provocative, and out of bounds. Although it is fair to take the UVF's position with a grain of salt (given its own role in the killings), it is clear that the protocols for resolving disputes can only go so far when one of the key protagonists is uninvolved.

The durability of the cessation was also in question because of the absence of Johnny Adair from the negotiations. Although Adair returned to prison shortly after the 19 August festival, he was always known to have a strong cadre of supporters who were more loyal to him than to the UDA as a whole. Indeed, nothing in the cease-fire agreement indicated that Adair's followers had renounced him or his revanchist vision. Thus, while the joint statement announcing the feud was regarded as hopeful to the extent that the LVF would no longer be allowed to use the better-organized structures of the UDA/UFF for its operations, the statement offered no guarantees that hardliners within the UDA would not continue to do so.

Three days after the joint statement was issued, the first signs of internal UDA discontent—and the use of violence to resolve it—surfaced when James Rockett, a UDA man, was found dead from a gunshot wound in an estate in North Belfast. The murder was widely regarded as an internal UDA hit. And although the dispute was believed to be over unauthorized drug dealing, that it came in the wake of the UDA's attempt to clean up its image indicated that the leadership was choosing inhumane methods to enforce the organization's "new" direction.

In May 2002, Johnny Adair was again released from prison. Not surprisingly to many of those living on the Shankill, tensions mounted upon his return, only this time the majority of it was internal, between Adair and other brigadiers in the UDA. As with the 2000 feud, the LVF was involved. After his 2002 release, Adair rekindled his former relationship with the LVF, working to establish new drug markets in the Portadown area with its help (Lister and Jordan 2003). Within a few months, an internal UDA feud would erupt. It would be bloody, with three murders and seven attempted murders occurring before its hostilities would end. At its conclusion Johnny Adair would be expelled from the UDA. He was returned to prison shortly after his ignoble standing down in 2003. After his release two years later, he would go directly to Bolton, England (where his family had relocated). Adair's evacuation to Bolton was likely related to intimations by UDA brass that he would be killed if he returned to the province (Lister and Jenkins 2005).

Explanations

Peter Mandelson set the tone for the depiction of internecine Loyalist feuding at a press conference he gave at Belfast International Airport on 21 August as he returned to the province from a vacation. He was blunt in his assessment of the events up to that point: "What we are witnessing has nothing to do with politics and/or the peace process. It is nothing more or less than squalid murderous gang warfare. It is about certain individuals trying to assert personal control over local communities and we are not going to have it" (as quoted in Henderson 2000).

Mandelson's comments heralded the arrival of two tropes that would come to dominate descriptions of the 2000 feud and those that followed. The first, the gangster trope, became an all-purpose moniker to describe individuals involved in Loyalist feuding. The term "gangster" brings to mind a host of (often American) images, from urban, African American rap stars in Los Angeles to sharply dressed mob bosses in Chicago or New York. In Northern Ireland, the gangster motif drew on the latter, referencing real-life figures like Al Capone and fictional movies like *The Godfather*. The second trope—apolitical criminality—was used to explain the motivations of the so-labeled gangsters.

It is unlikely that Mandelson intended to create a "mobster" ethos around the feud. Indeed, while Mandelson's re-arrest of Adair signaled a "get tough" approach common to the policing of organized crime, he also signaled his willingness to negotiate by announcing his intention to schedule talks with the political representatives of the two paramilitaries. Regardless of his intentions, the tropes soon caught on, becoming the prevailing explanatory framework for the feud. Indeed, the frame became so ubiquitous that people of varied political stripes used the tropes even as they made divergent arguments about the role of the "gangsters" and the meaning of their criminal activity.

The gangster trope was frequently deployed in newspaper accounts of the feud. In an *Irish Examiner* story, for example, journalist Joe Oliver interviewed a BBC reporter who had been allowed to "hole up" in a UVF club on the Shankill for a few days. The reporter, who Oliver does not identify by name, used mafia lingo to describe what he saw: "It resembled a scene from *The Godfather*. All these men were either getting out of their sleeping bags or shaving in mirrors of the club. The food seemed to have been stockpiled and brought in by family members. There were several lookouts at both exits and maps covering the Shankill area pinned up on the walls. They were definitely preparing for a siege" (Oliver 2000). An investigative piece in the *Sunday Observer* in 2003 on the internal UDA feud two years later also relied on the gangster trope to chart the rise and fall of its key protagonist, Johnny Adair. The journalists were liberal in their use of terms like "the Shankill Godfather" and "Loyalist warlord" to describe Adair. In a particularly vivid passage, they even describe how one of Adair's outfits was appropriately "gangster."

> On 2 July, a snappily dressed Adair was part of a loyalist delegation that met John Reid, Tony Blair's third appointment as Northern Ireland Secretary. "Has the man from the UDA become the Man at C&A [a European retailer]?" asked a Sunday newspaper as it pored over his costume. In fact, Adair was considerably more up-market. As he stepped into the East Belfast Mission Hall for the meeting, he was wearing a pinstripe Hugo Boss suit, a yellow tie with a fashionably large knot and a baby-blue shirt. He looked every inch the stylish Mafia boss. (Lister and Jordan 2003, 28)

Journalists seemed intrigued by the similarities between Loyalists and so-called mafia bosses, and they were not alone in their fascination with the metaphor. In his book *Godfathers*, Jim McDowell cites a "senior police source" who tells him that "some of these boys aren't as stupid as they look. Sometimes, they are as slick as the real mafia 'Godfathers' in America" (2001, 172).

Politicians also embraced the gangster trope, often to frame divergent views of the feud. On 30 August, the office of then first minister David Trimble issued a terse statement promising to deal with "the mafia sub-culture" that had spawned the feud:

> I have no doubt there are elements within Loyalism and within Republicanism who are trying to tighten their grip on local communities. This is a major challenge for Her Majesty's Government and the RUC. The people of Northern Ireland will expect them to respond in a firm and decisive manner. Tomorrow morning I will be speaking to the Deputy Chief Constable and I will discuss with him what steps are being taken to deal with the mafia sub-culture that has spawned from years of illegal paramilitary activity in parts of Northern Ireland. (Trimble 2000)

Anti-agreement politicians also relied on a gangster trope to frame the feud, although they blamed the gangsterism on pro-agreement forces rather than paramilitary culture. Speaking to the media in the week of the initial fracas at the Rex Bar, for example, Conservative Party chairman Michael Ancram remarked, "We have been saying for some time that if you release squalid, murderous gangsters back onto the streets this type of thing was likely to happen" (as quoted in Hyland 2000).

Not surprisingly, the depiction of Loyalists as gangsters was accompanied by an equally common description of their motivations as criminal or apolitical. As I note above, Peter Mandelson was insistent that participants' motivations were "personal" and "squalid" rather than "political." Most investigative journalists were in agreement. In *Godfathers*, Jim McDowell argues that the 2000 feud was rooted in the UDA/UFF's decision to involve itself in the illicit drugs trade. As he explains:

> By the time Adair got out of jail . . . the UFF had taken a decision to exploit the illegal drugs business. It would do two things. It would help bolster the income of prisoners coming out of jail who still needed financial help. And, it would line the pockets and make rich some of the men at the top: especially on Adair's "home patch" of the lower Shankill in Belfast. But it was a policy that was later to spark a bloody and brutal internal war: an internecine feud between Adair's UFF and the other major paramilitary bloc on the loyalist side, the Ulster Volunteer Force. (2001, 157)

McDowell (2001), for example, traces the feud's first murder, of UVF man Richard Jameson in Portadown, to drugs. He argues that Jameson had been opposed to LVF drug dealing in the Portadown area and had been collecting information on the group's activities. It is unclear from the account to whom Jameson planned to pass along his information—to the police or to senior commanders in the UVF—but his murder is painted as punishment for collecting the information at all:

> UVF man Richard Jameson, according to sources close to his family, started building up a dossier on the County Armagh LVF drugs dealers. . . . Eventually the LVF started to "get heavy" with him. They visited his home. They threatened him. The hoods delivering the threat were captured on a security video camera at his home. Richard Jameson defied the LVF. He paid with his life. A car carrying two gunmen followed his jeep home one night. Close to his front door, they shot him dead. (McDowell 2001, 160)

McDowell summed up the motivations of the feud by quoting Richard Jameson's brother Bobby: "They're not the LVF. They're the DVF—for the Drugs Volunteer Force" (159).

Investigative journalists would also describe the UDA feud two years later as a battle over drug turf, highlighting the connections to the LVF as well. Lister and Jordan speculate in the *Observer Magazine* that Johnny Adair saw the suicide of his friend and high-ranking LVF associate Mark "Swinger" Fulton, in June 2002, as an opportunity to consolidate his "business" interests in the Portadown area:

While Adair was upset at his friend's death, he also saw it as an opportunity. According to one close associate, "I was talking to Swinger four months before he died and that was the first time I realized what Johnny was up to with the LVF. Johnny was running up and down to Portadown and he would have gone to all these different dos. So my reckoning was that he was definitely working deals with them on the drugs. And I think when Swinger died, Johnny saw that as his move to take over the whole patch." (2003, 28)

Other commentators, like Fintan O'Toole, focused on the apolitical (rather than criminal) aspects of the feud. Writing about the cultural festival that had set off the feud, O'Toole remarks that Adair's cultural repertoire was more Hollywood pastiche than traditional defense of Protestantism. As he explained:

Adair doesn't march his stormtroopers down the Shankill Road to the tune of God Save the Queen or Rule Britannia, but to the sound of Tina Turner. The slogan on their T-shirts isn't "for God and Ulster" but "Simply the Best," the title of Tina's gooey pop hymn to some standard-issue fantasy man. Over this T-shirt, Johnny's sweatshirt proclaims, not the dignity of Protestant Britain, but the virtues of Nike Athletic. The tattoo on his arm isn't of Carson or Paisley, but of Mickey Mouse. The main cultural influences at work, in other words, are not Britishness and Protestantism, but Hollywood, Top of the Pops and the Sun. This is a makeyup mentality in which the flotsam and jetsam of movies, pop songs, brand names and tabloid TV get washed up on the shores of a narrow little mind. (2000)

O'Toole concludes by chastising Protestants for not defending their tradition from such abusers.

The respect for different traditions enshrined in the Belfast Agreement will only mean something when those who profess to belong to those traditions are willing to defend them, not just against external enemies, but against those within their own ranks who parade a grotesque parody of culture. (2000)

As the flavor of these varied commentaries suggests, the prevailing view of both feuds was that Loyalists had issues other than politics on their mind. For McDowell (2001) and Lister and Jordan (2003), control over a burgeoning drug market was a key motivation for feud participants. For O'Toole (2000), the feud was about a narrow-minded bigot who liked mixing his cultural metaphors. In none of these accounts is the possibility of a political dimension to the feuds seriously considered. Neither McDowell (2001) nor Lister and Jordan (2003), for example, explore the motivations of those who fought Adair. Indeed, while McDowell acknowledges that Richard Jameson was opposed to LVF drug running, he makes no effort to explain Jameson's opposition as a matter of UVF policy, which is explicitly "no drugs."[5] The unintentional result of such analysis is that all Loyalist actors are branded criminals. Likewise, while O'Toole is correct that Adair's cultural referents are as much Disney as British, his demand that Protestants reject such cynicism is especially confounding given that the UVF leadership was busy doing just that.

Indeed, many of the people on the UVF side who were intricately involved in the feud saw their participation as a response to Adair's political cynicism. When I interviewed Billy Mitchell in 2003, for example, he complained about the media's depiction of the feud. "Everyone put that down to marking out territory between the UVF and the UDA." It was not a correct analysis he told me. Indeed, as early as 2 September, the UVF had issued a statement asserting a political dimension to the feud. Writing in the *North Belfast News*, Billy Mitchell chastised those who described the feud as a turf war over drugs and racketeering:

> The current regrettable conflict that is tearing the heart out of the loyalist community has been put down as a "turf war" being waged between two criminal gangs to see who can gain overall control of a criminal empire that includes drugs, racketeering and prostitution. This simplistic and wholly inaccurate analysis is commonplace within the media and certain sections of church and state. (2000)

The feud, Mitchell argued, was not due to competition over illicit assets but a struggle over the future direction of Loyalism. The seeds of the feud, he noted, were planted in 1996 when the mid-Ulster division of the UVF broke from the main organization over the impending peace accord.[6] The division's leader, Billy Wright, would go on to form the LVF as a means of fighting the forthcoming agreement. Mitchell also claimed that the split was fostered by members of the Portadown Unionist establishment who hoped to derail the UVF's involvement in the peace agreement. As he explained:

> For those who have short memories, the first indications of fractured relations within Loyalism after the declarations of the ceasefire in 1994 was the rise of

[5] An internal UVF discussion document states: "The UVF and the RHC [Red Hand Commandos], as organizations, believe that involvement in the illicit drugs trade is incompatible with the principles of loyalism and neither organization is involved in, nor endorses, such activities" (Ulster Volunteer Force 2002, 49). As I mention in the next two chapters, the UVF had trouble enforcing this policy, due in part to the flexible command chain in the UVF and the autonomy it provides. The no-drugs mandate is also difficult to enforce because issuing a stand-down order (that is, essentially firing offenders) can create as many problems (for example, with feuding or splinter groups) as it solves.

[6] The UVF leadership stood down its entire mid-Ulster division after a series of sectarian murders indicated the division was not complying with the letter or spirit of the organization's cease-fire.

dissident voices within the mid-Ulster UVF. It is common knowledge that a split was engineered by certain anti-peace politicians who had tried and failed to get the UVF not to declare a ceasefire. (2000)

Mitchell also argued that the UVF's decision to ignore anti-agreement voices in Portadown and elsewhere led to a

> concerted campaign of vilification and violence against the Progressive Unionist Party because it was seen that the bulk of the UVF membership was willing to listen to the political analysis of the PUP. The vilification and felon-setting has come from both anti-agreement unionists and anti-agreement para-militaries. This campaign has intensified during the past two years, resulting in the killing of six people who were associated with the PUP or who accepted the political analysis of the PUP. (2000)

Mitchell also challenged the media to back up its claims that the feud was a turf war over criminal assets. Pointing to the feud's innocent victims, he asked:

> What about the thirty odd families that were violently expelled from the turf of the Lower Shankill Estate? Were these men, women and children all expelled from their homes because they were competing for a slice of criminal action? If this was a turf war over drugs, prostitution and rackets the media needs to tell us how many prostitutes the [displaced] elderly disabled pensioner whom we saw on television last Monday was pimping for? They need to identify how many businesses were paying protection money to the young lady who had her wedding plans wrecked when her home was looted and her savings pilfered. They need to provide evidence that people like Gusty Spence were expelled from their homes because they controlled rival drug empires to those of their attackers. (2000)

For some, Mitchell's argument is clear, well reasoned, and bristling with common sense, but for others his affiliation with the UVF casts doubt on his assertions. His conclusion is not, however, a difficult one to reach when the political views of the feud's key protagonists are examined on their own merits. No one disagrees, for example, that the LVF was opposed to the Belfast Agreement. In the run-up to the agreement, the group threatened those who openly supported it (BBC 1998). And when the LVF finally signed on to the accord in 1998, its own press release on the matter insisted that the LVF "wish[ed] to go on record that they were never part of the sell-out" (Loyalist Volunteer Force 1998). Their participation seemed designed, above all else, to encourage no votes in the historic election (BBC 1998).

Moreover, while Johnny Adair has never publicly decried the peace accord in the way that his associates in the LVF have—indeed at times he pretended to champion it—the depth of his connection with the LVF would have been unlikely had he sincerely supported the accord.[7] Adair's naked sectarianism also makes his support of the accord an unlikely proposition, given the "parity of esteem" the accord established between the two communities. In fact, Johnny Adair is alleged to have had links with British neo-Nazi groups, whose views of Catholics are often no better than their views of Jewish people. Adair's deepest ties are believed to have been with the neo-Nazi group Combat 18. Journalist Henry McDonald (2003) even alleges that members from the UK branch in Bolton were present when Adair's marchers unfurled an LVF color guard in front of the Rex Bar.

The connection to far right groups continues today. When Adair's family and followers were forced to flee Belfast in late 2002 (or face execution by the UDA), Combat 18 in Bolton is alleged to have helped them find housing (Atkinson 2006). And, in a bizarre tribute to Adair upon his 2005 release from prison, a German neo-Nazi group from Dresden came to celebrate with him at his wife Gina's abode in Bolton (Lister and Jenkins 2005). None of this history definitively proves that Adair was anti-peace, but it makes a convincing circumstantial case that is hard to ignore, especially in light of his prime targets in the 2000 feud. Indeed, whether Adair was anti-peace because he feared it would lead to a united Ireland or because he thought peace would be bad for his burgeoning drug empire, his actions had the effect of quashing a pro-peace line within his turf on the lower Shankill.

Indeed, it is C Company's attacks on PUP members, many of them no longer active in the UVF, that are most indicative of the ideological dimension of the feud. Loyalist community workers from the "class of Long Kesh" had begun to engage in cross-community work (see Springfield Intercommunity Development Project 2005), and the PUP had an established platform that called for working-class unity across sectarian lines. If the feud had been merely a battle over drug turf—that is, an attempt to take over UVF drug markets—C Company would have targeted the competing dealers in the UVF. Without a doubt, there are drug dealers in the UVF— many of my informants admitted as much, albeit off record—but C Company targeted political Loyalists like Billy Hutchinson and Gusty Spence. Neither has been linked to criminality, but both have gone on record condemning drug dealing on political grounds. Plum Smith was targeted for the same reason.[8] When I interviewed him about the feud, Plum told me, "I was a target, I had to go on the run." When I queried why, Plum responded,

---

[7] Although Republican and Loyalist paramilitaries have been known to cooperate on criminal matters (see McDowell 2001), the LVF–UDA C Company connection was more than one of convenience. The two groups shared an ideological outlook as well. A mural was even painted to commemorate their coming together.

[8] Community workers associated with the UDA also went into hiding during the height of the feud. Del Williams, who helps run the Loyalist Prisoners Aid Network, told me in our interview: "I went back to Wales for two weeks. I mean, I just took the car and went on the road and went out of it. And, then I came back [to Belfast], and stayed in my house for two weeks."

Well, I went public about the drugs, you see. Because they [C Company] had a drug house down there [on the lower Shankill] where they were selling drugs to kids of all ages. And they were selling them to our kids. And I did an interview [about it] . . . we were complaining because the police were doing nothing.

Some C Company members have also acknowledged that politics was behind their targeting of the UVF leadership. For example, Gallaher and Shirlow (2006) found that in the run-up to the 2000 feud, C Company was actively recruiting young men from the upper Shankill on the grounds that the UVF and the PUP were betraying the Loyalist people. As one of their informants, a former C Company member, explained:

The blacknecks[9] [UVF] are keeping us out of their area, for they know that the wee lads want to join us. 'Cause they know that we are talking sense and that we will lead them into a true loyalist culture. They're afraid of us, and the fact that we are more popular than them. They know that the wee lads know that they are betraying loyalism. (As quoted in Gallaher and Shirlow 2006)

Mark Langhammer, the local councillor in the district where Mark Quail lived (one of the young men shot during the course of the feud), confirmed the inter-paramilitary competition for recruits as well. As he explained to me:

That's a cycle that is going on at the minute. From what I can gather from young people in me own constituency, when you ask them "well, why did you join the UDA or the UVF?" they'd say, "it's because I wanted to stand up to the UDA or the UVF." You know, whichever [paramilitary] was the opposite [from the one they were in].

Although Councillor Langhammer has little sympathy for political paramilitarism, preferring that the paramilitaries be disbanded altogether, when I asked him what he thought the 2000 feud was about, he did note the divide between the UDA and the UVF vis-à-vis the peace process. As he put it:

I suspect it was about all those things—about turf, about personalities, about drugs, about possibly elements in the UDA who felt that the elements in the UVF were taking a "pro-Fenian" line. That would probably be the way it would have been put. So, those feuds, because, because the UDA doesn't have politics, doesn't have a political position, doesn't have an ideology, and it's only at the grassroots level about winning the area [from the UVF], or about, you know, ruthless sectarianism in the area, it will always be prone to feuds.

[9] Steve Bruce remarked in a review of this manuscript that UVF men were often called blacknecks because they favored black attire (pants and turtlenecks) for paramilitary "jobs." The UDA was more partial to camouflage.

Given the evidence I've outlined, it is not difficult to concur with Mitchell's assessment of the feud as political. Indeed, most of C Company's targets were persons associated with the political wing of the UVF. And the feud's effect on political discourse within Loyalism was (for a time) stifling; dissent from a revanchist line was cast in do-or-die terms. This conclusion does not negate the prevalence of drug dealing, however—quite to the contrary. There is a substantial record indicating Adair's involvement in the drug trade. Indeed, Peter Mandelson was able to thwart Adair's appeal of his 2000 return to prison by using RUC intelligence linking Adair to drugs, among other nefarious activities (BBC 2001). The point here is that drug dealing and revanchist politics are comfortable bedfellows. By presenting itself as the true protector of Loyalism, C Company was able to put itself above the law. And as the "ultimate" guarantors of Loyalist culture, its leaders obviously felt free to set their own law.

What Loyalist Feuding Says about Criminality and Low-Intensity Conflict

Many scholars argue that criminality is part and parcel of low-intensity conflict (Kaldor 1999; Mueller 2004; van Creveld 1991). If they have no legal means of support, guerillas and paramilitaries must necessarily rely on illicit activity, such as racketeering or trafficking in illegal goods, to fund themselves. These enterprises create a temptation to skim off the top. And when spats arise (usually over proceeds), differences are often settled with gunfire. Not surprisingly, such an environment has a tendency to blunt ideological concerns, pushing them to the background if not erasing them altogether. A bare minimum of legitimacy is, however, necessary, so fighters often continue to define their goals as political. Indeed, they often adopt more strident positions, reasoning that such rhetoric will keep civilians in line and substantive politics (which are bad for illegal business) at bay. Under this framework, which is found in the political violence literature (for example, Kaldor 1999; Kaplan 1994; Mueller 2004; Münkler 2004; van Creveld 1991), the 2000 feud would be an inevitable event—the result of natural disputes over criminal assets and their distribution.

As my analysis shows, however, while paramilitaries may go to war over criminal turf, they may also battle over the legitimacy of criminality within the ranks. That is, the tensions between political and criminal elements can also lead to fighting. In Northern Ireland the arrival of peace created a context for such arguments as some members chose to explore politics while others preferred to continue the war and reap the benefits associated with it. This finding has conceptual/theoretical implications that apply not only to the Northern Ireland case but to other conflicts as well. Two stand out as particularly relevant.

First, the 2000 feud impels us to remember that paramilitaries are often internally divided organizations. In the case of Loyalism, members can and do espouse different ideas about what is best for the Protestant people. And although these varied ideals are all particularist (their concern is, after all, for the future of Protestants), they are not equal. This proposition may seem obvious, but many conflict scholars eschew any form of particularist politics, and a good number reject any involvement by paramilitaries in post-peace political structures (see especially Kaldor 1999). In Northern Ireland many commentators feel the same way. Indeed, when Loyalist feuds erupted, critics tended to decry Loyalism's self-destructive streak and bemoan the lack of leaders available to draw them back from the brink. In this well-worn narrative all Loyalist paramilitary men are carbon copies of one another. With such a narrowly construed narrative, it should surprise no one that containment is seen as the only viable solution to Loyalist recalcitrance. However, Loyalists are not all alike, and there are real interventions that can be made from within its boundaries. Painting all Loyalists with Adair's brush only discourages, even undermines, the real and important actions that political Loyalists take every day to transform Loyalism, and the roles they could take in its future transformation.

Highlighting the differences between political and revanchist Loyalism is also important because it throws into sharp relief the paradoxical position in which political Loyalists found themselves after 1998. In Northern Ireland, the peace process was built on the assumption that political carrots would encourage Loyalists to close up shop. Although the process worked for Republicans (however belatedly), it has taken longer and produced incomplete results for Loyalists. Indeed, the UVF's stand-down order in 2007 notably lacked a promise to decommission its weapons. As Steve Bruce (1992) has argued, pro-state terror groups always have more difficulty establishing a political program than their anti-state counterparts do. They need different incentives to close down. In the absence of such incentives, Loyalists like Adair were able to continue, even expand their organization's criminal and sectarian enterprises, often for personal gain and satisfaction. Meanwhile, political Loyalists were expected to reign in their criminal elements even though they had no political carrots to offer them as an alternative and lacked any tools save violence to control them.

Not surprisingly, Loyalist feuding left political Loyalists with a deep sense of pessimism. In their 2004 report for LINC's series of conflict transformation papers, Edwards and Bloomer found politicos in a glum mood. When they interviewed Plum, for example, he observed:

> Loyalism cannot be reconstructed—too much has happened since. I was at a meeting in Fernhill House about six months ago—the last time I walked up that road was to announce the ceasefire and the world's press was there, Loyalism was on a high, six months ago there was no-one. [It was] clear we are

moving backwards—the reasons are clear enough—gangsters, drugs . . . resulting in all Loyalists being viewed in similar vein. That image . . . has really damaged Political Loyalism. (2004, 20)

Tom Roberts was similarly pessimistic:

The current defeatism within unionism has made the PUP pro-Agreement position increasingly difficult—I don't think there now is such a thing as a pro-Agreement Party, some were and are simply pro aspects of the Agreement which suited/suits them—in today's political environment the Agreement couldn't be negotiated. (Edwards and Bloomer 2004, 30)

The diminishing capacity of political Loyalists to operate effectively within paramilitary structure was brought home in 2005 with the onset of yet another feud, this time between the UVF and its nemesis the LVF. The 2005 feud represented the first time the UVF launched an offensive feud in the post-agreement period.

The UVF–LVF Feud of 2005

The 2005 feud between the UVF and the LVF[10] began on 1 July with a midday murder. The victim, James Lockhart, was sitting in a lorry outside a demolition site when he was shot by a masked gunman (Chrisafis 2005).[11] Lockhart was believed to be a member of the LVF, and his name had recently appeared on a Shankill wall. Having your name tagged on a wall is usually a bad sign. The "Loyalist bush telegraph," as Chrisafis (2005) dubs such graffiti, is a sure sign someone has been targeted for a punishment beating, or worse, execution. Two weeks later, the UVF struck again, shooting and killing Craig McCausland as he sat at home with his child and partner (Gordon and McCambridge 2005). McCausland's family denied he was a member of the LVF.

A week later three hundred UVF men descended on an estate in the Garnerville area of East Belfast with the stated goal of expelling families associated with the LVF from the estate (McKittrick 2005). The UVF argued that LVF drug dealing in the area had gotten out of hand and the PSNI had failed to do anything about it (Hutton 2005).

[10] A smaller feud erupted between the UVF and the LVF in 2004 but was quickly resolved. Although I treat Loyalists feuds as discrete entities, hard feelings from previous feuds often feed new ones. Indeed, if one were to take a more lengthy view of Loyalist feuding, it would be possible to categorize discrete Loyalist feuds as part of an ongoing feud that had lulls between the fighting.

[11] In a strange twist, Lockhart was working for a construction crew tearing down the Avenue One bar that UDA boss Jim Gray had owned. The location appears to have been a coincidence as the UDA was not involved in the feud.

The next week the UVF killed again (Breslin 2005). Its victim, Stephen Paul, was not believed to have been a member of the LVF, but he was reported to have gotten into an argument with a UVF man in the weeks before his death. The PSNI responded to the escalating feud with a series of raids in North Belfast. Rioting ensued in the Crumlin Road area in the wake of the raids, and the PSNI argued that it was orchestrated by UVF men in the area. Forty officers were injured in the fracas (McCambridge 2005). Two weeks later another man, Michael Green, was murdered (Cunningham and Erwin 2005).

On 14 September, Peter Hain, the Northern Ireland secretary, announced that the UVF was in breech of its cease-fire. The group was "specified" and lost its privileges associated with participation in the agreement.[12] Perhaps because the killings were so lopsided—all of the LVF's attempted murders during the feud failed—tensions began to fizzle. The feud formally ended in late October when the UVF and the LVF announced a truce (Erwin 2005). A few days later the LVF announced that it was standing down its membership (CAIN 2006b).

A number of the feud's patterns are troublesome as they concern the UVF. First, unlike previous feuds, the UVF appears to have started this one. Indeed, the UVF adopted an offensive posture from the start. In its sixth report, the Independent Monitoring Commission made special note of the UVF's aggressive behavior.

> We believe that, while the recent escalation of the feud may have boiled up as a result of local animosities set against the history of longstanding rivalry, the UVF leadership has decided that now is the right time to finish off the LVF. In the case of the LVF, we believe their violence against the UVF and its supporters, though coherent and fuelled by rivalry and animosity, is more by way of response than initiated as a campaign designed to achieve a purpose other than survival. (2005, 8)

Although the UVF regards the IMC as illegitimate *and* uninformed, it has not rejected the IMC's own characterization of its actions. Indeed, the UVF basically acknowledged as much. After Michael Green's murder, for example, a UVF man told two reporters, "They [the LVF] have to disappear; they have abused this society for too long" (Cunningham and Erwin 2005). A senior UVF man also told the *Belfast Telegraph* that the feud would go on until the LVF was gone "once and for all": "We don't want to be looking over

---

[12] Under the terms of the Good Friday Agreement, the Northern Ireland Office (NIO) may periodically review the status of the respective armed parties' cease-fires. If a group is deemed in violation of its cease-fire, the NIO can "specify" the group as in breech and remove all political benefits attached therein. Paramilitaries wanting to rejoin the process must meet requirements established by the NIO. Once requirements are fulfilled, the NIO can "despecify" the group and return its political privileges.

our shoulders, or under our cars, every morning fearing an LVF attack, so it has to be sorted now" (as quoted in *Sunday Life* 2005).

Second, although the political rift that gave rise to the LVF still partially explains the differences between the UVF and the LVF (the IMC admits as much), politics appears to have had a smaller place in this feud. Indeed, a look at the UVF's choice of targets is revealing. Of the four men it murdered, two were not directly involved with the LVF, and none of them was a senior (decision-making) member of the organization. Had the UVF's fight with the LVF been primarily about politics, it stands to reason that the UVF would have attacked the LVF's leadership, or at the very least avoided persons who were not clearly members of the LVF.

Edwards and Bloomer argue that structural changes led to the UVF's sloppy targeting. As they note, "perhaps one of the main reasons why low-level LVF players were targeted, instead of the organisation's leadership cadre, is that the UVF, like most other paramilitary groupings, have become rusty in their operational effectiveness" (2005, 16). They also suggest that retirements at the leadership level permitted the "absence of a strong disciplinary code among volunteers" (17). The retirement of "seasoned veterans" also allowed local commanders the freedom to "become involved in drugs trafficking and other nefarious criminal activities" (17).

The UVF's expulsions from the Garnerville estate are also disturbing, especially when one recalls the UVF's anger at C Company expulsions from the lower Shankill in 2000. To be fair, the UVF has claimed that it conducted its expulsions because LVF men in the estate were selling drugs to Protestant kids in the area. And some residents were clearly happy to see the LVF families leave. One woman told a reporter she felt "liberated," explaining:

> They [LVF men] were partying all night, drinking and taking drugs, and keeping up residents who had to get up for work in the morning. But if anybody makes noise during the day when they're asleep, they would come out and say the LVF are going to do you in. People here were totally sick of it. It is terrifying. You don't know when somebody's going to rap your door and tell you to get out, or trail your sons or your husband out and give them a hiding. I made complaints to the police and had been in touch with the community police and as far as I can see the police's hands are tied. (As quoted in Hutton 2005)

Even if one accepts the "paramilitary as police" role, however, the UVF's claims to moral authority in the area are undermined by its own dealing. As one UVF man told a journalist with the *Guardian*, "there is dealing on both sides" (Chrisafis 2005). This statement does not mean, of course, that all three hundred men were drug dealers engaged in a hostile takeover of lucrative turf. Some probably were disturbed by the drug dealing. As long as even some UVF men engage in drug dealing, however, the leadership (which set the UVF's no drugs policy in the first place) will be subjected to cynicism about its efforts to clean up the Loyalist house. The added layer of segregation, this one internecine, is also troubling. Working-class people in Nationalist and Loyalist communities already have a bisected social space that they must navigate. Another layer of segregation only magnifies such problems.

Although the UVF's actions rest in a morally gray area, the blame cannot be cast entirely within the organization's borders. Indeed, it is naïve to think that Loyalist paramilitaries could police themselves in ways consistent with human rights. Paramilitaries are, as Steve Bruce states, "in the violence business" (1991, 127). The paramilitaries can and should do their part—by closing down—but they will need help from both the PSNI and the governments to make it stick. For its part, the PSNI must accept responsibility for policing Loyalist criminality. Likewise, the governments should enact formal demilitarization schemes to absorb as many former combatants as possible. This is especially important in light of the UVF's stand-down order in 2007. Indeed, the order's durability will depend on it; without such aide individual Loyalists may well carry on their war under new flags of convenience.

In the next chapter I examine post-accord attacks against immigrants in Belfast and paramilitary involvement in them. As I demonstrate again, political Loyalists found themselves in an awkward spot as they tried to police their criminal elements. And, as my analysis demonstrates, active intervention from the governments and police will be crucial to cleaning up the remnants of Loyalist paramilitarism.

7   *Immigrants, Paramilitaries,*
and Turf

Immigration to Ireland and Northern Ireland is a recent phenomenon. In 1845, on the eve of the potato famine, the population of the island stood at approximately eight million people. Five years later, it had declined by over a third, with one million people succumbing to starvation and disease and another two million emigrating, mostly to America (American Immigration Law Foundation 2001; O'Grada 1995). In the century and a half that followed, both Ireland and Northern Ireland continued to send émigrés to locations across the globe. In the south, most migrants left for economic reasons: the Republic's economy was unable to sustain all of its working-age population. Irish rituals were even adapted to reflect the place of out-migration in the culture. The American wake, a funeral fete for émigrés about to cross the Atlantic, was given in recognition that most would die in America. In Northern Ireland, emigration rates were much lower because of industrialization in Belfast and smaller cities like Derry. Residual tensions from partition, however, meant that few outsiders wanted to relocate to the province's humming industrial zones, so in-migration was minimal. After the Troubles erupted, net out-migration became the norm. During 1971–72, the most violent period of the conflict, the province recorded an out-migration of 20,400 persons (Hutchinson and Simpson 2000). During the 1980s, net migration to Scotland and England alone was around 9,000 persons a year (Mulholland 2002).

In the early 1990s, things began to change in both Ireland and Northern Ireland. In the Republic, the economy took off, attracting light manufacturing, hi-tech firms, and professional services related to both. Pundits took to calling Ireland the Celtic Tiger (O'Hearn 1998; Sweeney 2000).[1] In Northern

---

[1] Irish economist David McWilliams is credited with dubbing Ireland "the Celtic Tiger" in 1994. He used the term to liken Ireland to countries like Malaysia, South Korea, and Singapore, which had been labeled "East Asian Tigers" in the late 1980s for their phenomenal export-led growth (Wikipedia 2005b).

Ireland growth was less striking but still significant. The cease-fires in 1994 and the peace accord four years later gave a measurable boost to the province's sagging economy. For the first time in living memory, people on both sides of the border began to witness an utterly unfamiliar phenomenon—positive net migration. In Northern Ireland the 2001 census counted 157,410 new migrants to the province (Northern Ireland Statistics and Research Agency [NISRA] 2001c).

Immigrants to Northern Ireland are a diverse lot; most are nonwhite and come from cultural traditions quite different from those of the province's two ethnoreligious blocs. In-migration is a recent phenomenon, however, so the total number of immigrants remains low. Indeed, although it is not a perfect measure of immigration,[2] the percentage of ethnic minorities in the province today continues to indicate overwhelming racial homogeneity. According to the 2001 Census, over 99.15 percent of the population is white. Even Belfast, where most new migrants land, is still 98.63 percent white. The largest ethnic minority in the province is Chinese, followed closely by migrants from South Asia (NISRA 2001b).

Despite their low numbers, a backlash has developed against the province's nonwhite residents/migrants. The backlash is manifested in a variety of ways, from discrimination in housing and employment to harassment, physical assault, and attacks on homes. The problem is a rapidly growing one as well. In 1998–99, the PSNI recorded 93 racial incidents in the province.[3] Five years later, in 2003–4, the number had risen to 453 (Northern Ireland Affairs Committee 2005). The occurrence of racial incidents has been geographically concentrated, with most attacks occurring inside Belfast, and within the city, in its southern quadrant where almost one-third of all attacks occurred in 2003–4 alone (Northern Ireland Affairs Committee 2005).

The backlash against the province's new migrants is disturbing but not without precedent. Similar strife has arisen in other western European capitals dealing with heightened numbers of immigrants in the post–cold war period (Lahav 2004; Sassen 2000). What makes the backlash unique in Northern Ireland is the involvement of paramilitaries in the process. To date, the majority of involvement has been by Loyalist rather than Republican paramilitaries (Rolston 2004).

Loyalist paramilitary involvement has taken many forms. In some cases, members have participated in harassment and intimidation on an individual

---

[2] The limited numbers of immigrants in the last 150 years and the nonwhite status of most new migrants mean that immigration trends can be roughly captured in data on ethnic minorities.

[3] The PSNI is required to collect and report data on a fiscal-year basis, which runs from 1 April to 31 March. Thus, yearly crime statistics do not coincide with the calendar year. The PSNI collects data about abusive behavior aimed at minorities under the category "racial incidents." It defines the category as "any incident which is perceived to be racial by the victim or any other person" (Northern Ireland Affairs Committee, House of Commons 2005).

basis. In other cases, groups within Loyalist paramilitaries have linked up with racist and neo-Nazi groups to conduct intimidation campaigns. On occasion, entire paramilitary companies have become involved in the attacks.

In this chapter I examine the role of paramilitaries in the intimidation of ethnic minorities/new migrants in the province. Paramilitary participation in these campaigns demonstrates the relative weakness of political Loyalists vis-à-vis their revanchist peers. Indeed, despite the best efforts of political Loyalism to steer members away from criminality, some obviously prefer to continue the "war," even bringing it to new "enemies." That Loyalism's new "enemies" pose no threat to the union is troubling. Such attacks indicate the declining importance of ideology for the remnants of the Loyalist brigades. Moreover, as I document in this chapter, political Loyalists and other leaders unhappy with the attacks were unable to effectively, and palatably reign in these criminal elements. In short, it was impossible for paramilitaries to police themselves in ways that are congruent with accepted norms.

I begin by briefly summarizing battles for turf in the post-accord era, focusing specifically on Belfast. Turf wars generally occur with the greatest frequency in working-class areas or in housing estates run by the Northern Ireland Housing Executive. Not surprisingly, most new migrants come to the province with limited means, so their ability to find housing (either on the open market or through the Housing Executive) is usually limited to these same areas. To understand the mechanics and form of paramilitary campaigns against ethnic minorities, we must examine these attacks in this wider context. In the second section I introduce Donegall Pass, a neighborhood in South Belfast that had the highest number of racial incidents in the city during the period of my research. I then turn in the third section to a paramilitary-led campaign during the winter months of 2003–4 to "cleanse" immigrants from "the Pass." Members of both the UVF and the UDA were accused of launching the attacks, but the UVF company in the area was considered the primary perpetrator. Given the potential for reprisals against sources, I do not name the seven individuals I have quoted or paraphrased in this chapter. It should be noted, however, that none of the immigrants subjected to the attacks provided information for this chapter. Any limitations or errors in the story line and subsequent analysis are the sole fault of the author. And any attempts to rebut this chapter should be directed solely at the author. In the fourth section I detail the response of the leadership in the UVF to the attacks in the area and discuss the limits that working within a paramilitary structure placed on political Loyalists trying to stop them.

The Growing Importance of Turf in Post-Peace Belfast

VIOLENCE AND SEGREGATION

Segregation between Catholics and Protestants is an enduring phenomenon in Northern Ireland, dating to the plantation period of the seventeenth century (Doherty and Poole 1997). Segregation has always been high, but levels have ebbed and flowed over time. Decreases are usually correlated with periods of relative calm, while increases are associated with upswings in violence (Doherty and Poole 1997). Not surprisingly, levels of segregation increased during the Troubles. A report conducted at the start of the conflict, for example, estimated that as many as 8,000 families in mixed areas were forced to flee their homes for homogenous estates in 1971 alone (Darby and Morris 1974). Given this ebb-and-flow pattern of segregation, many commentators expected segregation to slacken (albeit slowly) after the historic 1998 peace accord was signed.[4] Some evidence suggests that such a trend is taking hold. James Anderson (2004) observes, for example, that high-end apartment buildings in Belfast's new development corridors appear to be fairly integrated. Workplaces are also becoming less segregated.

In poor areas of the city, however, and especially in those places where the conflict was fought, segregation appears to be intensifying rather than declining (Jarman 2002; Shirlow 2003; Shirlow and Murtagh 2006). This trend is especially apparent in estates owned and operated by the Northern Ireland Housing Executive. A recent report on social housing by the Northern Ireland Affairs Committee noted a steady increase in segregation on its estates, a trend seemingly impervious to both the 1994 cease-fires and the 1998 accord: "Whilst there has been a marked improvement in the housing provision in Northern Ireland creating a sound basis from which individuals and communities can actively participate in social, economic, political and cultural life, difficulties persist. Housing has become more segregated over the last 20 years; more than 70% of NIHE estates are 90% Protestant or 90% Roman Catholic" (2004, Ev 55). These are remarkable figures given that the Housing Executive uses an artificially high threshold to indicate segregation. Indeed, if NIHE had used the threshold set by most scholars, that an area is segregated when the majority group reaches between 70 and 80 percent of the population, the percentage of segregated estates would have been even higher.

Jarman suggests that post-conflict segregation in Belfast tends to manifest itself spatially in one of two ways. In some cases, Catholic and Protestant

---

[4] Doherty and Poole note that although segregation in Northern Ireland has tended to decrease during periods of relative calm, it does not tend to decline to pre-violence levels. Thus, "the overall trend [in segregation] is inexorably upward" (1997, 526).

areas become homogenized and agglomerated, creating "large single identity zones such as the Greater Shankill and the Falls Road area" (2002, 21).
In other cases, however, the segregation occurs at the estate level, creating a
checkerboard pattern of Catholic and Protestant estates. The emergence of
this checkerboard pattern has led not only to the creation of more distinctly
Catholic and Protestant estates but also to more total boundaries between
the two groups. These boundaries, known as interfaces in Northern Ireland,
are often sites of conflict.

Interfaces, and conflict at them, have a long history in Belfast (Boal
1969). Some of the earliest battles of the Troubles occurred at interfaces between Catholics and Protestant neighborhoods. Many interfaces, especially
those that were early hotspots for conflict, have been separated by physical
barriers, known euphemistically and not a little sarcastically as peace walls.
The Beverley Street interface, which separates the lower Shankill from the
lower Falls, for example, was bricked in as early as 1969 (Jarman 2002).
Likewise, the Springfield Road interface, which was built in 1985 (Jarman
2002), is divided by a twelve-foot brick wall with a twenty-foot iron mesh
fence on top of it (see fig. 15). Although few people expected these peace
walls to disappear after the 1998 accord, even fewer expected their numbers to increase in its wake. Between 1994 and 2000, however, the number
of peace walls in Belfast almost doubled, rising from 15 to 27 (Jarman
2002). The creation of more interfaces, and ultimately peace lines, has negative ramifications for the city because the interfaces tend to create or exac-

Fig. 15. Interface on the Springfield Road.

erbate conditions of social deprivation. A number of studies demonstrate, for example, that persons living on interfaces tend to have higher levels of long-term unemployment, poorer health, and more limited education than do residents of similar economic means in non-interface areas (Jarman and O'Halloran 2000; Jarman 2002; Shirlow 2003).

Increasing segregation is also visible on the symbolic landscape. In the wake of the 1994 cease-fires, both Catholic and Protestant neighborhoods sought to more firmly claim areas of the city as their own. The result has been an explosion in turf-marking activity in the last ten years (BBC 2000d). Councillor Mark Langhammer noticed the increase in his council district shortly after the 1994 cease-fires. As he explained:

> Now, one of the things that I noticed very, very soon after the cease-fires ten years ago was that there was an explosion of marking-out activity. On both sides, but predominantly the Protestant side. I call it dog-leg activity. It's like a dog marking its territory. So there was flags, there was emblems, there was murals, there was all of that stuff. And there was an increase in activities. Now, as a pretty low-level, local councillor, I noticed that in my constituency mailbag, if you want to call it that. Because I was dealing with more intimidations, I was dealing with more what we call SPED [Special Purchase of an Evacuated Building] cases, which is where the housing authority buys back a property for an intimidated person. I was dealing with many more of those than I did before.

As Langhammer's comments suggest, turf marking is often associated with violence.

While the endpoint of turf-related violence is often intimidation out of one's home, such situations often have their genesis in rioting. Someone throws a stone or hurls an insult at a person on the other side. He or she responds in kind, and soon their shouting draws the attention of neighbors on both sides of the interface. The street fills with onlookers, and new participants join in. If tensions escalate, as they often do, stones are quickly abandoned for more lethal weapons, like petrol bombs. Such riots are routine affairs in some parts of the city, leading many community workers to label the phenomenon as recreational rioting (Jarman 2002). Although it may be difficult to think of rioting as something one does for fun during free time, the term captures the nonpolitical nature of such riots. As Jarman explains: "The term 'recreational rioting' is suggestive of the origins of the violence— as a social activity, occurring out of boredom and bravado rather than having a more political basis" (2002, 29).

Rioting occurs all year long but tends to increase during the late spring and summer, coinciding with the marching season and summer holidays. Most rioters are young people, and rioting is increasingly a routine, social behavior rather than a phenomenon tied to a political event, such as a contentious parade. As one interface resident explained in Jarman's study, "Outsiders come in [to this area] even when there are no parades, just to have a go" (2002, 33). Boredom is a factor as well, and it is compounded by the social marginalization of interface areas that provide few alternative activities for young people during the summer holidays. A recreational rioter in Jarman's study recounted, for example, that "we have a place [on an interface] where we all hang out, where we go every night in good weather and sit and smoke. No one lives there so we get less bother from our own community, though we often get told to move on by the police. As well as that there's the chance of a riot [happening] there too" (32).

While rioting is increasingly a social, even routine affair for young people, it can have a devastating impact on interface residents. Rioters may begin by throwing stones but often progress to lobbing petrol bombs. A few interfaces, such as the one on Springfield Road, have walls that are high enough to impede the use of explosive devices (the higher the wall the more likely a device is to explode on the thrower's side), but many interfaces have low walls (less than twelve feet high), and new interfaces tend to have no barriers at all. When petrol bombs start flying, residents at unprotected interfaces often have no choice but to evacuate their homes. Evacuation often leads, however, to a downward spiral in conditions on an interface. When a house is evacuated, rioters often take over the premises, using the second story as an elevated launching pad for hurling incendiary devices. Not surprisingly, evacuated houses used in this way become targets for rioters on the other side, which puts neighboring houses in the line of fire and encourages even more residents to evacuate their homes.

Persons fleeing their homes because of rioting are allowed to apply to the Housing Executive for temporary, emergency housing. Given the high occupancy rate of Executive housing (especially in safe areas), many evacuees are given shelter in hotels. Although some of the city's most luxurious hotels, including the Hilton and the Europa, are used for temporary housing, the hotels often place onerous restrictions on their temporary guests. Beverly Davidson-Stitt, a Loyalist community worker in East Belfast who works with the Protestant Interface Network, recalled the experiences of a woman forced to evacuate her home because of rioting[5]:

> This friend of mine was put in, wouldn't you think, in the Europa hotel. They were put into the Europa hotel. Five of them in one room with two beds. They wouldn't get the children breakfast. Now, all they were permitted to have was a bed. They weren't there as guests to use the hotel. They were away in what

[5] Davidson-Stitt explained that her friend's experience with evacuation spurred her involvement in community work. "It [the riot] was on a Sunday night, and [my husband] and I go down to see if she was ok. They'd moved her out and she was in a church hall, along with all the other residents, her and the wee ones. And just sittin' in that church hall and seeing all those wee children—wee tots crying, and mommies crying, distraught—I just thought, I really have to help here." The next day she and her husband started calling the Housing Executive and other social services in the community to help the evacuees.

would be like, what I would class as servants quarters really, where staff stay. They wouldn't give the kids breakfast in the mornings. They weren't allowed there all day. So they had to leave there in the mornings at 9 o'clock and be out all day. They were allowed to come and sleep at night. Community centers would have made food for them so that they could have something to eat. Otherwise the children would have had nothing because they had no homes to go to.

Although most recreational rioters tend to be teenagers, paramilitaries have been involved in the process as well. Their involvement in rioting has taken one of two forms. In some cases paramilitaries have orchestrated riots in order to intimidate the other side to leave an area. Such rioting is accompanied by targeted intimidation, including harassing phone calls, paramilitary graffiti on homes, and threats in local shops. These sorts of campaigns have usually been conducted in mixed areas but have been occasionally aimed at areas inhabited solely by the other side but considered of strategic importance to the attackers.

In other cases, paramilitaries have encouraged rioting and other antisocial behavior on interfaces in an effort to consolidate existing turf and preempt offensive maneuvers by the other side. This activity has been especially common in areas in which the population is in numeric decline (which is most often the case in Loyalist estates). In these instances, paramilitaries have encouraged young people to riot along an interface. While such rioting may lead members of their own community to evacuate their homes, the paramilitaries bargained that the Housing Executive would not place members of the other community in the area. Although cleared, an area is nonetheless considered more securely Loyalist or Nationalist. In 2004, in testimony before the Northern Ireland Affairs Committee, the Housing Executive explained the barriers that paramilitary manipulation placed on their ability to use such vacated housing:

> Paramilitary organisations on both "sides" of the community are still actively involved in unofficial "policing" and violent inter- or intra-community unrest often simmers or breaks out. These social divisions have a number of impacts on the housing system, and in particular on the capacity of social housing agencies to manage their existing stock and provide accommodation to those in need. For example, there may be a high level of unmet need in particular inner metropolitan areas near to viable dwellings which have been rendered unoccupied by violence or the threat of violence. Social housing managers have to take into account the wishes of applicants, as well as sensible expectations about the risk that would attach to anybody housed in the "wrong" neighbourhood. Any analysis of stock availability, including vacancy rates by sector and geographic location, must take the realities of intense social conflict into account. (Northern Ireland Affairs Committee 2004, Ev 126).

LOYALIST INTERPRETATIONS OF TURF WARS

Loyalists generally assert that they engage in turf battles for defensive rather than recreational or strategic reasons. They contend that Republicans are trying to take over "their" territory and that they must defend their space at all costs. The changing geography of Belfast is, however, more complicated than tropes of Protestant siege and Catholic aggression suggest. As I mention in chapter 3, middle-class Protestants have left the city at high rates over the last twenty years. Those left behind in Protestant working-class areas live in a situation of decline. Loyalist estates are often marked by empty houses, few shops, and a bleak "feel." Brendan Murtagh (2002) has called this process "residualisation." The sense of decline in Loyalist areas is contrasted by demand for housing in Catholic areas and bustling energy on its streets. Indeed, the legacy of discrimination in housing means that Catholics are less willing (or able) to move to the suburbs than their Protestant counterparts, making available housing more scarce in Catholic areas of the city than in Protestant ones. Unfortunately, as Jarman notes, the Loyalist response to the situation is often reactionary:

> Nationalists are therefore perceived to be gaining ground (both in a territorial and a political sense) and unionists are losing ground as the boundaries begin to shift. It is thus increasingly important to defend the boundaries of one's area and ensure that the land does not pass into the hands of the "other." Even if there is no demand for housing within one's own community ownership of the land must be maintained and the boundaries must not change. (2002, 16)

It is not surprising that Loyalists feel a sense of loss as well as deep resentment at the plight of their neighborhoods. Murtagh's (2002) discussion of residualization makes it clear that living in such neighborhoods is often a depressing and difficult venture. Nor is it astonishing that Nationalists would want more space so that their children can relocate nearby when they leave the nest to start their own families. While the differing views of the two communities are to be expected (given the legacy of conflict), the turf battles that attend them are not and have often been manufactured by paramilitaries. On the Loyalist side (the focus of this book), such battles represent the spatial manifestation of a rigid, revanchist identity politic in which Protestant/Loyalist space can only exist when its other is absent from it. Indeed, these turf battles have little to do with the old geopolitical goals of Loyalism—maintenance of the province's union with Great Britain. Rather, the rigid dictates of revanchist Loyalism drive these battles, requiring residents to defend Protestant space against Catholic incursion at all costs. Indeed, attacks are deemed defensive even when the houses being "defended" are empty and even if Protestant families have to be burned out to make a street uninhabitable for Catholics.

The revanchist identity politic that drives these turf battles frames the matter as a zero-sum game and as Republican driven, essentially denying that Loyalists have any culpability. In its more subtle form, this politic is given voice in rhetoric about the greening of Belfast. In its more common, conspiratorial form, an ethnic cleansing trope is used. In the wake of rioting in 2002 at the Cluan Place/Short Strand interface, for example, a Loyalist Web page called Residentgroups warned readers of Republican plans to cleanse Belfast of its Protestant population and highlighted the strategic importance of defending key Loyalist strongholds like Cluan Place.

> To capitulate to the republicans would be to add Cluan Place to the long list of Belfast areas ethnically cleansed of Protestants in the past 30 years—New Barnsley, Grosvenor Road, Cliftonville Road, Upper Meadow Street, Spamount Street, the "Bally" streets of Oldpark, and many more. Cluan Place must remain a Protestant and Unionist area, otherwise the message will go out that no part of Belfast, not even in the stronghold of the East is safe from republican takeover. In recent times, republicans have tried unsuccessfully to add Whitewell estate, "Tigers Bay" and Glenbryn to that list. Cluan Place is also strategically placed, situated as it is adjacent to Ballymacarrett Orange Hall, and close to Templemore Avenue, meeting place of the Orangemen of No. 6 District on the Twelfth. Like its close neighbour, Thistle Court, another small Protestant enclave subjected to bombardment by republicans, Cluan Place represents a symbol of Unionism, Protestantism and loyalism in the Short Strand triangle, and republicans find this very hard to accept. (Residentgroups 2005)

Loyalist groups are not the only ones to accuse Republicans of ethnic cleansing. Politicians have entered the fray as well, introducing the ethnic cleansing trope into official (and mainstream) discourse. Nigel Dodds, an MP for the Democratic Unionist Party, used the phrase publicly in August 2004 in comments he made to the press after violence at the Torrens interface led ten Protestant families to flee their homes. Republicans, he told the press, were engaged in a campaign of ethnic cleansing. He lamented: "This is the most tragic story to emerge from the entire Troubles, in terms of the displacement of a community. This isolated Protestant community has been systematically targeted by republicans over many years. The people living there simply can't take any more" (BBC 2004a).

In tracing this discourse of ethnic cleansing I do not intend to suggest that Loyalists are solely to blame for such turf battles. Indeed, while Gerry Kelly, then a Sinn Fein Assembly member for the Torrens area, rejected Dodd's charge of ethnic cleansing, he admitted that Nationalists had engaged in attacks in the area: "Attacks in this community happen both ways. There were attacks on Torrens and we have put our case time and again. There are people out volunteering [on our side] and trying to prevent these attacks— usually from kids." Kelly also acknowledged, however obliquely, the Nationalists' desire for housing: "Torrens had ongoing problems of negative housing and unionist politicians were involved in planning the move. We need to dispel some of these claims [of ethnic cleansing] that are becoming mythical in proportion" (*Irelandclick* 2004a). My intention in tracing the ethnic cleansing trope is to demonstrate that the backdrop to interface violence on the Loyalist side of the equation—declining population brought on by deindustrialization and Protestant middle-class flight—is largely ignored by revanchist leaders. In its place is a rigidified identity politic that requires a house to be occupied by a Protestant or sit empty if a Protestant cannot be found to reside in it. This discourse is relevant to this chapter because it is into just such situations that new immigrants unwittingly move and through which their presence is interpreted.

Donegall Pass

Donegall Pass is what urban geographers usually call an inner-city neighborhood (see fig. 16).[6] The neighborhood is located approximately three-quarters of a mile south of the Belfast city hall. A brisk walker can traverse the distance in less than fifteen minutes. Its main road, Donegall Passage, is bisected by Shaftsbury Square, off of which flow two of the city's main spoke roads, the Malone and Lisburn roads.

Donegall Pass is part of the Shaftsbury Square ward, but it is also a distinct area within it, with clear boundaries on all sides. To its north, the Donegall Pass area is bordered by the central business district and to the east by the Ormeau Road, a main thoroughfare into the city from east of the Lagan River. A railway line demarcates its southern border, providing a physical barrier between it and the university district. Its western edge is given form by the M1 motorway. Although the northwestern portion of the area abuts Sandy Row, another Loyalist neighborhood, the two areas are distinct because Sandy Row is governed by the UDA while the Pass is controlled by the UVF.

Donegall Pass is decidedly working class, and not surprisingly it is staunchly Loyalist. Union Jack flags fly above many households, and a number of Loyalist murals cover the gable ends of houses and businesses. The content of the murals alerts passers-by that the area is controlled by the A Company of the Second Battalion of the UVF South Belfast Brigade. A few murals also commemorate UVF heroes and "war" dead (see fig. 17). Another mural celebrates the area's flute band, the Young Conquerors (see fig. 18).

---

[6] In the United States this term usually has a negative connotation, bringing to mind images of poverty, violence, and dereliction, although in Northern Ireland, as in much of Europe, it does not have such a connotation. More often than not, the term is used straightforwardly, as a geographic marker. Indeed, although Donegall Pass is socially deprived today, before the Troubles it was a thriving working-class neighborhood with few negative associations linked to it.

Fig. 16. Donegall Pass and the Village. By Nuala M. Cowan, Department of Geography, George Washington University.

Fig. 17. UVF mural commemorating UVF dead, Donegall Pass.

Despite the staunchly Loyalist ethos advanced by these symbols, a walk down Donegall Pass indicates a neighborhood in transition. Just east of Shaftsbury Square, two Chinese restaurants sit on opposite corners. A peek in the windows of one of them during lunchtime presents an ethnic pastiche, but a professionally dressed one. On the next block sits a Buddhist Center and a travel agency advertising cheap flights to Asia. On the north side, near the end of the street, is the gasworks building, which used to house the main source of power generation in the city. Today the building is part of a business park and is mixed use. At the intersection of the Ormeau Road (the A24) sits the city's newest luxury hotel, the Radisson, and a new high-rise office building. The area west of Shaftsbury Square is more residential. The main road crosses the rail line into the Village, a run-down area of terraced homes.

Immigrants settled into the Donegall Pass area for a number of reasons. An obvious point of attraction is the area's centrality. Its proximity to major transportation hubs (the bus and train stations) is especially attractive for immigrants dependent on public transport. Cheap rental housing is also plentiful in the area. During the Troubles, the area's proximity to the city center (a focal point of IRA bombing) made it an unattractive area in which to live, and those who could afford to leave did so. When things began to calm down in the early nineties, much of the empty housing was purchased

Fig. 18. UVF mural for the Young Conquerors Flute Band.

by investors and developers, who offered it as low-cost rental housing. Rental prices have remained low, however, because the area is more dilapidated than other centrally located neighborhoods, such as the nearby university district.

Donegall Pass is also situated near two hospitals, the Belfast City Hospital and the Great Victoria Hospital, both of which employ increasing numbers of immigrants. Indeed, a shortage of nurses and hospital workers in the mid-nineties led hospitals like Great Victoria to recruit health-care workers from overseas, drawing qualified applicants from countries such as the Philippines that have workers with high levels of education but job markets that are saturated. As is often the case with immigrant enclaves, the Pass's attraction as a destination for new immigrants has developed a self-sustaining momentum. Indeed, as immigrants establish themselves in an area, they often send word to family members back home to follow. These second-in-line migrants generally settle with or near their relatives rather than engaging in an independent search of their own for housing.

The literature on migration abounds with current and historical examples of the tensions that arise when immigrants arrive in working-class or run-down areas of a city (Lahav 2004; Ignatiev 1996; Vargas 2004). In many ways, Donegall Pass is no different from the hundreds of other places in the world where such changes have occurred or are under way. As in other places, there are deep cultural differences between the Pass's new migrants and its indigenous, Loyalist inhabitants. They speak different languages, worship different gods, and in many cases eat different foods. There are also socioeconomic differences between the Pass's new migrants and its older inhabitants. New migrants often work in professional jobs (such as nursing), and few are unemployed. Loyalist inhabitants, by contrast, work in low-end service jobs or subsist on state aid. The Shaftsbury Square ward of the city, in which Donegall Pass is located, is ranked as the fourteenth most deprived ward in the city (NISRA 2001a).

On their own, these patterns of cultural difference and socioeconomic variance can create a volatile mix. In Northern Ireland, and in Donegall Pass in particular, this mix has been made all the more explosive by the presence of paramilitaries.

Cleaning out the Immigrants

In January 2004 journalist Angelique Chrisafis, writing in the *Guardian* newspaper, dubbed Belfast the "race-hate capital of Europe":

Northern Ireland, which is 99% white, is fast becoming the race-hate capital of Europe. It holds the UK's record for the highest rate of racist attacks: spitting and stoning in the street, human excrement on doorsteps, swastikas on walls, pipe bombs, arson, the ransacking of houses with baseball bats and crow bars, and white supremacist leaflets nailed to front doors. (Chrisafis 2004)

Chrisafis also made a link between the racist attacks and Loyalist paramilitaries. Indeed, the title of her article, "Racist War of the Loyalist Street Gangs," left little to the imagination. Inside the article she expanded on the point:

> In the past weeks, fear has deepened. Protestant working-class neighbourhoods are showing a pattern of orchestrated house attacks aimed at "ethnically cleansing" minority groups. It is happening in streets run by Loyalist paramilitaries where every Chinese takeaway owner already pays protection money and racists have plentiful access to guns.

Chrisafis also quoted a Belfast estate agent who suggested that paramilitaries had told him not to rent to ethnic minorities.

> [The] agent said yesterday that he had been visited by a group he thought were paramilitaries telling him not to rent another house to "Chinese, blacks, or Asians." Ten of his tenants were forced out last year.

The estate agent, William Faulkner, later told other reporters that the UVF was behind the purported ban (Kearney 2005; McGuigan 2004).[7]

Chrisafis singled out the Village in Donegall Pass as a particularly problematic area of the city, noting:

> The Village in south Belfast is a run-down network of Loyalist terraces where unemployment is high, union flags sag from lampposts and almost every family has a link to Loyalist paramilitaries. In post-peace process Northern Ireland, communities like this are more segregated than ever—through choice. Last year, five student houses, home to mixed Protestants and Catholics, were attacked until they were vacated. The siege mentality against "outsiders" is rife. (2004)

Chrisafis's description of the attacks and their background highlights two characteristics that make the violence against minorities/immigrants in Northern Ireland unique to the rest of Europe. The first is the orchestrated nature of the attacks, which suggest paramilitary involvement; the second is the presence of racketeering in the area, which suggests a structural reason for the enmity between native and non-native in the area.

Indeed, although there had been violence against minorities in Donegall Pass before 2003, the sharp uptick in racial incidents that year appears to

---

[7] In 2005 *Daily Ireland* reported that the UVF burned the estate agent's office twice since he went public with his allegations (Kearney 2005).

be directly related to a dispute over racketeering. Five of the seven sources interviewed for this chapter told me, for example, that attacks increased in number and intensity after the owner of a Chinese restaurant agreed to serve as a PSNI witness in a racketeering case against the UVF commander in the area.[8] One of these sources also suggested a backstory that not only explains why the restaurant owner decided to approach the PSNI when he did, but demonstrates how entrenched paramilitary policing was in the area as well. The source claimed the restaurant owner called on the local UVF commander to resolve a dispute in the area and that the owner only went to the PSNI after a disagreement about the commander's resolution of the matter. Although only one source provided details on the backstory, another corroborated the general outlines of it, noting that "it seems to fall into place from all the information I have." The source who informed me of the backstory was not a member of the UVF or connected to it; the source who corroborated the story was connected to the UVF.

The story began when two Chinese restaurants in the area, hereafter Restaurant A and Restaurant B, became involved in a clash over a Chinese gambling ring.[9] In late 2002, members of this ring began gambling in Restaurant A. One night the following spring, members of the gang lost a significant amount of money gambling in the restaurant. Charging foul play, they threatened the owners of Restaurant A, who promptly forced the party to leave and banned them from returning to the area. A few nights later, however, the gamblers returned to the neighborhood and set up shop nearby, in Restaurant B.[10]

The owners of Restaurant A were angry; not only had the gang members returned, but they had relocated to a nearby competitor's dining room. Restaurant A retaliated by launching an attack against Restaurant B, defacing the establishment's façade and vandalizing the owner's car. After the attack the owner of Restaurant B contacted the local UVF leadership to sort out the problem. The UVF "investigated" the situation and levied two "punishments." It ordered a stop to the gambling and directed Restaurant A to shut down for two weeks.[11]

---

[8] The other two sources did not reject the racketeering charge. One was unaware a racketeering arrangement had sparked the trouble. The other argued that although racketeering was a problem, racist attitudes did more to explain the attacks than a spat over racketeering.

[9] I do not use the real names of these restaurants because doing so could inflame UVF members implicated in the attacks and lead to more assaults against immigrants. It is important to note that none of the information provided here comes from the restaurant owners or from those associated with them.

[10] Although my other sources were unaware of the gambling dispute between Restaurants A and B, none seemed surprised by it. As one explained, "I do understand there is some fighting between two rival restaurants [in the area]. It's to do over territory, maybe gambling."

[11] In the world of paramilitary racketeering, criminal activity by nonparamilitary actors is usually strictly forbidden unless the paramilitary first approves of it and is given an opportunity to share in the profits.

The owners of Restaurant B were initially happy with the UVF's ruling. The following week, however, relations soured when the UVF hiked its protection fee. As the source stated: "They closed the restaurant [Restaurant A] for a few weeks. And like I mentioned, you know, after they did the punishment, they asked [Restaurant B] for more money. . . . You know, if you use their services, it's not free." From all accounts, Restaurant B paid the higher extortion fee, but the owner was angry enough to contact the PSNI and agree to testify in a pending government case against the UVF for racketeering.[12] The UVF's South Belfast Brigade soon found out about Restaurant B's plan, however, and it was then that the attacks against immigrants in the area intensified.[13] Between April and December 2003, 212 racial incidents were recorded in the province—almost as many as the number (226) recorded for the previous year as a whole. By March 2004, the number of attacks stood at 453. An alarming number of these attacks, 147 of them, occurred in South Belfast, in Donegall Pass (Police Services of Northern Ireland [PSNI] 2005).

Attacks ran the gamut from harassment and intimidation to physical assaults on immigrants' homes. The goal was to drive migrants out of the area. A particularly nasty attack in December caught the attention of the press. The BBC ran a story on the assault the following day.

> Two Chinese families—one with newborn twins—and one of African descent have since fled their homes following the attacks in the loyalist Village area between 1900 and 2000 GMT on Saturday. In the most serious incident, the gang of up to four men broke into a house at Broadway Parade. They assaulted two pregnant Chinese women then broke a man's nose by smashing him in the face with a brick. Windows were broken in two other houses in the area shortly afterwards. Police say the occupants of all three houses, some of them young children, have left their homes for their own safety. (BBC 2003a)

All of my sources described the attacks as retaliation against the restaurant owner. As one source explained, "pressure was put on the Chinese community to get the owner to withdraw [from the suit]." Another said the attacks sent a message that "if he didn't drop the case there would be repercussions for the Chinese community." The source who provided the backstory also

---

[12] Another source suggested that the restaurant owner knew someone in the PSNI who asked him to participate in the racketeering case.

[13] A 2005 report on hate crimes by the Northern Ireland Affairs Committee confirms that attacks against Chinese people intensified after the owner of a Chinese restaurant made an official complaint to the PSNI about racketeering. The report does not, however, mention the initial spat between the two restaurants or the involvement of the UVF commander in sorting it out. The report asserts: "Tensions were provoked following a threat made against a Chinese restaurant owner who reported a case of extortion which resulted in two local men facing trial. Prior to the trial, pressure was placed on this businessman and the Chinese community, in an attempt to coerce the businessman from proceeding with the case" (Northern Ireland Affairs Committee 2005, Ev 222).

suggested that one of the houses subject to attack was targeted because the owner of Restaurant B was running an illegal business from the premise. The source claimed it was a safe house operation for illegal migrant women brought to Northern Ireland to give birth and obtain UK passports for their children. By striking out at the safe house, the source told me, the UVF was sending the owner of Restaurant B a message (we know about your plans to testify for the PSNI) and a warning (testify at your own peril).

In testimony he gave before the House of Commons' Northern Ireland Affairs Committee the following year, a spokesman for the Northern Ireland Council for Ethnic Minorities (NICEM) made much the same point, albeit with considerably less detail.

> Firstly, paramilitaries being involved in racketeering is not a new issue within the Chinese community and certain Asian communities running businesses in the local area. The high profile attack in the Donegall Road area last December related to revenge by the UVF. That involved racketeering in which a Chinese restaurant owner became the prosecution witness for the PSNI. As a result, the Chinese were attacked and targeted. (Northern Ireland Affairs Committee 2005, Ev 21)

Another source suggested that the houses were attacked because the estate agent in charge of renting them, William Faulkner (whose comments to a newspaper are excerpted earlier in the chapter), was not paying his weekly racket. The source suggested the agent had been asked to pay five pounds per property per week and had balked at the fee, refusing to pay it.

Whatever the genesis of the December attack, it was not a lone incident. Indeed, attacks against ethnic minorities continued, in fact increasing steeply in the following months. In 2004–5, 813 racial incidents were recorded in the province, an increase of 79.5 percent from the previous year, and 159 of them occurred in the Donegall Pass area (PSNI 2005). The increase may be due in part to the momentum such phenomena tend to develop, but it also reflected a concerted campaign to legitimate past attacks and encourage more on the grounds that Loyalist turf was under siege. Indeed, in March 2004, a few months after the December attacks on the safe house, a flier was distributed in the neighborhood with the ominous-sounding title "Yellow Invasion: Who's "Pass" is it?" The one-page leaflet began by noting the historically Protestant roots of the area:

> Donegall Pass is no longer a Protestant/loyalist area, it is commonly known as "Chinatown" throughout our city and the people of the Pass are in the midst of losing the already small foothold they have in their community forever.

Chinese migrants were also described as invaders who were taking Protestant housing away from Protestant people:

These immigrants occupy a vast amount of our houses stopping any Protestant families moving in that would be more beneficial for the betterment of our community in all aspects of community life. The overwhelming mass of Chinese immigrants in Donegall Pass are driving our youth to move out of the area where they were reared, because they see no future for them in the Chinatown/Donegall Pass. The Chinese only take from our community and provide nothing for it.

The leaflet also painted migrants as an enemy on a par with the IRA:

The influx of the yellow people into Donegall Pass has done more damage than 35 years of the IRA's recent campaign of Republican propaganda and violence waged against the Protestant community of Donegall Pass. It is eroding the Britishness and Ulster Protestant culture and heritage from our area more than the IRA could have ever hoped to do.

The manifesto concluded with a call to arms:

The time has come to fight back before it is too late. Rid our community of these Chinese immigrants and clear the way for Protestant families to move in and our young people to remain and contribute in helping to make our community a better place to live. Reclaim your area—give the Pass its Protestant and Ulster culture and heritage back.

While the "yellow invasion" leaflet was unsigned, the chief constable for the PSNI, Hugh Orde, quickly denounced the document as the work of Loyalist paramilitaries. Although he would not identify which paramilitary was involved, he was adamant that at least one of the Loyalist paramilitaries was behind the document. As he explained: "It's self-evident. That's exactly where it comes from. . . . I won't attribute it [which paramilitary] at the moment. But the tone of the statement would make anyone with commonsense clear that it's from a Loyalist paramilitary group" (Keenan 2004). My source for the backstory was more specific. He/she described the "yellow invasion" leaflet as the work of a commander in the UVF's South Belfast brigade.

There is also some evidence that the local UVF battalion responsible for the attacks had made common cause with a British neo-Nazi group. Rolston (2004) alleges, for example, that the UVF commander in the Pass had links to Combat 18. Rolston (2004) speculates that the group, which has long tried to establish connections with Loyalists in Ulster, turned to the UVF after the UDA's 2002 internal feud led to the ouster of its former affiliate Johnny Adair. As I mention in chapter 6, Combat 18 was involved in both Adair's attempt to take over UVF turf on the mid- and upper Shankill in 2000 and his later attempts to usurp the UDA central command in 2002.

Unfortunately, the involvement of paramilitaries in attacks on minorities and immigrants in the Donegall Pass area of South Belfast has been difficult to prove. In 2004–5 only 15.9 percent of racial offenses were prosecuted (PSNI 2005). Compounding this low prosecution rate is the fact that many other cases do not make it to court because witnesses are too intimidated to testify. Indeed, even the racketeering case in which the owner of Restaurant B agreed to participate fell apart when he failed to show up in court to testify. As one source explained, "I understand the owner left the restaurant and moved to another part of Northern Ireland because he feared for his life." Another source suggested that the man left the province.

In the following section I detail political Loyalists' efforts to stop the attacks. Before doing so, however, it is worth considering the nature of paramilitary racketeering pre- and post-1998 because a rackets dispute explains the sudden upsurge in racist attacks. During the Troubles, both the UDA and the UVF were involved in racketeering. The UDA tended to extort protection money from builders, whereas the UVF focused on smaller businesses in Belfast (Bruce 1992). Although racketeering was never popular, most business owners paid up. They did so because nonpayment often meant having your shop or building site burned out. Both groups were able to justify their actions at least in part by reminding Loyalists that there was a war on.[14] Since the advent of peace, however, racketeering has become increasingly difficult to justify. Indeed, in 2003, when the racist attacks began to increase, the UVF was in a cease-fire, and its sworn enemy, the IRA, was in the process of winding down its military operations.

After 1998 the UVF defended its continued racketeering with two lines of argument. Some leaders argued that fund-raising for weapons and other military gear was essential because, the IRA's dismantlement notwithstanding, other Republican paramilitaries continued to exist. Other leaders argued that Loyalists had to continue to fund their arsenals because if the conflict were to reignite, the IRA was better positioned to restock its arsenal than the UVF was. The breadth of IRA connections to international arms dealers dwarfs those of either of the Loyalist paramilitaries.

Although these claims are not inaccurate—most people believe the IRA could rearm itself quickly—they largely skirt the issue. While the UVF was still in operation, it could easily have used membership dues to keep its arsenal up to date. (Indeed, the UVF's decision to stand down without decommissioning its weapons suggests it thinks this is possible). The continuation of racketeering after 1998, therefore, begs an obvious question. What was the purpose of racketeering in the context of peace? The answer is complicated. The proceeds from some rackets, or percentages of them, went back to the leadership, and likely for the reasons outlined earlier. But evidence also suggests that commanders and other midlevel leaders were skimming

---

[14] Bruce (1992) notes that the UDA's confederate system permitted more abuse of rackets than did the UVF's more centralized command structure. UVF abuses were also limited because it confined its operations to Belfast. According the Bruce (1992), the UVF's rural brigades were strongly opposed to racketeering.

increasing amounts off the top. They also took advantage of the perks associated with racketeering. One source recalled seeing the perks in action. "I was in [name of restaurant withheld] and the local paramilitary man came in. He went straight into the kitchen. He left with a bag of carryout. He may have paid in the back, but I didn't see him paying at the counter, you know." Paramilitary men also used rackets to buttress their criminal enterprises. Many Loyalist paramilitary men, for example, have been selling ecstasy and other club drugs in nightclubs that pay protection fees. Although a drug bust could lead authorities to shut a business down, most owners permitted the sales because they would be threatened with bigger extortion fees or other forms of intimidation if they did not (McDowell 2001). In short, the ideological rationale of racketeering—funding the cause—was replaced with the more banal motive of profiteering. Moreover, it is worth noting that when the UVF did stand down, it failed to list fundraising among the activities, such as recruitment, military training, and intelligence gathering that it would halt.

When questions about the legitimacy of racketeering arise, paramilitary men have often sought to legitimize their behavior by manufacturing new threats, reasoning that people will look to them for protection. This tactic has had two effects. First, it diverted attention from the problems at hand. Indeed, in Donegall Pass the issue ceased to be whether paramilitary racketeering was legitimate and became instead whether Chinese people had a right to live in South Belfast. Second, scapegoating has created a general climate of fear, which has helped paramilitary men maintain power even as their legitimacy has waned. If Chinese people can be seen as invaders, then so too can other outsiders, including Ugandans, Poles, and even college students. In such a climate anyone can be subject to attack, and submission is seen as the best strategy for avoiding it.

This logic represents a particularly virulent form of particularism in which others are deemed so dangerous that they can be dealt with only through violence and expulsion. Indeed, the "yellow invasion" leaflet defined the Chinese as a threat tantamount to that posed by the IRA, even though the immigrant population in Belfast is both small and unarmed. The comparison is, as one informant forcefully stressed to me, an indication of how far the ideology of Loyalism has moved from its traditional base.

Although racketeering set the stage for the initial imbroglio, racism was also clearly a factor. As one informant explained to me, "it [racketeering] doesn't explain why Ugandans were attacked, Bangladeshis were attacked, or why Poles were attacked later [in 2006]." To some degree, the racist leafleting resonated among residents of the area. It was, after all, seen as fertile ground for the far right (some would say fascist) British National Party (BNP). As the report on hate crimes from the Northern Ireland Affairs Committee states:

At least some of the attacks would appear to have been motivated by what might be termed "casual" racism, which may have been stirred up by leafleting campaigns by British racist groups. A member of the British National Party visited Belfast towards the end of 2003 and the BNP clearly see Northern Ireland as a potentially fruitful recruiting ground. The links between racist organisations in Great Britain and aspects of loyalism have been fairly well documented. (2005, Ev 63)

In short, the residualization (to use Murtagh's term) of Loyalist neighborhoods provides a fertile base from which to stir racist sentiments and organize recruitment drives.

Progressive Loyalism Responds

When journalist Angelique Chrisafis dubbed Northern Ireland the "race-hate capital of Europe" in January 2004, she suggested that Loyalist neighborhoods were choosing to be segregated. At the end of her article, however, Chrisafis described Belfast as waiting for the paramilitary leadership to do something about the attacks, implying that the campaigns were driven by rogue elements within the paramilitaries and that those elements could be reigned in by the leadership. As she writes in the conclusion of her article: "But most of all, Belfast waits for the loyalist paramilitary leadership, which controls the working-class communities and young lads who live in fear of punishment beatings, to make a statement or move which shows the attacks will not be tolerated" (2004).

Although the UVF has since stood down, it is worth considering a key question Chrisafis's article raises about the nearly ten-year period in Northern Ireland where peace and paramilitaries co-existed—who's job was it to police the paramilitaries? On the one hand, many people in Loyalist neighborhoods despise the paramilitaries. They want nothing more than to see them eliminated, or at the very least neutralized. As Councillor Mark Langhammer has cogently observed, "the privacy of the polls are the only place where working class Protestants can punish paramilitaries, and they never fail to take the opportunity to do so" (2003). On the other hand, people living in Loyalist estates are suspicious of the police, and when problems arise they often turn to paramilitaries to solve them. In so doing they not only legitimate paramilitary power but even buttress it.[15] Nor are immigrants immune to this paradoxical behavior. Indeed, it is telling that when Restaurant B had trouble with Restaurant A, it contacted the UVF to take care of the problem. It is important, therefore, to assess not only the efforts of

---

[15] See Brewer, Lockhart, and Rogers (1998) and Knox (2002) for detailed analyses of the contradictory view of paramilitaries in working-class areas.

paramilitary leaders to solve the problem of minority attacks in Donegall Pass but their effectiveness as well. Indeed, this issue has wide relevance as it is likely to occur in any post-conflict country that does not actively dismantle its armed groups after peace.

Although Chrisafis's report suggested that the Loyalist paramilitary leadership was doing nothing about the violence in Donegall Pass, plenty of evidence indicates that some Loyalist leaders were "doing something." David Ervine, for example, worked with local community groups to calm things down. One source, who works in a community group serving minorities, stated, "We have been working with him to solve a lot of the problems. Basically, he was trying to ease the tensions."

After the brutal attacks in December, the PUP also issued a joint statement with the Northern Ireland Council for Ethnic Minorities condemning the racial incidents in South Belfast:

> The Northern Ireland Council for Ethnic Minorities (NICEM) and the Progressive Unionist Party (PUP) make the following statement today. We unequivocally condemn the recent racial harassment and racially motivated attacks in the Donegall Road village. We witness the increase of these attacks on the most vulnerable groups in our society with dismay. We contend that everyone has an inherent responsibility to help stop these attacks.

Echoing the Belfast Agreement, the statement went on to declare the importance of being able to live free from intimidation:

> Everyone has the rights to be free from fears, intimidation and harassment in both working and family life. Good relations are built upon with understanding and respect. In order to promote a multi-racial and intercultural society in Northern Ireland, we must accept and embrace differences and diversity in an inclusive manner. Different traditions and cultures are an invaluable asset to our society and should not, indeed must not, be considered a threat.

The statement also rejected, albeit implicitly, the discourse of ethnic cleansing that has often been leveled against Nationalists and migrants searching for housing in Loyalist neighborhoods. Rather, it laid out a more accurate history of the housing issue in the area, highlighting the role of Protestant middle-class flight as well market forces in attracting newcomers.

> We must recognize that the village area is suffering from severe social deprivation and poverty. Previously the area mainly accommodated students at Queens and staff from both the hospitals nearby. The area became run down and a lot of vacant houses were sold to private homeowners and developers. As a result a substantial number of private rented houses are available in the area with modest rent and easy access to the city centre and workplace. Over time, different groupings of black and minority ethnic people have moved into the area.

In the fifth paragraph NICEM and the PUP approached the issue of blame. They began by pointing the finger at white supremacist groups working in the area:

> Formerly, only minor incidents of intimidation and harassment were the common experience of the black and minority ethnic people living in the village. However, for the last year, the recent White Nationalist Party, an offspring of the BNP in England, has been disseminating the inflammatory information on the black and ethnic minorities living in the area, such as asylum seekers, refugees, or migrant workers describing them as "people who are swamping your area." This in turn created a climate of fear among the indigenous people of the area causing them to consider those who were black and a minority ethnic as a serious threat to their well being.

In the next paragraph NICEM and the PUP also acknowledged that "individual members" of Loyalist paramilitaries had been involved in the attacks, although mention was made only in passing, in the middle of the paragraph:

> Since the proliferation of this propaganda, vicious and orchestrated attacks have been carried out. These are evidenced in two separate incidents, in June and July, of pipe bombs being thrown into the homes of different black families, living on the same street no less. In addition, there were the high profile attacks before and after Christmas of last year on families of minority ethnic backgrounds. We recognize that individual members of the loyalist paramilitaries have been involved in these attacks, as well as unaffiliated indigenous people. We also recognize that the majority of the indigenous people in the area are adversely affected, do not want such atrocious acts to be profuse in their community, and long for a much sought after peace.

After laying out its analysis of the genesis of the problem, the PUP and NICEM proposed a fourteen-plank course of action. One-third of the suggestions were specifically targeted at the PSNI. Suggestions included encouraging more systemized responses to racial incidents, eliminating institutional racism within the PSNI, providing high-quality interpretation services, and requiring anti-racism training for police trainees.

In addition to the press release, Loyalist leaders also took to the streets. A month after the UVF's purported December attack on the immigrant safe house, both David Ervine of the PUP and Frankie Gallagher,[16] a spokesperson for the Ulster Political Research Group, participated in an anti-racism rally held in downtown Belfast. They also attended a rally against racism on

---

[16] The reader will recall from the discussion in chapter 3 that Frankie Gallagher adopted a revanchist approach to class politics. His willingness to stand against attacks on immigrants is evidence not only of the personal level at which tensions between revanchist and political Loyalism can play out, but of the contingencies of the political landscape.

29 October later that year. Both rallies were organized by the Anti-Racist Network (ARN). The participation of Loyalists in these events did not go unnoticed by its organizers. Writing in the *Blanket* about the October rally, for example, ARN's chairperson, Davy Carlin, was mostly positive about their participation:[17] "[it] was an 'unprecedented' incident when I was holding an Anti Racism banner and the combined leaderships of Northern Ireland's loyalism were behind it. That is, David Ervine, as well as Tommy Kirkham, Frankie Gallagher, Frank McCoubrey, Jackie McDonald etc. Therefore I have found during eight years as an activist that politics on many occasions can not only be inspirational but interesting at times" (Carlin 2004a, 2004b).

Given that the rally included a variety of left-leaning groups often affiliated with Republicanism and was attended by top Sinn Fein leaders, Ervine's and Gallagher's participation was a brave move. Indeed, although Ervine and Gallagher escaped "direct fire" for their involvement, Loyalist participation in the march inspired animosity in some Loyalist quarters. After the January march, for example, a group named Redwatch put up a Web page that not only posted photographs and the home addresses of the march's organizers but requested information on unidentified participants in the group's photo gallery of the march. The Web page did not mince words in regard to Loyalist participation: "People saying they were Loyalists attended this Demo. Notice there are no Union flags on this 'parade,' plenty of red ones though. How can so-called Loyalists mix with these Fenian scumbags and still call themselves British? They are a disgrace to this country and should hang their heads in shame!!" (Redwatch 2005).

For its part, the UVF leadership responded by rebuking those behind the attack. In February 2004, the UVF leadership announced that it was standing down its top brass in South Belfast (McCambridge 2004; Rolston 2004). The man, alleged to be in his late thirties, had only been in control of the company since May 2003 when the previous company commander had been jailed. The illicit nature of paramilitary activity tends to inhibit standdown orders because the expelled often seek revenge by turning to the police. Stand-down orders can also lead to splintering or factionalism. These disincentives make a stand-down order significant. As Rolston (2004) notes, "as symbols go, the sacking of a local warlord is a particularly powerful one" (2004).

---

[17] Carlin was criticized by other groups on the left, which charged that he was unwittingly making common cause with bigots (Carlin 2004a, 2004b). Indeed, the Irish Republican Socialist Party (IRSP) viewed Loyalist participation in the march as hypocritical: "The sight of the leaders of the UDA and of the UVF turning up at an anti-racist rally recently in Belfast was enough to turn many sick. These are the same individuals who give cover and succour to the murder gangs who petrol bombed Catholic homes, drove large number of Catholics from mixed areas, and engaged in a sustained murder campaign against Catholics in an effort to destroy republicanism" (Irish Republican Socialist Party 2004).

Loyalist community workers in South Belfast also tried to calm tensions on the ground locally. A source connected to the UVF told me, for example, that he was asked to investigate the claims of estate agent Faulkner that a UVF commander in the area was charging exorbitant protection fees. The source explained that the UVF leadership wanted to assess whether Faulkner was telling the truth so it could make a determination on its commander's behavior. The source concluded that the estate agent was making a false claim:[18] "He may be paying money to another paramilitary organization. He wasn't paying to the UVF, but, he was accusing the UVF of collecting it." Fact-checking missions by paramilitary go-betweens are especially important in areas like Donegall Pass, where the police have too little credibility to get to the bottom of many issues. And although the source ruled that Faulkner was lying, it is clear that the UVF wanted to get its facts straight before taking action.

There is no doubt that key leaders within Loyalism have made a concerted effort to end the violence in Donegall Pass. Some have done so at great personal and political risk. Joining a parade with Sinn Fein leaders was a hugely symbolic step for Loyalist leaders. And standing down a commander is no mean feat in paramilitary circles. The risk and high symbolism of these acts notwithstanding, they failed to solve the problem in Donegall Pass.

Indeed, one source expressed skepticism about the extent of political Loyalism's efforts, remarking that the "yellow invasion" leaflet was printed and distributed *after* the UVF man was stood down. The source suggested that the timing of the document—which he/she suggested appeared after the sacking—indicates that the UVF did not actually stand the man down. Moreover, in mid-August 2004, almost six months after the UVF's announcement, residents in Donegall Pass told the *South Belfast News* that the UVF man was still in control of the neighborhood and had orchestrated attacks against his critics there (*Irelandclick* 2004b). Residents also claimed that members of the Young Conquerors, the area's UVF flute band, were carrying out the attacks for the man and were often drunk while doing so. Residents alleged that the Young Conquerors had beaten a French resident in the area for walking around in his home without clothes. In another instance, they alleged that the group's members killed seagulls flying in the area. One resident told the paper, "the local UVF are running wild and this

---

[18] The Belfast press has also discredited William Faulkner, albeit for different reasons. In January 2004 the *Sunday Life* reported that Faulkner had been arrested in 1994 in Scotland for selling ecstasy tablets worth £60,000 (Breen 2004a). A subsequent article reported that Faulkner was indebted to a number of parties in the province (Breen 2004b). Faulkner argued that his background had no bearing on the UVF's behavior and suggested that the group had tipped off the *Sunday Life* about his past. However, the *Sunday Life* denied the UVF was the source of its story, noting that Faulkner "wrongly suggested that the UVF had told us about his appearance in the debtor's magazine" (Breen 2004b).

area is going to become a ghetto unless someone sorts these people out" (*Irelandclick* 2004b).

It is possible the UVF did not stand the man down, but both journalistic accounts (McCambridge 2004; Rolston 2004) and the remainder of my sources suggest that the man was formally let go and that he was acting alone (that is, unaffiliated) in the months thereafter. One of my sources also suggests that the stood-down commander was not the same person responsible for posting the "yellow invasion" document. Although the veracity of the stand-down order is an important issue (and one I cannot conclusively ascertain here), the more relevant point is that residents and journalists alike assumed that ultimate responsibility for stopping the attacks lay with the UVF leadership rather than with the PSNI.

Criminologists identify two types of internal affairs paramilitaries have tended to police since the push to peace began in 1994: civil offenses and political "crimes" (Knox 2002; Silke 1998). The first category includes burglary, vandalism, and rape, which have long been policed by the paramilitaries. That paramilitaries continued to police such offenses after 1998 is the result of both the continuing mistrust of the Police (a legacy of the Troubles) and the failure of the new PSNI to win the confidence of these same communities. Paramilitaries also policed political affairs. These crimes generally include offenses against the paramilitary itself, including "unlawful" racketeering, criticism of paramilitaries, and collusion with the PSNI (Silke 1998; Knox 2002).

The UVF's decision to stand down its commander represents a form of civil and political policing. Although the former commander's crimes were clearly antisocial, they were also political in that they violated the UVF's cease-fire order. The UVF responded to the commander's crimes by acting as police, judge, and jury. The group is not, however, a normal arm of law or justice. It operates independently of a court system, and its punishments would not pass legal muster by human rights standards accepted in London or Brussels. Indeed, the typical paramilitary sentence in post-conflict Northern Ireland—a punishment beating—usually involves breaking an offender's kneecaps with a blunt object or a gun.

The UVF's punishment for its former commander was nonviolent. Unlike hundreds of other people who have been subjected to Loyalist paramilitary policing, the commander was merely relieved of his job. His continued power in the area, however, raises an important question—what should be done to halt the commander's actions, and more importantly, who should do it?

As I note above, many people expected the UVF to take care of the matter once and for all. However, if the UVF leadership had decided to solve the problem of the rogue commander once and for all (i.e., beyond its initial stand-down order), its punishment likely would have been violent. If he was lucky, he would have received a punishment beating. If he was unlucky, he could have lost his life. The commander's actions, both before and after his purported standing down, put the UVF leadership in a difficult position. If the UVF meted out a violent punishment, it could be charged with human rights abuse. If it did nothing, it could be accused of sanctioning the commander's actions or, at the very least, of letting the attacks happen. In effect, the leadership had no good options. The best solution, of course, is to let the police take care of the man. But the police seem unwilling or unable to do the job. Indeed, one source suggested that the police have abdicated local policing to the paramilitaries: "Police seem quite happy with the arrangement. They wouldn't say so, but it [paramilitary control] keeps some crime down in the areas, and if a window gets busted out, they [the police] don't have to respond. It's not having to get sucked up in all that paperwork."

The rogue commander's actions also demonstrate the structural limitations that operation within paramilitary confines placed on political Loyalists in the PUP. Although there is no indication that the PUP supported the rogue commander's actions, its relationship with the UVF limited how vociferous its critiques could be. The joint condemnation of the attacks by the PUP and NICEM is a case in point.[19] On the issue of blame, for example, a full paragraph was devoted to detailing the role of outside racist groups in fueling the problem, whereas only a clause, in a larger sentence midway through a paragraph, covered the role of Loyalist paramilitaries in the crime. The press release even suggested that only individual paramilitary members were involved in the attacks. The evidence, however, clearly points to the involvement of a local leader with foot soldiers at his disposal. Still, even if one paramilitary man was acting alone, without the consent of the leadership, it was one man too many.

The solutions called for by the PUP and NICEM are also telling. Over one-third of the solutions were aimed at the PSNI and reforms within it. Although such reforms are without a doubt necessary, the joint press release contained no suggestions for reforming the paramilitary structures that give rise to organized and systematic violence, of which the attacks against minorities in Donegall Pass are a clear example. It has been over a decade since the 1994 ceasefires, and almost as many since the historic Belfast agreement. While most people did not expect paramilitaries to disappear overnight, it is unclear what their purpose was when the attacks were occurring. What is clear is that racketeering, intimidation campaigns, and attacks on minorities are far from Loyalism's traditional casus belli—maintaining union with Great Britain.

---

[19] Problems in the PUP/NICEM joint press release are not an indictment of NICEM. Indeed, the organization needs the support of people who have credibility in areas where attacks happen. And this need clearly and understandably inhibits what the group can say about internal paramilitary matters.

Of relevance here is what all this meant for political Loyalism. By 2003 political Loyalism's flagship venture, the Progressive Unionist Party, had hit a wall. In the 2003 Legislative Assembly elections, one of the PUP's two members, Billy Hutchinson, lost his seat in a tightly contested election. Many people credit his loss to Protestant exasperation with continuing Loyalist violence. Indeed, a relentless campaign for justice by the Protestant father of a UVF murder victim appears to have been a decisive factor in Hutchinson's loss (Edwards and Bloomer 2004). As I detail in the next chapter, the father, Raymond McCord, waged a public campaign to bring his son's killer to justice, and along the way he battered the reputations of both the UVF and PUP.

After the 2003 election, many commentators speculated that the PUP would soon disappear. The rumors intensified in the wake of the UVF's 2005 feud with the LVF, with commentators suggesting that the PUP could only survive by delinking entirely from the UVF. At its annual meeting in 2005 the PUP chose to maintain a connection to the UVF, but several months later it proved itself ready for a new political alliance. In May 2006, Reg Empy, head of the UUP, announced that his party would form an Assembly group with the PUP (Walker 2006). Had the alliance stuck, it would have increased the number of ministerial seats for the UUP and decreased those of Sinn Fein.[20]

Although the move was driven by raw political considerations—how can we take seats away from Sinn Fein?—reaction from Nationalists and Unionists alike demonstrated the shrinking good will people were ready to grant the PUP after almost a decade of post-accord UVF existence. The DUP were particularly offended. Peter Weir called the move "grubby" and suggested that the UUP had "compromised their integrity" (Weir 2006), whereas Sammy Wilson deemed it "cynical." The SDLP's Alban Maginness intoned, "the bottom line is that the UVF is not on ceasefire" (McAdam 2006). Internal critics weighed in as well. Lady Sylvia Hermon, the UUP's only MP at Westminster, said the alliance had caused her "great distress" (Walker 2006).

In the next chapter I explore these sorts of reactions in more detail. Suffice it to say here that although the UVF and the PUP deserve their fair share

---

[20] In September 2006 the Speaker of the Northern Ireland Assembly chose to rescind recognition of the UUP/PUP Assembly group. Then UUP leader Reg Empey decried the move in a formal statement: "In May we acted in good faith under the standing orders, to maximize unionist representation, and at that time the Speaker accepted our position. However, following an intervention by the DUP Deputy Leader, Peter Robinson, she has changed her mind. This we regret, as the consequence is a promotion of Sinn Fein into second place in the Assembly, a position which was not given to them by the electorate in 2003." Empey also accused the DUP of doing Sinn Fein's bidding: "One may well ask why is the DUP doing Sinn Fein's dirty work for it? . . . It appears to us, that the DUP is prepared to see anybody elected or promoted as long as it damages fellow unionists in the UUP. There is no other logical explanation" (Empey 2006).

of criticism, there is not a little hypocrisy afoot among critics of the alliance. Indeed, the Belfast Agreement was predicated on bringing paramilitaries into government and away from violence. The signatories knew going into the agreement that they would be dealing with former terrorists. The real problem has never been sitting in government with former terrorists; rather, it has been the failure of the agreement to ensure that terrorists would become *former* terrorists and that their paramilitaries would be formally dismantled in a timely manner. This failure was especially relevant to Loyalist paramilitaries whose pro-state position made the paramilitary-cum-politician transition a difficult one. It was therefore not a little unfair to suggest that the PUP was responsible for policing the UVF. After almost a decade of peace, there has been little evidence that the PUP could do so. This responsibility should always have rested with the police, and been in concert with a government-run effort to reintegrate paramilitary men.

It is also fair to say that critics of the PUP often appear to have selective amnesia when it comes to dealing with the UVF–PUP connection. Unlike Sinn Fein, no one in the PUP's governing body sat on the inner council of the UVF (Edwards and Bloomer 2005). The PUP could not, therefore, be held accountable for the actions of a leadership council to which it does not belong. At most, the PUP was in a position to provide the UVF with information about the political ramifications of paramilitary actions and suggest alternative courses of action to them.

8   *What to Do with*
the Paramilitaries?

A Cease-Fire Murder

In March 2005 I interviewed Mark Langhammer, then a borough-level councillor (Labour) for Newtownabbey, an area just north of Belfast. Until then, most of my interviews had been with Loyalist paramilitaries, ex-prisoners, and community workers. Many of the men I spoke with seemed genuinely committed to peace, and it is clear that several had put themselves at great personal risk to promote a progressive notion of Loyalism. Although I found their efforts laudable, they were nonetheless difficult to square with ongoing Loyalist paramilitary violence. I wanted to speak with someone who would provide a contrasting view.

I sought out Councillor Langhammer because he is a fierce critic of Loyalist paramilitaries. In a white paper titled "Cutting with the Grain," Langhammer described Loyalist paramilitaries as "unhinged, apolitical and unpoliced" (2003, 3). He was equally dismissive of Loyalist political efforts, noting that the Ulster Political Research Group (UPRG) "has not produced any 'research' worthy of the name" (3). Langhammer is also no stranger to paramilitary violence. In September 2002 the UDA fitted the bottom of his car with a bomb. Fortunately, the device exploded while the car sat in the driveway, and no one was injured. The UDA had planted the bomb to protest Langhammer's support for a PSNI drop-in clinic in Rathcoole. As the *Belfast Telegraph* remarked, the clinic was "viewed as a challenge to the paramilitary power" in the area (Gordon 2005b).

Langhammer is also familiar with paramilitary violence because it has affected his constituents. When we met in 2005, Councillor Langhammer told me that paramilitary violence in his district had escalated since the peace accord was signed.

From the Good Friday Agreement on, my political constituency was the biggest killing field in Northern Ireland—there were more murders in my constituency than anywhere else, bar none.

One of the crimes he singled out for me was the murder of Raymond Mc-Cord.

Now, in my own constituency there was a murder in 1997 of a young man called Raymond McCord that was drugs related. Raymond McCord was murdered by members of the UVF who were also police informers. And the police knew about that. That's under investigation now. Or I should say that assertion is under investigation by the ombudsman.

The twenty-two-year-old McCord, a former radar operator in the Royal Air Force, was killed in November 1997. His body was discovered in a quarry in Ballyduff, Newtownabbey. Police surmise McCord was beaten to death and describe the manner of his death as "vicious and brutal" (Connolly 1997a).

The day after McCord's body was found, the *Belfast Telegraph* spoke to the murdered man's father, who is also named Raymond McCord. The senior McCord suggested that his son's murder could be the result of a long-standing UDA vendetta against him. In 1992 the UDA had ordered a punishment beating for the senior McCord. His legs, arms, and nose were broken and two of his ribs were cracked (Hall 1997).[1] The elder McCord spoke publicly about his attack at the time and claims that the UDA has never let him, or his family, forget it. Several years later the senior McCord recounted his ordeal to investigators with Human Rights Watch:

The UDA rules by terror in Protestant areas. I refused to join them when I was seventeen, and over the years they decided to make me an example. . . . The beating they gave me in February was the worst beating in my area in twenty years. I've charged them with my beating—I'm the first person in twenty years to do that. They attacked me outside a bar with flagstones. They dropped flagstones on my arms and legs and kicked my face while I was lying on the ground. Their usual weapons are baseball bats. (Hall 1997, 60)

When McCord spoke to the press after his son's murder, he acknowledged the murder could have been committed by someone else, but he "challenged Loyalist paramilitaries to deny involvement" (Connolly 1997a). Later that night the UFF issued a statement denying responsibility for the murder (Connolly 1997c).

A week later an anti-intimidation group told the *Belfast Telegraph* that it had been notified by reliable sources that people connected to the UVF were

---

[1] The *Belfast Telegraph* reported that the punishment beating occurred earlier, in 1990 (Connolly 1997a).

behind the junior McCord's murder. The group, Families against Intimidation and Terror (FAIT), urged the UVF to come clean about their involvement (Connolly 1997d). The Progressive Unionist Party, the political wing of the UVF, issued a statement later in the day which did little to clarify matters. A spokesman, Jim McDonald, told the paper, "I would condemn unequivocally the murder, no matter who carried it out" (Connolly 1997d).

In the years since the junior McCord's murder allegations about the rationale for it have slowly trickled into the public realm. The elder McCord has long suggested, for example, that his son was murdered because he lost a "drugs consignment" he was moving for a UVF leader (*Sunday Life* 2004a). McCord claims the man ordered the murder after his son was arrested for smuggling cannabis into the province. The leader wanted to keep his involvement in the drug trade secret from the UVF leadership (Murray 2005a). The elder McCord has also alleged that the UVF man was an informer with the PSNI (Cowan 2003; *Sunday Life* 2004b). Indeed, in 2001 McCord lodged a complaint with the Northern Ireland Police ombudsman's office claiming the police inquiry into his son's murder had been halted by the Special Branch when investigators discovered the main suspect in the murder was a police informer (Cowan 2003). In May 2002 Nuala O'Loan, the ombudsman, announced that her office was opening an official probe into the junior McCord's murder after an initial investigation suggested a more extensive review was necessary (Gordon 2002). In 2005 a Teachta Dála (TD) in the Irish Dáil, Pat Rabbite (Labour), also used parliamentary privilege to publicly identify, for the first time, the men alleged to be behind the murder:

> According to his father, the Mount Vernon UVF murdered Raymond McCord because he had been summoned by John "Bunter" Graham, the officer commanding the UVF on the Shankill Road, to account for his role in ferrying drugs for Mark Haddock. He was murdered to prevent Graham finding out about Haddock's unsanctioned drugs operations. At least two members of the gang who carried out the murder were Special Branch informers. They were Mark Haddock, who ordered the murder, and John Bond, who was present when Raymond McCord was murdered. . . . The central allegation is that Haddock was not charged with any crime because he was an informer who had to be protected. He was able to act with impunity while the police effectively colluded in his crimes. (*Dáil Éireann* 2005)

While the senior McCord waited for O'Loan's report, the UVF took action of its own. On 30 May 2006 Mark Haddock was shot at a home in Newtownabbey (McCambridge 2006). Haddock survived the attack but was badly injured. Three days after the shooting the *Belfast Telegraph* reported that the UVF leadership had ordered the murder (Rowan 2006).

On 22 January 2007 O'Loan released a report on her investigation into the murder of the junior McCord (2007). Her investigation found evidence that the RUC/PSNI's own intelligence files linked a police informer from a UVF unit in North Belfast to ten murders, one of which was the junior Mc-Cord. She concluded that the informer "was never fully investigated for the majority of these crimes" (27). Although TD Pat Rabbite publicly named the informer in 2005, O'Loan's report did not name him or the law enforcement officials engaged in collusion. As of 2007, the informer had not been arrested for the McCord murder.

Verbal Grenades

Raymond McCord's Battle

In the years since his son's murder, the senior McCord has kept his son's case in the public eye and in so doing has kept the issue of paramilitary violence there as well. He has, in effect, waged a one-man battle against the UVF. It has been a very public campaign, albeit one slow to get off the ground. As the *Belfast Telegraph*'s David Gordon observed after the attempted murder of Mark Haddock: "For many years, Mr. McCord told anyone who would listen that his son Raymond Junior was beaten to death in 1997 on the orders of an RUC Special Branch informer in the Mount Vernon UVF in north Belfast. Few people—outside of a small circle of journalists—took him seriously to begin with. All that changed when he took his grievances to Police Ombudsman Nuala O'Loan in 2002" (2006a).

The senior McCord had been quoted extensively by the press in Northern Ireland. A casual Web search returns hundreds of newspaper articles in which comments by McCord appear. The elder McCord has often used the papers to engage in public sniping with the UVF/PUP, and in the process he has kept his son's murder on the public radar.

In addition to periodic statements about his son's case, McCord has also become a favorite source of journalists in search of a comment about Loyalist paramilitary violence. McCord has often served as a de facto spokesperson for victims of Loyalist violence, speaking for victims and families who are too afraid to do so. When the *Belfast Telegraph* published a story, for example, on the UVF's decision to exile a ten-year-old boy from an estate in Newtownabbey,[2] the reporter quoted McCord rather than members of the boy's family.

---

[2] The UVF exiled the boy for breaking into and vandalizing a UVF social club. A UVF representative told the *Belfast Telegraph* that the boy had a long history of antisocial behavior: "The lad may only be 10, but he has engaged in all sorts of anti-social behavior and the people have had enough—that's why they went to the UVF. It is obvious the kid does have problems, and he has driven his father crazy, but the last straw was breaking into the club and smashing mirrors. The local UVF unit had to take a stand to show everyone this sort of thing won't be tolerated, regardless of what age people are" (Breen 2004c).

North Belfast man Raymond McCord, whose son Raymond jr was murdered by the UVF, condemned the group's hypocrisy. He said: "Why will the UVF not exile its members for engaging in extortion, murder and drug dealing? It's disgraceful what they have done to this kid. The 'brigadier' who sanctioned this kid's exile is nothing but a drunken coward, who wouldn't even speak to me when my son was murdered." (Breen 2004c)[3]

In 2003 the elder McCord took his battle to the electoral sphere, running as an independent for one of six available seats in the Northern Ireland Assembly for North Belfast. Of the other sixteen candidates, one was Billy Hutchinson, an incumbent representing the PUP and a former UVF prisoner. McCord ran on an explicitly anti-paramilitary platform, and although he failed to win a seat, some analysts suggest that his dogged campaign helped Hutchinson lose his (Edwards and Bloomer 2004).

THE UVF RESPONSE

The UVF took a low-profile approach in the face of McCord's one-man media challenge. It has offered few public denials of responsibility for the McCord murder, and most have occurred in conjunction with damaging news stories about the UVF's alleged involvement in it (Cowan 2003). The senior McCord asserts, however, that the group's relative public silence on the matter has been accompanied by an organized campaign to harass him and his family. The bullying often occurs in spurts. May 2000 was a particularly bad month. It began when vandals destroyed the younger McCord's gravestone (McCaffery 2000b). A few days later one of the junior McCord's surviving brothers, Gareth, reported that he was attacked by a "loyalist gang." He charged the attackers with "waging a hate campaign" against the family (M. Breen 2000). In the same week, the senior McCord also received a "sympathy card" in the mail with the names of his remaining family members listed on it (McCaffery 2000c).

Two weeks after the junior McCord's grave was vandalized, the UVF gave an interview to the *Irish News* (McCaffery 2000a). In it the group denied involvement in the younger McCord's murder and announced that it had tapped a go-between to begin talks with the senior McCord. The group told the paper:

The UVF in this area wants this put to bed, because this is impacting on the people in Mount Vernon and the Shore Road. It is leading to high levels of tension. Mount Vernon is getting enough bad press and we want it to stop. It is time to move on. We can understand he (Mr. McCord) has lost his son. Some

---

[3] McCord has also offered support to the victims of the Loughinisland massacre, an incident in which six Catholics watching a football match in a pub were allegedly murdered by the UVF (*Sunday Life* 2004b).

of us here are fathers—we know how it would be like to lose a child . . . but he is looking in the wrong place. (McCaffery 2000a)

The elder McCord agreed to meet with the go-between but suggested that the overture was probably a "publicity stunt": "I don't think this is genuine" (McCaffery 2000a).

The UVF–McCord "talks" never got off the ground, and the UVF continued its periodic campaign of harassment against the elder McCord. In the run-up to McCord's Assembly election, for example, the UVF magazine *Combat* published an article accusing McCord of threatening residents in his estate in Rathcoole and generally acting the part of a "bully."

The newspaper reading public will never know the truth about McCord's background of violence and bullying. The people of Rathcoole know only too well what it is like to be subjected to decades of threats, intimidation and violence by a man who is no stranger either to beating the victim—or playing it. (as quoted in Breen 2003a)

The senior McCord responded by telling the press:

The UVF leadership know I will be standing in the Assembly election and they don't like it one bit, because they know I will expose them for what they are— murderous thugs. . . . I admit that I am no angel, but I never murdered, petrol bombed or attacked the innocent Protestant people of North Belfast. (Breen 2003a)

The elder McCord has also received numerous death threats, which he alleges are from the UVF. In November 2003, for example, he told the *Belfast Telegraph*: "police told me that a call had been made to a Belfast newsroom that I would be shot" (Gordon 2003).

In November 2004 the press reported that the UVF had stood down its "senior most figure" in North Belfast along with several other lower-ranking members (*Sunday Life* 2004a). The senior figure was Haddock, although the paper did not print his name. The press speculated that the standing down was retribution for the man's role in the McCord murder (2004a). The UVF refused, however, to verify the claim, telling the press only that the standing down was not "linked to any single event" (2004a). The senior McCord suggested that he viewed the UVF announcement as long overdue: "I told them that Raymond was murdered over a lost UVF drugs consignment, but the man who has now been removed denied this, and told his own leadership lies. He probably told other lies, too, and they are now belatedly conceding that he misled them on Raymond's murder and many other events" (2004a).

The UVF's attempted murder of Mark Haddock two years later could be viewed as a response of sorts to McCord's campaign for justice. However, the group's decision was probably less an olive branch to McCord than revenge against Haddock. Indeed, the *Belfast Telegraph* reported that the UVF ordered the hit in response to "recent revelations about [Haddock's] informer activities" (Rowan 2006). Moreover, the UVF's intimidation campaign did not abate in the wake of the murder bid. A month after Haddock was shot, McCord's cousin Robert was attacked by a UVF gang from Mount Vernon. A local Loyalist told the press: "two carloads of men kicked the door in. They were from the Mount Vernon UVF and they singled out Raymond's cousin and demanded to know if he knew where Raymond was living. When he replied he had no idea, they stripped him to the waist and then gave him an awful kicking and burnt him with cigarette lighters" (Breen 2006).

THE PUP RESPONSE

For its part, the PUP has adopted a number of poses in response to McCord's public battle for justice for his son. At times the party has appeared conciliatory. After the junior McCord's grave was desecrated in May 2000, for example, Billy Hutchinson told the *Irish News*: "If UVF men are threatening him (Mr. McCord), or wrecking his son's grave they should desist from that. This man should be allowed to get on with his life and his son should be allowed to rest in peace. There is no way I would condone any such actions in a graveyard. The young lad is dead. His family should be allowed to grieve" (McCaffery 2000c). In November 2004, the PUP's David Ervine met with the senior McCord (Breen 2004d). In a statement to the press, McCord characterized the meeting as "positive," even though he took the opportunity to lash out at the UVF "chief of staff" for failing to meet with him as well (Breen 2004d).

At other times, the PUP has taken a more aggressive tone and, in the process, appeared as if it were trying to discredit the elder McCord. In March 2003, for example, Billy Hutchinson is alleged to have labeled McCord a "Walter Mitty" figure, implying that the elder McCord lived in a fantasy world similar to that of the fictional character in James Thurber's short story (*Sunday Life* 2003). McCord was furious when told of the comparison, telling the press:

> I can't believe the political mouthpiece of the terrorist organization which killed my son is calling me a Walter Mitty—I'm no such person. I just think they are trying to impose more hurt on my family by slagging me off, because they know only too well, that I know the people who murdered my son. (*Sunday Life* 2003)

Hutchinson denied he made the remark but did not reject its aptness:

> I actually feel sorry for Mr. McCord—he lost his son and I would hate to lose my son. But I would like to remind him that it was not me who described him as a Walter Mitty—it was a judge in a court of law. (*Sunday Life* 2003)

The senior McCord refused to back down, however, challenging Hutchinson to name the judge in question.

> I don't want to get into a row with Billy Hutchinson. But, I'd like him to tell me what judge, and in what court, I was called a "Walter Mitty." Billy Hutchinson is only trying to blacken my name because I'm standing in the elections. (Breen 2003b)

In November 2003 David Ervine also made comments that seemed designed to discredit McCord's campaign by smearing his son. In an interview with David Dunseith on the BBC radio program *Talkback* Ervine labeled the junior McCord a "convicted drug dealer" and implied, without directly saying as much, that the man's involvement in the drug trade, not a UVF vendetta, had led to his murder (Gordon 2003).

The elder McCord has long admitted his son was facing a drug charge at the time of his murder. But he insists that his son's involvement in drug running was on behalf of the UVF, rather than separate from it, as Ervine's comments suggest (Breen 2002). McCord also lashed out at Ervine for claiming that his son had been convicted of a drug offense (he had not) and for what the father saw as suggesting that this history somehow justified his son's murder. Ervine recanted his assertion and sent *Talkback* a written statement to be read on the air: "The PSNI have told us that they have no record of Raymond McCord having been convicted of any drugs-related offences. Mr. Ervine now accepts that his statement on this programme was incorrect. We do regret the distress caused to the family of Mr. McCord by this comment" (Gordon 2003).

At other times the PUP has seemed intent on avoiding McCord altogether. In October 2003 David Ervine was asked to comment on a death threat received by McCord. He told the press any murder would "shock and hurt" him, but added, "I'm no longer going to answer questions about Raymond McCord. He has a fixation with the media, and the media has a fixation with him" (*Breaking News* 2003). Two years later, when the *Belfast Telegraph* reported on another death threat against McCord, which he attributed to the UVF, Ervine sounded a note of exasperation: "Raymond McCord is the most written-about parent in the world, in a country where over 3,500 people died. I just can't see the logic or the rationale why the UVF would want to do anything to Raymond McCord. This situation has been going on for a very, very long time" (Gordon 2005c).

The Politics of the Dead

In Northern Ireland, as in other conflict zones, the dead often live on after their murders, given second wind by the political hay others make of their varied misfortunes. The fact that paramilitary murders happen routinely, coupled with the reality that many are never solved, means that those looking for redress (for the murder or the larger trend it represents) must often resort to politics. As the discussion of McCord's media battle suggests, he used the press to keep his son's murder in the spotlight and, in so doing, to keep public pressure on both the UVF and the PUP. Other groups have also used the junior McCord's murder for political purposes, including Republicans, human rights groups, and independent politicians.

Republicans, for their part, have paid close attention to the McCord murder because it seemed likely to (and eventually did) validate long-standing Republican accusations of collusion. *Forum Magazine*, a self-described "Republican Journal," devoted the lead article in its May 2004 issue, for example, to the matter of collusion and spent the majority of the article discussing the Raymond McCord investigation. The author of the piece concluded with the remark: "It is clearly in the public interest, and not just the interest of the families who have been pressing for an inquiry all those years, that this rotten murky underworld be openly explored, and shown up for what it is" (Hennessey 2004). Not surprisingly, Loyalists have generally denied that collusion exists. The senior McCord acknowledged as much when describing his changing views on the matter: "As a protestant from a unionist background, I always thought when I heard about this collusion it was republican propaganda. It's not republican propaganda, it's the truth" (Press Association 2003).[4]

Human rights groups have also used the McCord murder and others like it to advance a political agenda. The Human Rights Watch report in which the senior McCord was interviewed, for example, concludes by arguing that the scope of paramilitary violence in Northern Ireland means that paramilitary actions should be governed by the Geneva Conventions:

> A core principle of international humanitarian law is the protection of civilians in armed conflict, as well as others taking no part in hostilities including combatants who have been captured or are otherwise hors de combat. The four Geneva Conventions of 1949 regulate the conduct of parties to international armed conflict. Article 3, common to all four conventions, sets out minimum standards for the treatment of civilians and others taking no active part in the

---

[4] McCord's views on collusion have changed over time. In 2000 he told the press he rejected the term "collusion," even though he acknowledged links between Loyalist paramilitaries and the RUC: "I believe the ordinary RUC man on the street wants to see this man jailed. The ordinary policeman—which I have a lot of time and respect for—wants to solve crimes, but is not being allowed to do so. I don't support the theory that there is collusion between the RUC and paramilitary groups—I believe people high up in the security forces have the power to intervene. They turn a blind eye to murders committed by informers, because these people are more useful out of jail than they are in. The same applies to Pat Finucane and Rosemary Nelson— while I don't believe the RUC had them murdered, I believe the RUC let them be murdered" (O'Doherty 2000).

hostilities during armed conflicts "not of an international character." . . . Paramilitary punishment assaults and shootings thus violate the right to life, freedom from humiliating and degrading treatment, the right to due process and
the guarantee of a fair trial as codified in Common Article 3. (Hall 1997).

Such a position has potentially wide-ranging implications for the families of
victims of paramilitary violence. Should the position be formally adopted
by international organizations, families could not only bring their cases to
the international court (something they can currently do), but they could
hold their government accountable for failing to prosecute them.

The only substantial constituencies that have avoided public commentary
on the murder are Unionist and Loyalist politicians, albeit for different reasons. For their part, Unionists largely ignored the murder when it happened. Indeed, a search of the *Belfast Telegraph* archive for the whole of
1997 turns up six articles on the murder, and in none of them are Unionist
politicians quoted. Although Unionists cannot be expected to speak out
publicly about every murder, their silence is noteworthy given the vicious-
ness of the crime and its timing: during Loyalist paramilitaries' cease-fire
and in the midst of negotiations over what would become the Belfast Agreement. In contrast, several victims' groups, including FAIT and OutCry, im-
mediately denounced the murder publicly and commented on what it meant
for the ongoing negotiations (Connolly 1997b). Indeed, FAIT called on Mo
Mowlam to review whether Gary McMichael, then leader of the UDP,
should be allowed to participate in the negotiations (recall that initial reports suggested the UDA was behind the murder).

Unionists began making public comments about the murder only after
Nuala O'Loan's office agreed to investigate the elder McCord's allegations
in 2002. Still, the first time most Unionists addressed the murder in the
press was much later, during the spring of 2006. Their public outcry was
not, however, the result of a sudden, collective change of heart. Most commented on the murder because it had become part of a larger, then-
unfolding story about the UUP's decision to invite the PUP into its Assembly
group. The senior McCord met with a UUP delegation shortly after the announcement and emerged with a startling allegation: party member Michael
Copeland had offered McCord the chair of a new UUP victims' group in exchange for his silence on the alliance (Barnes 2006). Not surprisingly, the
DUP jumped at the allegation, condemning UUP "horse trading" and de-
crying the party's injurious treatment of the senior McCord. Jeffrey Donaldson (DUP) even took the matter to the floor of the House of Commons:
"Is my honorable friend aware that one of his constituents, Mr. Raymond
McCord, whose son was murdered by the UVF, met the leader of the UUP
on Monday morning? Before that meeting, another UUP Assembly Member, Mr. Copeland from East Belfast, made an offer to Mr. McCord of the
use of an office if he would keep quiet and not criticize the decision. The

UUP is now into bribing victims" (*Hansard Parliamentary Debates* 2006). Although McCord probably appreciated the DUP's rebuke of the UUP–PUP alliance, the more pressing concern for McCord, and others like him, is securing justice for murdered family members. In short, while public condemnations are appreciated, most families want to know that they will be followed by more substantive efforts to kick-start the justice process. For many victims of Loyalist violence, such efforts seem minimal.

Indeed, victims of Loyalist violence often charge that Unionist politicians are more interested in condemning Republican than Loyalist violence. Families point to the Unionist response to the January 2005 murder of Robert McCartney as an example. McCartney, a Catholic from the staunchly Nationalist Short Strand area of Belfast, is alleged to have been killed by IRA volunteers. His murder had nothing to do with politics (it was essentially a barroom brawl turned deadly), but his surviving sisters and fiancé claim that the IRA protected its volunteers and threatened witnesses with punishment beatings if they spoke to police. In the wake of the crime, Unionist politicians publicly lambasted the IRA and Sinn Fein. Indeed, at times it seemed as if they were racing one another to see who could be the first to release a press statement or provide a definitive comment for journalists. Ian Paisley and Nigel Dodds both denounced the murder in the House of Commons (*Hansard Parliamentary Debates* 2005a, 2005b). More importantly, Unionists also offered government assistance to the McCartney family. When the family traveled to the European Parliament to request EU funds for their campaign, the DUP supported the motion and used floor time to name three people who were believed to be involved in the murder. (McCord had to rely on a TD in the Irish Dáil to name his son's murderer, and he has received no offers of government assistance from Unionist politicians.)

Although the senior McCord has offered public support for the McCartneys' campaign, he questions why Unionist politicians have failed to offer the same sort of high-profile support (which would include public condemnation *and* government assistance) for the victims of Loyalist violence:[5]

> Myself and other victims are absolutely disgusted over the stance the Democratic Unionists and Ulster Unionists have taken on Robert McCartney. Why can't they look at things closer to home? They have failed the people who voted them in. I totally support what the sisters are doing. I went to visit them at their house, I've been on the phone to them and I hope they get justice. But why have

---

[5] This is not to suggest that Unionists never condemn Loyalist violence. Rather, a good deal of Unionist condemnation goes unreported by virtue of where it is delivered—from church pulpits, which tend not to get routine coverage by the press corps. However, the families of Loyalist victims want more than equal doses of public outrage. They certainly want public condemnation, but they want it backed by substantive efforts (pressure to bear, funding for inquiries, etc.) to bring justice for victims.

people within unionism stayed silent on the murders of our sons? The UVF has murdered something like 30 Protestant people since their so-called ceasefire. It seems to me that nationalist MPs have no qualms about fighting for their community but within unionism it's the complete opposite. The stance they have taken, and their hypocrisy, is staggering. (*Breaking News* 2005)

The senior McCord is not alone in making such charges. The mother of Andrew Robb, whose son was killed by the UVF during the 2000 feud, has also complained about what she sees as Unionist indifference to her son's murder. In the wake of McCartney's murder she told the *Portadown Times*:

Not one politician has helped me, yet all sides are—as they should—helping the McCartneys. There are real parallels here, but our cause doesn't seem to be as fashionable. The wrong people were killed that night, and the wrong information about the two boys was fed to the Press—yet we haven't had a modicum of justice. (V. Gordon 2005)

It is difficult to know with certainty why Unionist politicians have offered only tepid support for campaigns like those by the McCord and Robb families. In McCord's case, Unionists may well be leery of his ability to use the press to batter his opponents. He has certainly proven a capable adversary. Some of the reluctance may also be due, as Ms. Robb's comments suggest, to the way news coverage shapes the narrative of such murders. Indeed, the victims of internecine Loyalist violence are usually described in an unsympathetic light, as linked to paramilitaries or involved in the drug trade. It is difficult to stop such narratives once they appear in print and even more arduous to change their course. In that regard, the McCartney sisters were fortunate (if such an adjective can ever describe the survivors of a murder victim) that similar allegations were not made about their brother.

Unionist diffidence may also be related to a desire to avoid the topic of collusion, which is certain political quicksand. During most of the Troubles, Unionists denied that collusion even existed, and even those who did acknowledge its existence (and inherent dilemmas) preferred not to discuss it. Indeed, admitting that the police were acting in systematically unlawful ways would have not only legitimated Republican distrust of the police but undermined the Unionist law-and-order message. Whatever the reasons for Unionist diffidence, victims of Loyalist violence feel slighted, as if their pain means less than that of Republican victims.

Loyalists have, as I noted previously, responded slowly and inadequately to the McCord murder. The UVF denied involvement in the murder and launched a campaign of harassment against the McCord family. And when the UVF finally took action, seven years later, it refused to acknowledge the action as related to the McCord murder. For its part, the PUP vacillated among gestures that were evasive, conciliatory, and defamatory.

It is not common for paramilitaries to publicize their internal deliberations, but it is worth noting that Loyalists are not always so tight-lipped on the subject of Loyalist violence. Their condemnations generally focus, however, on the actions of rival paramilitaries. Indeed, the deterioration of relations between rival Loyalist paramilitaries since the 1998 accord has opened the way for an increase in such public missives. A notable example, and one relevant to the McCord murder, was the PUP's condemnation of the murder of Lisa Dorrian, a twenty-five-year-old shop clerk. Dorrian was last seen alive at a party on the Ards peninsula in February 2005. Although her body has never been found, and no one has been arrested in her disappearance, the PSNI believe she was murdered (McDonald 2005a), and they are investigating LVF involvement in her death (BBC 2005a).[6] In the wake of the alleged murder, Ervine met with the Dorrian family on several occasions. After one meeting Ervine told the press that the events surrounding her death resembled "a cesspit" and warned that "if you leave cesspits alone they multiply" (BBC 2005a).

Although Ervine's comments were meant to call attention to the Dorrian murder, so that witnesses might be encouraged to come forward and the PSNI to step up its investigation, his comments were also a jab at the LVF. Ervine told the press that he was certain "beyond a doubt" that the LVF were responsible for the murder (Heatley 2005).

It would be easy to suggest that Ervine was acting hypocritially. It is difficult after all to square his willingness to speak out about the Dorrian murder with his equivocation regarding the junior McCord's murder. Ervine's role was not, however, an easy one. Heading up the UVF's political wing required a delicate balance of candor and tact, and an ability to speak truth to power while also defending the organization from whence the party emerged. The growing influence of revanchist Loyalism within UVF ranks after the peace also tended to drown out the largely progressive message that Ervine and his peers in the PUP were espousing.

On Walking the Line

The American country music singer Johnny Cash's career-making hit of the mid-1950s, "I Walk the Line," a ballad about a troubled soul's effort to walk the straight and narrow for his lover, is an apt way to think about progressive efforts within Loyalism. In the nine years it took for the UVF to stand down, progressive Loyalists had to find ways to be truthful to Loyalism

---

[6] The Independent Monitoring Commission declines to assign paramilitary responsibility for Dorrian's murder. "We recognize that people may have expected us to refer here to the disappearance of Lisa Dorrian on 28 February 2005 and her murder and to the murder of Thomas Devlin on 10 August 2005. We have no reason to believe that either murder was carried out on behalf of a paramilitary organization" (2005, 5).

even as Loyalism seemed to be falling apart all around them. The allegations of unmet responsibility, hypocrisy, and irrelevance that swarmed around David Ervine and the PUP bring to the fore a fundamental question for that period: What was the most appropriate way for Loyalist leaders in the UVF and the PUP to deal with the criminal elements within their ranks? While my analysis here is on Northern Ireland, this question has relevance for other societies emerging from conflict. Indeed, many places coming out of civil war are too weak to force immediate demilitarization of their armed groups. As such, understanding the dynamic around this issue is of relevance beyond the province.

In Northern Ireland the general flavor of critique suggests that most people there thought that Loyalist leaders were responsible, at least in part, for reigning in their own criminal elements. A number of examples highlight the breadth of this view. As I note in chapter 7, when the UVF's South Belfast Brigade leader was organizing assaults on immigrants in the Village, journalist Angelique Chrisafis described the terrorized neighborhood as waiting for the paramilitary leadership "to make a statement or move which shows the attacks will not be tolerated" (2004). Even victims' families turn to paramilitary leaders to adjudicate their loved ones' murders. A few days after Robert McCartney was murdered, for example, his sister Gemma told the press, "If the IRA are an army, an army can order people to do something. They should order them to hand themselves in" (Harding 2005b).

The senior McCord took a similar approach to his son's murder. Indeed, he has focused as much of his energy on getting the UVF to take responsibility for the murder as on pushing the RUC/PSNI to solve it. A week before the UVF announced that it was standing down the members presumed to have been behind the murder, the elder McCord told *Sunday Life* that he wanted the group to expel the men. "As I've said before, I don't want the people who murdered my son to be executed—I just think they should be expelled from the organization" (Breen 2004d). McCord also called on the PUP leadership to resign, implying that they were complicit in UVF criminality: "It's about time Hutchinson and David Ervine resigned, because they can't say their henchmen are no longer involved in drugs, when it's clear for everyone to see" (*Sunday Life* 2003).

The mother of Lisa Dorrian has also suggested that she would accept help from Loyalist paramilitaries in her effort to find her daughter's body, although she insisted to the press that she did not want "paramilitary justice." "If they can help," she told the press, "I would be really grateful" (BBC 2005c).

Nor is the government immune to the view that paramilitaries are responsible, at least in part, for cleaning up their own houses. In November 2004, for example, then Northern Ireland secretary Paul Murphy met with leaders in the UPRG to review the UDA's effort to rejoin the peace process.

After several meetings, Murphy decided to "despecify" the UDA and indicated that he was pleased with the group's efforts to move away from criminality. Indeed, he pledged to work with the UPRG to help it clean up its internal affairs: "The government agrees with the UPRG when it says that the loyalist community's enemies are issues such as poverty, social deprivation, drugs and crime, and we will work energetically with them and others to tackle those problems" (Murphy 2004).

Although persons outside of paramilitary structure argued that paramilitary leaders should take care of their rogue elements, those within paramilitary structure took a different view of the matter. In my interviews with paramilitary men connected to the UVF, they argued that it was the PSNI's job to take care of criminality. When I queried Tom Roberts, for example, about whether the leadership was unable or unwilling to reign in criminal elements, he responded:

> I can categorically state that the UVF leadership is totally opposed to criminality of any description. And they would view it as a law-and-order issue. There is elements within the UVF that are engaged in criminality and the forces of law and order should deal with that. . . . Basically, it's a law-and-order issue. If they [PSNI] have evidence to suggest that they're [UVF members] engaged in criminal activity then let them deal with it.

When I asked Plum the same question, he responded, "I'm more interested in what the police are going to do." Plum also argued that the police ignore Loyalist areas on purpose, essentially allowing criminality to thrive. As I recount in chapter 7, Plum alleges that the PSNI knew about an open-air drug market that Johnny Adair's C Company was running in the lower Shankill and did nothing about it: "They [the police] were not moving in or making it difficult for them to sell there. They weren't going near to the drug house down there, you know."

Billy Mitchell also agreed that it was the PSNI's responsibility to police paramilitary criminality. And like Plum, he saw the failure of policing in Loyalist areas as deliberate. Writing in the *Blanket*, Mitchell said: "If the resources and the tactics that were used against paramilitary organizations were deployed against the criminal gangs, the problem should be easily eradicated. One wonders why this has not happened before now" (2002a). The example Mitchell gave in the article to illustrate his point was the same one Plum highlighted for me in our interview—PSNI ambivalence to drugs in Loyalist communities. Mitchell continued:

> There appears to be a willingness on the part of police to tackle those aspects of organized crime that hurt the business community but a clear lack of interest in addressing organized crime where it impacts adversely on working-class communities. It seems to be okay for criminals to poison the lives of working class kids with drugs but not okay to engage in activities that hurt the business

community. It also seems okay for the army of touts [informers] employed by the intelligence services to be given the freedom to engage in criminal activity so long as it is perpetrated against those living in marginalized communities. (Mitchell 2000a)

Mitchell also offered a theory to explain the PSNI's alleged indifference:

One could be forgiven for believing that organized crime, particularly the illegal drugs trade, is being deliberately used to destabilize certain working class communities and impose an insidious form of social control on those who, if empowered socially and politically, might dare to engage in class politics. (2002a)[7]

Without a doubt, many people will find such answers unsatisfactory, even conspiratorial. Paramilitaries can wage a thirty-year war, the thinking goes, so surely they could take care of their rogue elements. On the face of it, this reasoning is entirely logical, but the best method at the disposal of paramilitary leaders was no longer considered palatable in the post-peace era.

When I asked Billy Mitchell, for example, what the leadership could do to reign in their rouge elements, he responded, "in the early years somebody would shoot them." Shooting rogue elements was still an option after 1998, Billy told me, "but it's not a particularly nice way [to deal with the problem]." Obviously, it was also not in keeping with either the Loyalist ceasefire agreement or human rights standards. As Mitchell colorfully explained: "Unfortunately, to use Davy Ervine's language—this is his language not mine—he says 'in every organization you've got a pile of shite, and shite floats. It comes to the top.' . . . And then, Davey's other comment was, 'we go to clean the shite up, and we'll start smelling of it.' You know, you can't clean it without smelling of it."

David Ervine explained the problem to me by highlighting the fallout from Republican attempts to clean up their criminal element: "They [the UVF] did go through a process where they were going to do what the IRA did with DAAD—Direct Action against Drugs[8]—where the IRA executed drug dealers. The UVF decided they couldn't do that." When I asked Ervine why not, he cited two reasons. First, drug dealers (in and out of the UVF) work with hundreds of people to sell, move, or protect their goods. As he explained somewhat facetiously, the UVF "wouldn't have enough bullets"

---

[7] In their interviews with Loyalist paramilitaries, Edwards and Bloomer found a similar viewpoint: "There has always been support for the theory that the police allowed the drugs to come in to destabilize Loyalism, allowed the rogue elements to grow within Loyalist paramilitaries" (2004, 32).

[8] Direct Action against Drugs was a cover name for IRA units tasked in the midnineties with clearing out drug dealers in IRA territory. See McDowell (2001) for a detailed account.

to really solve the problem.[9] Nor, I suspect, would the UVF garner much public support in going after dealers if the IRA/DAAD experience is any indicator.[10] Most people do not like drug dealers, but they abhor paramilitary "justice" even more. More importantly, Ervine explained that adopting DAAD tactics would hurt the UVF politically. "The Paisleys of this world would say, 'I told you so, they're not ready for peace, they're not committed to peace.' " As Ervine concluded, "once upon a time, when people infracted the rules, they [the UVF leadership] would have shot them. They found that a little difficult to do against the backdrop of a peace process."

Plum offered a similar assessment, as the following excerpt from our conversation indicates:

CAROLYN: So you think the only options that you guys would have [in dealing with criminality] would be violent options?
PLUM: Yeah.
CAROLYN: And you don't want to deal with that?
PLUM: No. We're trying to move away from that.

Del Williams, a community worker with the Loyalist Prisoners Association, a UDA group, described a similar dynamic when I asked him to comment on the UDA's options for reigning in rogue elements like Johnny Adair.

CAROLYN: How does the UDA deal with those [criminal] elements?
DEL: Well, as it stands now, they can't.
CAROLYN: Because of the peace?
DEL: And that's why you've got all this defending Johnny, and "up the face of the UDA" . . .
CAROLYN: Well, how would the UDA have taken care of Johnny Adair pre-1998?
DEL: You'd have got one in the head.

The growing distaste for the "old" methods is no where more evident than in the public outcry that ensued when the IRA offered to shoot the men responsible for killing Robert McCartney, whose murder I discuss

[9] In some ways Ervine's analogy to DAAD allowed him to skirt my specific question, which was why the UVF did not do more to clean out its *own* criminal element. Indeed, McDowell (2001) notes that the IRA, under the DAAD banner, largely ignored its own dealers in favor of unaffiliated pushers or those among its competitor Republican paramilitaries. However, it is also reasonable to infer that if the UVF did try to clean up the dealers in its midst (by beating, maiming, or killing them), it would find it hard to stop at its own front door since many paramilitary drug operations are run in collaboration with persons outside the UVF. In that regard, Ervine's point about the problem inherent in the DAAD approach is relevant.

[10] McDowell (2001) suggests that the IRA launched DAAD to win Catholic hearts and minds by going after an already unpopular segment of society. Its hope, in doing so, was to secure votes for Sinn Fein in the run-up to peace. Most Catholics, however, found the group's behavior abhorrent.

earlier in this chapter (see O'Toole 2005 for the full IRA statement). Although the family used measured language to reject the offer,[11] politicians of all stripes lambasted the IRA proposal. The SDLP's Eddie McGrady described it as "appalling," while the UUP's Sir Reg Empy called it a "sick and desperate move." Paul Murphy, then secretary for Northern Ireland, responded that "there is no place for kangaroo courts or capital punishment in this country." The justice minister for Ireland, Michael McDowell, even weighed in, labeling the offer "bizarre" (all as quoted in Harding 2005a).

It is worth noting, here, however, that the public outcry over the IRA's offer stands in sharp contradiction to the general public's perception that paramilitaries could "do something" about their rogue elements. Indeed they could, but they could no longer do so in ways that appealed to the great majority of the province's residents, whether Catholic or Protestant. Like the McCartney family, the elder McCord rejected paramilitary justice for his son, requesting instead that the UVF stand down its members involved in the murder (Breen 2004b). However, standing down a member—the one nonviolent option paramilitaries have at their disposal—is often a risky move. The horizontal organization of paramilitaries means that central leaders have to be careful when and how they use such powers. If they stand down a popular member, he may decide to fight back and bring others with him. Indeed, Billy Wright formed the LVF after the UVF leadership stood down his unit in Portadown in 1996 (BBC 2000f). That organization went on to become a destabilizing force within Loyalism, as its role in both the 2000 and 2002 feuds indicates.

This does not mean, of course, that paramilitaries had no options for dealing with their criminal elements. They did and do (even post-standing down), but the methods are limited. When I interviewed Billy Mitchell, for example, he described a two-pronged approach that involved a combination of isolating criminals within the ranks and exposing them to police: "It's by isolating the criminals within the organization, and also making it clear to the police if a member of the UVF is engaged in criminal activities—arrest him. There's going to be repercussions. We won't support them, our prisoner groups won't support them." Mitchell also argued that paramilitaries should support community efforts to police their own neighborhoods. Writing in the *Blanket*, for example, he argued that "they [paramilitaries] can also help by openly supporting non-violent community pickets against known drug and vice dens" (2002a).

Mitchell also believed that communities bear some responsibility for working with paramilitary leaders to ensure that criminality is brought to their attention. As he noted in our interview:

[11] The McCartney sisters issued a statement that read in part: "For this family it would only be in a court, where transparency and accountability prevail, that justice will be done" (BBC 2005d).

One of the things that we are doing in some areas is bringing clergy and local councillors, civic leaders together along with the paramilitaries to develop sort of a panel, to address a lot of those issues. And that's what makes the paramilitaries accountable. In Ballymena, for instance, [it's] through a thing called Community Voice, with the clergy, the chamber of Commerce, local councillors. And representatives from the UPRG, the PUP are involved. So the onus is on the community to keep putting pressure on paramilitaries, to deal with this issue of criminality.

Despite the best efforts of progressive Loyalists like Billy Mitchell, Plum Smith, Tom Roberts, and David Ervine, among many others, their approach lacked needed muscle. Indeed, efforts to stand down criminal members proceeded slowly. It took the UVF seven years to stand down the members involved in the Raymond McCord Jr. murder. Moreover, when the UVF does decide to take care of its rogue elements permanently, the result is often violent, as the attempted murder of Mark Haddock illustrates.

It is unrealistic, however, to hold political Loyalists responsible for the actions of all Loyalists. Indeed, one wonders what the paramilitaries would have been like without these moderating voices, however few they numbered. Indeed, many political Loyalists wanted to stand down much earlier but feared that doing so while revanchism was on the ascendance would have propelled Loyalism into a chaos from which it could not easily extract itself (Edwards and Bloomer 2004). In an interview with Edwards and Bloomer, for example, Plum Smith explained:

It was always the plan that at some stage we would break the link, would grow as a political party—events on the ground have militated against this course of action e.g. the 2000 feud—we were thrust into that whether we liked it or not—Drumcree for a couple of years meant we had to keep the links with the paramilitaries—we wanted at one time to move to being exclusively political, recognizing our past and offering advice and insight to the UVF/RHC [Red Hand Commandos]—events still prevent it—we need to influence events on the ground and you can't do that without links to the paramilitaries. (2004, 30)

When I spoke with Plum in 2003 he also noted that "retirement" was not a good option because there was no guarantee that the police would come in and "mop up" the revanchist remnants left behind. In short, while political Loyalists were unable to secure the sorts of results many hoped of them, their decision not to sever their links to the UVF was a considered response to the situation then at hand. Their decision to stay put was designed to provide a bulwark against the rising tide of revanchism.

It is clear, for example, that David Ervine was as instrumental as the police in lowering the tensions in South Belfast after the initial dustup between the Chinese business owners and the local UVF brigadier in the area. Of course Ervine was not successful in stopping the harassment altogether, and the joint statement issued by the PUP and NICEM failed to acknowledge the depth of paramilitary responsibility in the imbroglio. However, the situation would probably have been much worse without his intercession at the paramilitary level. In short, although the PUP was often blamed for not doing enough, their efforts were often more useful than most people realized.

It also bears recalling that there were structural reasons why PUP influence over the UVF was limited. As Edwards and Bloomer observe, there were no PUP members in "leadership positions in the UVF . . . the PUP does not [therefore] have sufficient influence on the UVF to bring pressure to bear" (2005, 22). Despite these structural limitations, the PUP was routinely held responsible for UVF violence. Edwards and Bloomer point to the IMC as an example. They note that the IMC has consistently held the PUP responsible for UVF violence even though doing so ignores the reality of the UVF–PUP connection and the limitations inherent to it. Ervine made reference to the difficulty of his position in late July 2005, just as the bitter feud was developing between the UVF and LVF. Ervine, who had just learned that the Northern Ireland secretary Peter Hain was considering suspending PUP's Assembly allowances for a second year in a row, issued an irate rejoinder:

> I am willing to meet the Secretary of State and lay before him the reality of life within the leadership of the PUP who in some people's eyes seem to be responsible for all of the things that are wrong in this society. . . . It is against all the tenets of natural justice that people who are not responsible for what paramilitaries do are punished in this way. I am the leader of the PUP. If I have broken any laws or rules, I would like to be arrested and charged now.[12] (*Irish Examiner* 2005)

Negotiating with Criminals

Scholars who depict low-intensity conflict as criminal recommend against negotiating with armed groups or bringing them into political arrangements (Kaldor 1999). Doing so, the argument goes, provides criminals with a legitimacy they do not deserve. In Northern Ireland, peacemakers rejected this view. Indeed, the 1998 accord was premised on the idea that warring parties would be active participants to peace. The structure of the agreement established a system whereby the province's armed groups would be held accountable through their political intermediaries. In essence, the government would use carrots and sticks to reward or punish political parties for the actions of their affiliated paramilitaries.

---

[12] Gerry Adams issued a similar challenge to the Irish Taoiseach, Bertie Ahern, after he suggested that Sinn Fein had given the IRA a green light to conduct the January 2005 robbery of the Northern Bank. He told the press, "I think the Taoiseach has crossed the line. It's time for him to shut up or put up." "Arrest me," he challenged Ahern (*Times Online* 2005).

This approach has worked fairly well in the government's dealings with the IRA. Indeed, although Unionists complained loudly and mightily about the sluggish pace of IRA decommissioning, the government was able to extract real concessions from the group. The DUP's refusal to engage in government with Sinn Fein after it became the dominant Unionist party is a case in point. The party's demand that the IRA declare a formal end to its war put pressure on Sinn Fein to deliver real concessions from the IRA (three rounds of decommissioning in 2001, 2001, and 2003) and undoubtedly contributed to the IRA's unprecedented statement in July 2005 that it had "formerly ordered an end to the armed campaign" (Lavery and Cowell 2005). The political fallout from the McCartney murder and the Northern Bank robbery (in which the IRA is believed to have stolen over £26 million in December 2004) certainly gave impetus to the IRA's move, but the underlying structure of the agreement—using carrots and sticks with the IRA's political wing, Sinn Fein—provided a framework for it to happen.

This approach has not, however, worked as well with Loyalist paramilitaries. As I observe in chapter 1, the political parties associated with Loyalist paramilitaries have never been numerically strong. At its height, the PUP only had two Assembly members, and the UPRG and its predecessor have never had any. Thus, although the government might have a wealth of inventive carrots and sticks at its disposal, it has no effective means of delivering them to Loyalist paramilitaries.

For Loyalism this arrangement has been devastating. Most Loyalist paramilitaries, even pro-peace ones, feel no connection to the peace process. Indeed, although the Combined Loyalist Military Command was an integral player in the 1998 negotiation, the structure of the agreement has effectively isolated Loyalist paramilitaries since. And anti-peace elements, which were always suspicious of the agreement, have been adept at manipulating Loyalism's detachment from the process, branding political Loyalists as traitors, silencing political dissent, and expanding their criminal endeavors under the guise of defending Loyalism. Not surprisingly, the continuation of Loyalist paramilitary activity after the IRA stood down, coupled with its failure to deliver any concessions in the way of decommissioning, invariably led many commentators to adopt the view that negotiating with Loyalists was pointless. Their resignation is perhaps best illustrated by the fact that even Unionists who trusted and respected David Ervine condemned his attempted alliance with the UUP.

Although the UVF finally stood down in 2007, it is worth highlighting why talking to political Loyalists was a worthwhile endeavor in the years between the 1998 accord and 2007. Although political Loyalists were not nearly as effective as most people would have liked them to be, their efforts were also more important than most people realize. As I note in the previous chapter, one of my anonymous sources told me that the situation in the Village would likely have been much worse if David Ervine had not intervened to stop the first round of attacks. Likewise, political Loyalists were integral in negotiating an end to both the 2000 and 2002 feuds—something neither the PSNI nor the Unionist political parties were capable of doing. Finally, although it is difficult to quantify, it is clear political Loyalists played a crucial role in finally getting the UVF to stand down. Indeed, before Billy Mitchell died in 2006, he was working on an internal position paper which was going to call on the UVF to finally stand down (McIntyre 2006). Although neither he nor David Ervine lived to see the UVF's final stand-down order, their role in the process was made clear by the UVF's decision to ask Gusty Spence, the father of political Loyalism, to make the final announcement. In short, although the agreement made it difficult for political Loyalists to follow the paramilitary cum political trajectory (and to bear the fruits thereof), they still managed to influence paramilitary leaders and guide their relationship with civilians on the outside.

Cleaning up the Remnants

No peace agreement is perfect; it is possible, even easy, to find flaws in all of them. The great majority of criticism of the Belfast Agreement has centered on its consociational format, with critics contending that the structure of the agreement has worsened sectarianism (Farry 2006; Langhammer 2003, 2004; McCann 2005). Although there is some truth to this, as I demonstrate in chapter 5, the agreement was not designed to address sectarianism but to stop its violent manifestation. In that regard, the agreement has been relatively successful. The evidence in this book suggests that the greater problem with the peace process in Northern Ireland is that neither government established formal mechanisms for demilitarizing paramilitaries (Edwards and Bloomer 2005).

The result was that the process dragged on for far too long, especially for Loyalist paramilitaries. Indeed, Loyalist demilitarization is not yet complete given that the UDA has yet to stand down. And, while the UVF has stood down, it failed to specify how or even if it will decommission its weapons. Perhaps most importantly, a paramilitary stand down does not mean paramilitary men go away. As Frankie Gallagher reminded me in our interview: "People say, you know, you have to get rid of them [paramilitaries]. The problem is that they are the people from them areas. They didn't parachute in. They are part of the community. They are an integral part of the issue and problem and resolution of it. So you can't get rid of them. What you can do is get rid of the causes that put them there." An anonymous source made much the same point, "Paramilitaries were never divorced from the communities [they controlled]—they come from them."

In this section I detail several concrete things that could be done to aide demilitarization. Many of these ideas are specific to the UDA, which remains in business, but some of them have relevance to the UVF, given that some members may decide to stay in the violence business, albeit under different flags of allegiance.

Formalizing Voluntary Sector Work

Since the 1994 cease-fire, enterprising Loyalists, many of them ex-prisoners, have found jobs in the voluntary sector. Indeed, this sector has provided innumerable jobs for ex-prisoners, and it has enabled them to develop a number of professional skills, including writing grants, managing budgets, running workshops, and mediating neighborhood conflict. This sector is, however, unsustainable by virtue of its dependence on grant financing.

The goal of EU peace funds, especially those of PEACE I, is laudable. Indeed, the initial goal of EU PEACE money was to bring the socially excluded into the body politic, and early EU documents suggest that paramilitary members were a key part of that group (European Communities 1998). Given the grant-dependent character of voluntary organizations, I suggest that the Northern Ireland government institute job programs within the civil service specifically for ex-paramilitaries.[13] The government could approach this task by creating a separate agency for reintegration, or it could establish branches within existing agencies. An agency for reintegration could provide jobs through public works programs, or it could funnel applicants into jobs in existing agencies. The experience that paramilitary members have had with social service agencies, for example, makes them uniquely suited to understand the needs of those receiving assistance from these same agencies. If tailored properly, such jobs could be an avenue for former paramilitaries to give back to their communities. To ensure that paramilitaries are not involved in criminality, the government could require applicants to meet the same kinds of standards as those required of ex-prisoners released under the provisions of the 1998 accord. These measures would not attract all paramilitary members, but they would provide important job alternatives for some.

Obviously, some constituencies are likely to object to such a plan on the grounds that it benefits an unworthy group—paramilitaries. However, as Councillor Langhammer (2004) notes, the EU's bottom-up funding approach already has favored paramilitaries because, as the most organized "constituency" on the ground, they were and still are best able to apply for money. Indeed, giving peace monies to groups associated with paramilitaries fosters the perception among Protestants "that gangsters and sectarian thugs are subject to special favoured status" (2004, 6). However, integrating paramilitaries into the civil service would have to be done on an individual,

[13] Here I define the term "ex-paramilitary" broadly to include ex-prisoners as well as active members who are willing to leave the paramilitary structure.

person-by-person basis. This approach would weaken paramilitary structure because the "subsidy"—in this case, employment opportunity—would go to individuals rather than groups. Moreover, opening up civil service jobs to ex-prisoners would bring them into the wider community rather than ghettoizing them in work that buttresses paramilitary power and that benefits only one ethnoreligious bloc.

WARDEN-BASED POLICING

As I've observed throughout this book, paramilitaries have long served as de facto policemen in their communities. They have meted out punishments, sorted out disputes between business owners, and kept an eye on antisocial behavior. While paramilitaries can and do police their neighborhoods, however unfairly, it is not so clear that they are willing or able to police themselves. And it is even less clear that they can oversee their own demise. Indeed, the UVF's stand-down order acknowledged as much when it suggested not only that volunteers engaging in criminality here forward would be in "direct contravention of Brigade Command" but that it would "welcome any recourse [against them] through due process of law" (UVF 2007). When I asked Councillor Langhammer how he thought Northern Ireland should get rid of its paramilitaries, he pointed to the Patten Report,[14] which suggests bringing paramilitary members into the police force.

> That was what Patten originally was getting to. What he was looking for was effectively a two-tiered policing force, a policing service whereby you'd have the professional top tier, which is essentially the PSNI. And then you would have a sort of much more voluntary type of warden-based policing that would nonetheless be under the discipline of the PSNI. But, de facto, what you would be trying to do is to co-opt the best of the paramilitary.

This suggestion is not a popular one in Northern Ireland. Many people believe that such a program would give paramilitaries more, not less, legitimacy. In a speech he gave in 2003 to the UUP's annual conference, for example, David Trimble rejected the idea, albeit in relation to the IRA:

> But I have to underline that it is simply absurd for people to have any responsibility for policing if they are linked to a private army! So much as we would like to see it we cannot support the devolution of policing until Sinn Fein have resolved to support the police and the IRA have taken the inevitable step, consequent on such support, to wind up, or transmute their organization into

[14] Prime Minister Tony Blair tapped Chris Patten, the last British governor of Hong Kong, to head the Independent Commission on Policing in Northern Ireland. The commission's final report is often colloquially referred to as the Patten Report (Independent Commission on Policing in Northern Ireland 1999).

something entirely peaceful and democratic. So any timescale for devolution is a timescale for these other matters. (Trimble 2003)

For their part, many nationalists fear warden-level policing because they worry that it would represent a return to forces like the Ulster Special Constabulary. However, as Langhammer explained to me, warden-based policing provides a check on paramilitary elements that currently operate as de facto police but in a context of no checks or balances. And because warden-level policing would draw members from the neighborhoods being policed, the force would not be an all-Protestant one. Rather, Nationalist areas would have Catholic warden-level police, while Loyalist areas would have Protestant ones.

Warden-based policing would also address one of the most trenchant complaints about the old form of policing in the province—that the RUC had no connection to the neighborhoods it policed (Langhammer 2003). Although this problem was well publicized in Nationalist areas, it was a problem in Loyalist ones as well, especially after the 1985 Anglo-Irish Agreement. Members of the RUC were, as Langhammer states, "intimidated from Protestant districts" after the agreement (2003, 13). "The police had to police it," he explained to me in our interview. "Whenever there were these demonstrations against the Anglo-Irish Agreement, the police had to form this blue line." Recruiting from within paramilitary ranks, and gleaning the best and brightest from within them, would create "an organic connection with the people in Protestant working class districts" (2003, p. 13) that currently does not exist. Equally important, it would bring members of Loyalist paramilitaries, who have power and in some cases legitimacy, into the body politic of the post-peace government.

Warden-level policing would also, as Langhammer observes, diminish the PSNI's reliance on informants within paramilitary structures. Indeed, because the police no longer live in Loyalist working-class areas, they have to rely on hired eyes and ears to figure out what's going on. This kind of policing is fraught with problems, as the murder of Raymond McCord Jr. demonstrates. As Langhammer remarked, "if you're reliant on informers, you have to turn a blind eye to their activity, including drugs activity and criminal activity and so on."

Finally, it is possible that the institution of warden-based policing, if done well, could give peace-minded Loyalists leverage against the anti-peace revanchists in their ranks. Although the divide between political and revanchist Loyalists occurs between and within paramilitaries, there is also a demographic element to the divide. Younger members tend to be revanchist, whereas older members, especially those who served time in prison before 1998, tend to be pro-peace (if not pro-agreement). Indeed, Gallaher and Shirlow (2006) note that Johnny Adair's climb up the UDA ranks was fueled in part by a demographic of young Loyalists who thought the UDA leadership had gone soft with age. If warden-based policing were to hire from the ranks of political ex-prisoners, older members would have a form of leverage against their younger, revanchist counterparts.

POLICING CIVILIAN NEEDS

Although I advocate warden-based policing, I am aware that the great majority of paramilitary members would not be suitable for these jobs. Indeed, as I've just mentioned, more recent recruits tend to be more stridently anti-peace than their older peers. Moreover, as Langhammer observes, since 1998 Loyalist paramilitaries increasingly recruited from the bottom of the social ladder: "Recruits to Protestant paramilitarism in the 1970s, for instance, would often be drawn from a layer of society that was usually 'skilled trades,' often involved in 'respectable' loyal orders, almost invariably a member of a trade union and in work. Today, by comparison, paramilitaries recruit most heavily from a more lumpen layer—unskilled, unemployed, often with criminal history, rarely in a trade union" (2003, 9). This trend is not surprising when we consider what has happened to the Loyalist working class as a result of deindustrialization. Indeed, trade unions are no longer large enough to provide a viable recruiting base. Warden-level police could be successful, however, if it recruited from the ranks of ex-prisoners and those with a proven track record in the voluntary sector.

The rest of the paramilitary structure (or their remnants in the case of the UVF) must be strongly policed, and there are a number of ways to do so. Langhammer argues, for example, that the military should set up watch towers and other installations in Loyalist strongholds. He has also suggested that the PSNI be permitted to use "confession evidence" and selective internment to take criminals off the street (2003, 2004). Some on the political left may find the call for a strong policing presence problematic. When I interviewed Councillor Langhammer, he noted as much.

> When the UDA were at their ruck [in my district], I took the view that instead of pandering to them, a far more robust policing presence is required. I also took the view, which people would say for somebody on the left is an unusual view, I took the view that an in-your-face policing policy, some might call it a oppressive policing policy, uh, certainly a physical policing policy, was required because it would work with the UDA.

Langhammer explained that the nonideological nature of most paramilitary ventures made aggressive policing appropriate:

> The reason it [aggressive policing] would work with the UDA is because they don't have any politics. And those who have no ideological grounding are vulnerable to that type of repression.

Langhammer was careful to state that his suggestions do not apply to policing in Republican communities, where different dynamics are in play:

> The same couldn't be said on the Republican side, where they have ideology and they have politics. A repressive, physical policing regime would be more likely to do the opposite.

I second Langhammer's support for aggressive policing of Loyalist paramilitaries, although I believe confession evidence should be used only if it can be made consistent with human rights standards on the issue. I also argue that aggressive policing should be applied most heavily for drug offenses. Indeed, although Loyalist paramilitaries are involved in a number of crimes, including racketeering and smuggling, their involvement in the drug market has the greatest negative impact on the already weak social fabric of Loyalist communities. And until the social fabric is more robust, drug crime deserves the better part of PSNI effort. Indeed, the disorder that drugs create in Loyalist communities only strengthens paramilitary dominance there.

CLOSING PARAMILITARY SOCIAL CLUBS

Another way to tackle the paramilitary problem is to go after its infrastructure. And a key part of that infrastructure is the network of paramilitary social clubs that each group maintains for its members. As Langhammer remarks, they are the modus operandi of paramilitaries, and if they are closed down, paramilitary operations will be limited as a result (2003, 12). Although it may seem a stretch to assume that closing down a few well-placed bars will make a significant dent in paramilitary organization, social clubs are more than local pubs. They are private, "members only" spaces; nonmembers cannot casually "pop in" to a social club. Their exclusivity makes them ideal for planning operations.

I paid my first visit to a UVF social club in July 2003 when I interviewed David Ervine. My reaction to Ervine's suggestion that we meet in a social club was equal parts excitement and fear. I was excited because going to a social club would allow me to see a part of Belfast I would have been unable to see on my own. I was fearful because I did not know what to expect, and walking into a paramilitary watering hole was not a little unnerving. I also had a mundane fear—that I would unable to find the place. Ervine had given me an address, but social clubs are not easy to spot on the landscape. They are designed to be inconspicuous, so they rarely have windows or signs. I was afraid I would walk right by the place. Fortunately I found my way.

My experience in the UVF social club where we met was perfectly benign. Ervine's train was running late, so I sat by myself for an hour and read the paper. The barkeep was polite and informed me on several occasions that Ervine had called to report on his progress. In many ways, it felt like other bars I had been to in Belfast—low-key, neighborhood watering holes.

Social clubs are not, however, benign places. Their exclusivity makes them ideal places for paramilitaries to plan operations in relative secrecy. Moreover, as Langhammer and others (Bruce 1992) have noted, paramilitary operations are often planned, hatched, and executed after a few rounds in a social club. Such ill-formed plans tend to target civilians rather than combatants. Langhammer suggests that the Criminal Assets Recovery Agency could be used to close down social clubs and thus inhibit the trouble that comes out of them. The agency, formed in Great Britain as a part of the Proceeds of Crime Act, is designed to break up criminal enterprises by, among other methods, seizing assets that are not in keeping with a holder's income or station in life and that the holder cannot justify as having been acquired legally, such as through inheritance (Parliament, United Kingdom 2002). Some paramilitary social clubs could clearly be targeted by using the criteria laid out in the Proceeds of Crime Act.

None of these ideas is a panacea for the problem of continued paramilitary violence in Northern Ireland. Taken together, however, they could, along with other suggestions, buttress the political impetus of progressive Loyalists while undermining the dominance of revanchists in the Loyalist paramilitary structure. I turn now to more theoretical considerations.

Implications for the Political Violence Literature

In this last section, it is worth considering what this study of Loyalism can contribute to wider debates about political violence. Two contributions come to mind. I discuss them in turn.

THE IMPORTANCE OF DISTINGUISHING BETWEEN CRIMINAL AND POLITICAL VIOLENCE

When independence struggles emerged in Latin American, Africa, and Asia during the sixties, many cheered the balaclava-wearing fighters who fought in them. In the academy, scholars labeled these groups revolutionary (rather than terrorist) and referred to their violence as political. Guerillas did not kill indiscriminately or wantonly, these scholars argued; instead, they used violence much like states did—to secure political goals. Guerillas would certainly make mistakes, but no more so, per capita, than states do.

In Northern Ireland, even unsympathetic scholars accepted that the IRA had political goals and that its violence was designed to meet political objectives (O'Malley 1984). Analyses of the group often focused on typical political science concerns: the group's emergence, the reasons for its internal schisms, the effectiveness of its strategy, and the limitations of its tactics. Although fewer scholars examined Loyalism, the ones who did acknowledged political motivations behind Loyalism (Aughey 1989; Bew, Gibbon, and

Patterson 1979). Indeed, even though most of these scholars agree that Loyalist political efforts are more stunted than those of Republicans, their explanation for the difference—that pro-state terrorist groups have less impetus to create politics because their goal is to defend an existing politic—assumes that a political position undergirds Loyalist violence. Indeed, political frameworks as varied as Marxism and liberalism have been used to explain Loyalist paramilitary violence (see McGarry and O'Leary [1995] for an excellent overview).

Since the fall of the Berlin wall, the term "political violence" has fallen out of favor. Today, most low-intensity conflicts are deemed anarchic and their fighters characterized as criminal (Ignatieff 1998; Kaldor 1999; Kaplan 1994, 2001; Münkler 2004; van Creveld 1991). Profiteering is defined as the primary impetus for such fighters. This argument has been made in reference to old conflicts, such as the one in Colombia, and to newer ones in Chechnya, Rwanda, and Sierra Leone. Indeed, even Islamic fundamentalism, which has a clear political program (implementation of Sharia law and the creation of a caliphate), is described in terms that suggest it has at best an unsophisticated agenda. The goals of so-called Islamic radicals have been labeled "uncivilized" and "pre-modern," with the implication being that such groups have only rudimentary political ideals (Enzensberger 2002).

The rise of the "apolitical" trend in the literature has coincided with the end of formal hostilities in Northern Ireland. However, paramilitary violence continued after the 1998 accord, and the apolitical trope has become a popular framework for explaining it, although few refer to the academic literature when doing so. To some degree, the trope fits. As I note in chapter 6, it is difficult to categorize Johnny Adair's empire building on the lower Shankill as political. However, it is a mistake to define all Loyalists by reference to Johnny Adair. Indeed, the UVF's response to Adair's aggressive behavior in the summer of 2000 was political. It was an attempt to limit the spatial extent of Adair's criminal network and to defend the UVF's decision to enter the Belfast Agreement. To be sure, the UVF's response was violent, and it is quite possible that some of its killers were driven by other motivations.[15] However, the UVF leadership, which presumably organized the murder bids, saw its actions as defensive—as protecting the organization's political gains. The violence may have been counterproductive, and it was certainly not standard political discourse, but it was political nonetheless.

Acknowledging the difference between political and revanchist Loyalism is important for practical reasons. Designing a demilitarization program for Loyalist paramilitaries requires an intimate knowledge of the structure meant to be dismantled. Indeed, full recognition of the political/revanchist

---

[15] Mark Haddock is believed to have been involved in two of the feud-related murders during 2000 (Dáil Éireann 2005). His status as a special branch informer calls his personal motives into question, given that serving multiple interests can complicate one's motivation.

divide could have helped the state understand why many political Loyalists were hesitant to stand down and how to negotiate with them to meet that end. As I observed earlier, political Loyalists were ready to stand down many years ago, but they feared that doing so in an environment where paramilitary criminals had few checks placed on them was untenable. Political Loyalists were motivated by two primary concerns. First, many simply did not want to leave their organizations in shambles. Many Loyalists believed they were engaged in a just mission. They wanted to stand down with personal *and* organizational dignity. Second, political Loyalists are also worried that if they did step down or cut their ties, the PSNI would not aggressively police the criminal elements left behind. These were not unreasonable concerns. Nuala O'Loan's report (2007) on the circumstances surrounding the death of Raymond McCord Jr. indicate both the depth of collusion and its pernicious impact. And other evidence not found in the report suggests that collusion may have contributed to murders that would otherwise not have happened. Indeed, former detectives Johnston Brown and Trevor McIlwrath allege that Haddock killed Sharon McKenna, a Catholic taxi driver, "to 'prove' to the UVF that he was not an informer" (Gordon 2006b). They further state that the Special Branch, by stymieing their inquiry into the McKenna murder, effectively permitted Haddock to go on to commit other murders, including that of Raymond McCord Jr. (Gordon 2006b).

Even though the UVF has finally ended its armed campaign, collusion must still be addressed—not only because the victims deserve justice but because effective policing in Loyalist areas requires it. As Langhammer puts it with specific reference to the UDA, "the PSNI is not closing down paramilitary activity, and the relationship of its Special Branch with the UDA in particular is of real concern. As a result, the 'blind eye' policing on the ground is of the 'three wise monkeys' variety, and it can only really be because of fear of what might come out in the wash" (2001). Although Loyalist paramilitaries are not often of the same mind as Councillor Langhammer, the comments of Loyalists excerpted in this and earlier chapters indicate that they have found something on which to agree.

In Defense of Particularism, or Why Cosmopolitanism is Inadequate

Like the wider social sciences they inhabit, political violence scholars have embraced questions of identity. Although much of the vast literature on identity is positive, scholars of political violence tend to be uneasy about identity politics. Indeed, many point to the fact that most contemporary conflicts are fought over contrasting identity claims, whether of ethnicity or religion. Critics are also wary of peace accords that entrench particularist identity in post-conflict political structures. Critics of consociational agreements are a case in point (Farry 2006; Wilson 2005). Scholars argue that the only effective antidote to identity-fueled violence is the creation of cosmopolitan identities that subsume ethnic and religious attachments under broader, unifying labels.

In this book, I have taken a different approach. Seeing a society still deeply divided along ethnoreligious lines, I argue that neither Catholic nor Protestant particularist claims will disappear over night. The elimination of particularism is an important goal, but the path there is often paved with particularist stone. Only when identity positions are viewed as "safe" by those who inhabit them can true cosmopolitan identities emerge. In the current context it makes more sense to evaluate differences among Loyalist particularisms rather than discounting all of them outright.

Within Loyalism it is clear that political Loyalism's identity politic is substantially different from that proffered by revanchist Loyalism. Not only do political Loyalists reject sectarianism and racism, but they reject criminality as well. Were conditions different—if, for example, the PSNI aggressively policed Loyalist criminals—political Loyalists could also be turned from violence. Despite these differences, it is common, even popular, for advocates of cosmopolitanism in Northern Ireland—both its liberal and socialist supporters—to dismiss Loyalism out of hand. At times these criticisms amount to little more than "tacit partisanship" (O'Leary 1999, 78). Eamonn McCann's pithy dismissal of the PUP, which I detail in chapter 3, is a good example. There is no economic basis for a resurgence of old Loyalism (that is, an industrial base dominated by Protestant workers), and there is no evidence that the PUP wants to bring such a regime back, but McCann argues that the PUP's socialist credentials are sullied by an attachment to Loyalism. McCann fails to level similar charges against socialists from the Republican camp. Nor does he make an effort to distinguish the real and important differences between political and revanchist Loyalisms.

Much of the world would undoubtedly like to see Loyalism simply disappear. It has never garnered the international sympathy of Republicanism, and the support it has garnered—from neo-Nazis in Britain and fundamentalist preachers in the United States—has often proved more a source of embarrassment than solidarity. It is unfair, however, to ask Loyalists to abandon their identity. Marking difference is an essential part of human identity formation. Defining difference as unacceptable and dangerous need not accompany it. Loyalists need the chance to define themselves in ways that denote their difference from Republicans, and in ways that are nonviolent and nonhateful. Only then can a truly cosmopolitan identity emerge. In this regard, demilitarization is the most effective path for getting there; without the threat of paramilitary violence lurking in the background, groups traditionally sidelined by paramilitary dominance (such as religious groups, women's associations, and organic intellectuals) can develop their own political identity projects. And, for its part, political Loyalism, unburdened of the paramilitary monkey on its back, will finally have the chance to prove whether it can attract a large Protestant constituency.

Loyalist paramilitaries appear to be winding down, collapsing under their own weight. However, reintegration should remain an important policy imperative. As several sources hastened to remind me, Loyalist paramilitary men are from the neighborhoods they control. They will not go away, even when the structures that support them melt away. Many will simply continue their violence under different banners—personal fiefdoms or criminal syndicates. Only a combination of effective policing and state-run schemes will truly dismantle the structures through which residual violence is produced. In that regard its many successes not withstanding, Northern Ireland can serve as a warning to other places coming out of conflict. Full peace requires systematic demilitarization, no matter the form of agreement by which it arrives.

Reference List

Adams, Gerry. 2005. Statement by Gerry Adams, then President of Sinn Féin, following the withdrawal of prosecutions in connection with an alleged IRA spy ring at Stormont in October 2002. Archived on the CAIN Web site. http://cain.ulst.ac .uk/issues/politics/docs/sf/ga081205.htm. Accessed August 2006.

Adamson, Ian. 1974. *Cruthin: The Ancient Kindred*. Belfast: Nosmada Books.

Adamson, Ian. 1991. The Ulster People. Bangor: Pretani Press.

American Immigration Law Foundation. 2001. The Making of a Melting Pot: Irish Immigration to America from 1700 to the Early 1800s. Immigration Policy Report. http://www.ailf.org/ipc/policy_reports_2001_Irish2.asp. Accessed July 2005.

Anderson, Benedict. 1991. *Imagined Communities: Reflections on the Origin and Spread of Nationalism*. London: Verso.

Anderson, Chris. 2002. *The Billy Boy: The Life and Death of LVF Leader Billy Wright*. Belfast: Mainstream Publishing.

Anderson, James. 2004. *Political Demography in Northern Ireland: Making a Bad Situation Worse*. Belfast: Centre for Spatial Territorial Analysis and Research, Queens University. http://www.qub.ac.uk/c-star/pubs/ESRC%201%20CRC% 20Presentation.pdf. Accessed March 2005.

Anderson, James, and Ian Shuttleworth. 1994. Sectarian Readings of Sectarianism: Interpreting the Northern Ireland Census. *Irish Review* 16: 74–93.

An Phoblacht. 2000. Unionists Block St. Patrick's Day Carnival. 6 January. http://re publican-news.org/archive/2000/January06/06stpa.html. Accessed April 2005.

Anthony, Andrew. 2005. The Price of Peace. *Observer Magazine*, 6 March.

Atkinson, Graeme. 2006. Metareligion: Combat 18. http://www.meta-religion.com/ Extremism/White_extremism/Combat_18/combat_18.htm. Accessed September 2006.

Aughey, Arthur. 1989. *Under Siege: Ulster Unionism and the Anglo-Irish Agreement*. London: St. Martin's Press.

Bambery, Chris. 1987. *Ireland's Permanent Revolution*. London: Bookmarks.

Barnes, Ciarán. 2006. Ervine Third Choice of UUP. *Daily Ireland*, 19 May. http://www.irelandclick.com. Accessed July 2006.

BBC. 1998. LVF Calls Truce to Back No Vote. 15 May. http://news.bbc.co.uk/1/hi/ events/northern_ireland/94588.stm. Accessed June 2005.

———. 1999. Northern Ireland Assembly Appoints Ulster Scots Translator. 18 September. http://news.bbc.co.uk/1/hi/northern_ireland/450725.stm. Accessed April 2005.

———. 2000a. Belfast Parade Brings Tight Security. 2 September. http://news.bbc.co.uk/1/hi/northern_ireland/908018.stm. Accessed June 2005.

———. 2000b. Fraud Probe on Ex-Prisoner Office. 21 September. http://news.bbc.co.uk/1/hi/northern_ireland/935258.stm. Accessed June 2005.

———. 2000c. Johnny Adair: Feared Loyalist Leader. 6 July. http://news.bbc.co.uk/1/hi/northern_ireland/821698.stm. Accessed June 2005.

———. 2000d. Loyalist Paramilitary Flags Explosion. 21 June. http://news.bbc.co.uk/1/hi/northern_ireland/799804.stm. Accessed August 2005.

———. 2000e. Loyalist Statement in Full. 15 December. http://news.bbc.co.uk/1/hi/northern_ireland/1072634.stm. Accessed July 2005.

———. 2000f. Murder as Loyalist Feud Boils Over. 11 January. http://news.bbc.co.uk/1/hi/northern_ireland/598794.stm. Accessed June 2005.

———. 2000g. Two Killed in "Loyalist Feud" Shooting. 21 August. http://news.bbc.co.uk/1/hi/northern_ireland/890016.htm. Accessed June 2005.

———. 2001. Adair to Remain in Jail. 9 January. http://news.bbc.co.uk/1/hi/northern_ireland/1105449.stm. Accessed June 2005.

———. 2002. "IRA Spy-Ring" Inquiry Call. 12 November. http://news.bbc.co.uk/1/hi/northern_ireland/2447141.stm. Accessed March 2005.

———. 2003a. Pregnant Women in "Racial Attack." 21 December. http://news.bbc.co.uk/1/hi/northern_ireland/3338091.stm. Accessed July 2005.

———. 2003b. Prisoners Attacked in Jail. 26 August. http://news.bbc.co.uk/1/hi/northern_ireland/3183329.stm. Accessed February 2005.

———. 2004a. Families Flee after "Intimidation." 26 August. http://news.bbc.co.uk/1/hi/northern_ireland/3599318.stm. Accessed July 2005.

———. 2004b. IRA Says Photos "Never Possible." 9 December. http://news.bbc.co.uk/1/hi/northern_ireland/4080697.stm. Accessed September 2005.

———. 2005a. Dorrian Family Talk to PUP Leader. 31 May. http://news.bbc.co.uk/1/hi/northern_ireland/4594961.stm. Accessed June 2005.

———. 2005b. Fact Files: Paramilitaries: Loyalist Volunteer Force. No date provided. http://www.bbc.co.uk/history/war/troubles/factfiles/lvf.shtml. Accessed August 2006.

———. 2005c. Loyalists May Act over Murder. 18 May. http://news.bbc.co.uk/1/hi/northern_ireland/4557765.stm. Accessed July 2006.

———. 2005d. McCartney's Response to IRA Statement. 9 March. http://news.bbc.co.uk/1/hi/northern_ireland/4333589.stm. Accessed August 2006.

———. 2005e. NI Receives Peace Funding Boost. 3 June. http://news.bbc.co.uk/1/hi/northern_ireland/4605181.stm. Accessed July 2005.

Bell, Geoffrey. 1984. *The British in Ireland: A Suitable Case for Withdrawal.* London: Pluto Press.

Bell, Jane. 2005. Capitol Move to Promote Ulster's Interests Stateside. *Belfast Telegraph*, 15 March, Jobfinders section, 1.

Bew, Paul, Peter Gibbon, and Henry Patterson. 1979. *The State in Northern Ireland, 1921–1972: Political Forces and Social Classes.* Manchester: Manchester University Press.

Billig, Michael. 1995. *Banal Nationalism.* London: Sage.

BIRW (British Irish Rights Watch). 1998. Conflict Related Deaths, 1998. http://www.birw.org/Deaths%20since%20ceasefire/deaths%2098.html. Accessed July 2006.

Boal, Fred. 1969. Territoriality on the Shankill–Falls Divide, Belfast. *Irish Geography* 6: 130–50.

Boserup, Anders. 1972. Contradictions and Struggles in Northern Ireland. *Socialist Register* 11: 157–92.

Boulton, D. 1973. *The UVF, 1966–1973: An Anatomy of Loyalist Rebellion.* Dublin: Torc Books.

Breaking News. 2003. Loyalists Want Me Dead, Says UVF Victim's Father. 23 October. http://archives.tcm.ie/breakingnews/2003/10/23/story118560.asp. Accessed July 2005.

———. 2005. Unionists "Hypocrites" over McCartney Death: Victim's Father. 16 March. http://www.breakingnews.ie/2005/03/16/story193970.html. Accessed July 2006.

Breen, Martin. 2000. Gang Attack Murder Victim's Brother. *Belfast Telegraph*, 6 May.

Breen, Stephen. 2002. Grieving Dad to Confront UVF Bosses over Murder. *Sunday Life*, 28 April.

———. 2003a. "I'm No Bully," Says UVF Victim's Dad. *Sunday Life*, 2 November.

———. 2003b. McCord Blasts NIO over Probe. *Sunday Life*, 30 March.

———. 2004a. Ecstasy Shame of Race-War Estate Agent. *Sunday Life*, 11 January.

———. 2004b. Ex-Con's Rage over Debt Query. *Sunday Life*, 29 February.

———. 2004c. UVF in Turmoil: Child Abusers, Terrorists Order Boy of 10 into Exile. *Belfast Telegraph*, 13 June.

———. 2004d. UVF Must Apologize. *Sunday Life*, 21 November.

———. 2006. McCord's Cousin Beaten by Gang. *Sunday Life*, 11 June.

Breen, Suzanne. 2000. Army Back in Belfast. *Irish Times*, 22 August, A1.

Breslin, John. 2005. Victim's Life Highlights Squalid World of Loyalist Violence. *Irish Examiner*, 1 August.

Brewer, John. 1998. *Anti-Catholicism in Northern Ireland, 1600–1998: The Mote and the Beam.* New York: St. Martin's Press.

Brewer, John, Bill Lockhart, and Paula Rodgers. 1998. Informal Social Control and Crime Management in Belfast. *British Journal of Sociology* 49 (4): 570–85.

Broder, David. 2000. South Carolina's Shame. *Washington Post*, 29 March, A25.

Bruce, Steve. 1986. *God Save Ulster! The Religion and Politics of Paisleyism.* Oxford: Oxford University Press.

———. 1992. *The Red Hand: Protestant Paramilitaries in Northern Ireland.* Oxford: Oxford University Press.

———. 1998. *Conservative Protestant Politics.* Oxford: Oxford University Press.

———. 2004. Turf War and Peace: Loyalist Paramilitaries since 1994. *Terrorism and Political Violence* 16 (3): 501–21.

———. 2005. Religion and Violence: What Can Sociology Offer? *Numen* 52: 5–28.

CAIN (Conflict Archive on the Internet). 2006a. Abstracts on Organizations—I. http://cain.ulst.ac.uk/othelem/organ/iorgan.htm. Accessed July 2006.

———. 2006b. Abstracts on Organizations—L. http://cain.ulst.ac.uk/othelem/organ/lorgan.htm. Accessed July 2006.

———. 2006c. Background Information on Northern Ireland Society—Religion. http://cain.ulst.ac.uk/ni/religion.htm#ni-rel-03. Accessed June 2006.

———. 2006d. A Brief Note on Decommissioning. http://cain.ulst.ac.uk/events/peace/decommission.htm. Accessed July 2006.

———. 2006e. A Draft Chronology of the Conflict—2000. http://cain.ulst.ac.uk/othelem/chron/choo.htm. Accessed July 2006.

——. 2006f. A Glossary of Terms Related to the Conflict: Acceptable Level of Violence. http://cain.ulst.ac.uk/othelem/glossary.htm#A. Accessed August 2006.

——. 2006g. A Glossary of Terms Related to the Conflict: Lundy. http://cain.ulst.ac .uk/othelem/glossary.htm#L. Accessed June 2006.

——. 2006h. A Glossary of Terms Related to the Conflict: Official Irish Republican Army. http://cain.ulst.ac.uk/othelem/organ/oorgan.htm. Accessed June 2006.

——. 2006i. A Glossary of Terms Related to the Conflict: Special Category Status. http://cain.ulst.ac.uk/othelem/glossary.htm#S. Accessed May 2006.

——. 2006j. A Glossary of Terms Related to the Conflict: Ulster Special Constabulary. http://cain.ulst.ac.uk/othelem/organ/uorgan.htm#usc. Accessed May 2006.

——. 2006k. Sutton Index of Deaths: Crosstabulations. http://cain.ulst.ac.uk/sutton/crosstabs.html. Accessed August 2006.

——. 2006l. Sutton Index of Deaths: Geographical Location of the Death. http://cain.ulst.ac.uk/sutton/tables/Location.html. Accessed July 2006.

——. 2006m. Sutton Index of Deaths: Status of the Person Killed. http://cain.ulst.ac .uk/sutton/tables/Status_Summary.html. Accessed July 2006.

Calhoun, Craig. 2003. "Belonging" in the Cosmopolitan Imaginary. *Ethnicities* 3 (4): 531–68.

Carbin, Jenn. 2003. Paint and Suffering. *Philadelphia City Paper*, 22–28 May.

Carlin, Davy. 2004a. The ARN—A Movement. Part 2. *Blanket*, 15 November. http://lark.phoblacht.net/dc15112g.html. Accessed July 2005.

——. 2004b. 8 Years in the Belfast SWP—A Fraternal Parting. *Blanket*, 15 November. http://lark.phoblacht.net/dc15112g.html. Accessed July 2005.

Casciani, Dominic. 2001. Ardoyne Stories: Peace Lines and Divisions. BBC News, 3 September. http://news.bbc.co.uk/1/hi/northern_ireland/1522743.stm. Accessed July 2005.

Cebulla, Andreas, and Jim Smyth. 1996. Disadvantage and New Prosperity in Restructured Belfast. *Capital and Class* 60: 39–59.

Chandler, David. 2003. New Rights for Old? Cosmopolitan Citizenship and the Critique of State Sovereignty. *Political Studies* 51: 332–49.

Chrisafis, Angelique. 2004. Racist War of the Loyalist Street Gangs. *Guardian*, 10 January.

——. 2005. Belfast Murder Sparks Fears of New Loyalist Feud. *Guardian*, 2 July.

Cochrane, Feargal, and Seamus Dunn. 1999. *International Study of Peace/Conflict Resolution Organizations (ISPO)—Northern Ireland Report*. Coleraine: University of Ulster Centre for the Study of Conflict.

Collier, Paul, and Anke Hoeffler. 2002. Greed and Grievance in Civil War. Washington, D.C.: World Bank. http://www.worldbank.org/research/conflict/papers/greedand grievance.htm. Accessed February 2005.

Community Foundation for Northern Ireland. 2005. http://www.communityfounda tionni.org. Accessed June 2005.

Community Workers Co-operative and the Northern Ireland Council for Voluntary Action. 2004. Designing Peace III. http://www.nicva.org/pdfs/p_PeaceIII_050504 .pdf. Accessed June 2005.

Connolly, Frank. 2000. Loyalist Feud Spins out of Control. *Sunday Business Post*, 12 November.

Connolly, Paul. 1997a. Animals Killed My Son: Heartbroken Dad Tells of Family Sorrow. *Belfast Telegraph*, 10 November.

——. 1997b. FAIT Fears a New Wave of Murders. *Belfast Telegraph*, 12 November.

——. 1997c. RUC Probe Murder of RAF Man. *Belfast Telegraph*, 11 November.

———. 1997d. UVF Should Come Clean on McCord Murder: FAIT. *Belfast Telegraph*, 17 November.

Cooke, Dennis. 1996. *Persecuting Zeal: A Portrait of Ian Paisley*. County Kerry: Brandon Book.

Coulter, Colin. 1999. *Contemporary Irish Society*. London: Pluto Press.

Coulter, John. 2004. Reclaiming Irish. *Blanket*, 27 December. http://lark.phoblacht.net/jco201052g.html. Accessed April 2005.

Cowan, Rosie. 2003. Lack of Cash Halts Ulster Murder Inquiry. *Guardian*, 5 May.

Crawford, Colin. 2003. *Inside the UDA: Volunteers and Violence*. London: Pluto Press.

Crean, Aiden. 2002. PSNI Accused of Double Standards. *Andersontown News*, 15 November. http://www.irelandclick.com.

Crothers, Jim. 1998. *Reintegration: The Problems and the Issues*. EPIC Research Document no. 2. Woodvale Road, Belfast, Northern Ireland: EPIC.

Cunningham, Dominic, and Alan Erwin. 2005. UVF Killers Pledge to Wipe Out Enemies as Fourth Man Dies. *Irish Independent*, 16 August.

Dáil Éireann. 2005. *Parliamentary Debates* 608 (5): 1491–93. Adjournment Debate, Northern Ireland Issues. 27 October. Available online at http://debates.oireachtas.ie/Xml/29/DAL20051027.PDF. Accessed August 2006.

Darby, John. 2006. Post-Accord Violence in a Changing World. In *Violence and Reconstruction*, ed. J. Darby, 143–60. South Bend, IN: University of Notre Dame Press.

Darby, John, and Geoffrey Morris. 1974. *Intimidation in Housing*. Belfast: Northern Ireland Community Relations Commission.

Democratic Unionist Party. 2005. "Peace Funding on Probation" Says Allister. http://jimallister.org/default.asp?blogID=229. Accessed June 2006.

Department of Finance and Personnel. 2000. Minister Welcomes Trust Investigation into Prisoners' Aid Group. Press release. http://archive.nics.gov.uk/dfp/000921b-dfp.htm. Accessed July 2005.

Department for Social Development in Northern Ireland. 2005. Urban Regeneration: Programmes and Measures. http://www.dsdni.gov.uk/urb-reg/comp-dev-schemes.asp. Accessed March 2005.

Dillon, Martin. 1990. *God and the Gun: The Church and Irish Terrorism*. New York: Routledge.

Directorate-General of Regional Policy. 1999. Northern Ireland Community Support Framework, 2000–2006. http://europa.eu.int/comm/regional_policy/funds/prord/document/ukcsf_en.pdf. Accessed May 2005.

———. 2000. EU Programme for Peace and Reconciliation in Northern Ireland and the Border Region of Ireland. http://europa.eu.int/comm/regional_policy/country/overmap/pdf_region/fp2mc_en.pdf. Accessed May 2005.

———. 2005. Summary Description of the PEACE II Programme. http://europa.eu.int/comm/regional_policy/country/prordn/details.cfm?gv_PAY=UK&gv_reg=ALL&gv_PGM=2000RG161PO001&LAN=5. Accessed May 2005.

Doherty, Paul, and Michael Poole. 1997. Ethnic Residential Segregation in Belfast, Northern Ireland, 1971–1991. *Geographical Review* 87 (4): 520–36.

Economist. 2005. Bang-Bang-Bling-Bling. April 14, 30.

Edwards, Aaron, and Stephen Bloomer. 2004. The Political Strategy of Progressive Loyalism since 1994. Conflict Transformation Paper no. 8. Belfast: LINC Resource Centre. http://www.linc-ncm.org/CTP_8.PDF. Accessed July 2006.

———. 2005. Democratising the Peace in Northern Ireland: Progressive Loyalists and the

Politics of Conflict Transformation. Conflict Transformation Papers no. 12. Belfast: LINC Resource Centre. www.linc-ncm.org/CTP_12.PDF. Accessed July 2006.

Ellis, Peter Berresford. 1989. Revisionism in Irish Historical Writing: The New Anti-Nationalist School of Historians. C. Desmond Greaves Memorial Lecture of the Connolly Association, London, 31 October. http://www.etext.org/Politics/INAC/historical.revisionism. Accessed May 2006.

Elshtain, Jean Bethke. 2001. New Wars, Old Violence. *International Studies Review* 3 (1): 175–89.

Empey, Reg. 2006. Statement by Reg Empey, then leader of the Ulster Unionist Party (UUP), on the decision not to recognize the UUP Assembly Group Association with David Ervine (PUP), 11 September. Archived on the CAIN Web site. http://cain.ulst.ac.uk/issues/politics/docs/uup/re110906.htm. Accessed October 2006.

Enzensberger, H. M. 1994. *Civil Wars: From LA to Bosnia.* New York: New Press.

———. 2002. Blind Peace: A Postscript to the Iraq War. *Telos* 125: 116–20.

Erwin, Alan. 2005. Dossier on Loyalist Paramilitary Murder Sent to UN and US. *Irish Examiner,* 2 August.

European Communities. 1998. *Peace and Reconciliation: An Imaginative Approach to the European Programme for Northern Ireland and the Border Counties of Ireland.* Luxembourg: Office for Official Publications of the European Communities.

Farry, Stephen. 2006. Inside Out: An Integrative Critique of the Northern Ireland Peace Process. Lecture at the United States Institutes of Peace, 15 June, Washington, D.C.

Fearon, Kate. 2002. The Conflict's Fifth Business: A Brief Biography of Billy Mitchell. Belfast: LINC Resource Centre. http://www.linc-ncm.org/No.2.pdf. Accessed July 2005.

Fenton, James. 1995. *The Hamley Tongue.* Belfast: Ulster-Scots Academic Press.

Finlay, Andrew. 2001. Defeatism and Northern Protestant "Identity." *Global Review of Ethnopolitics* 1 (2): 3–20.

Finlayson, Alan. 1999. Loyalist Political Identity after the Peace. *Capital and Class* 69: 47–76.

Fitzgerald, Garret. 1972. *Towards a New Ireland.* London: Charles Knight.

Fleming, Sean. 2004. A Living Tapestry of Tongues. *Blanket,* 6 August. http://lark.phoblacht.net/tapestryoftongues.html. Accessed May 2005.

Foot, Paul. 1989. *Ireland: A Rational Case for Withdrawal.* London: Chatto and Windus.

Frazer, William. 2005. FAIR Response to Victim's Strategy Consultation Document. http://www.victims.org.uk/victimsstrategy.html. Accessed July 2006.

Freedland, Jonathan. 2000. Internalising the Troubles. *Guardian,* 23 August.

Friel, Laura. 1999. Unionist Hypocrisy Elects Belfast Mayor. *An Phoblacht,* 8 June. http://republican-news.org/archive/2000/June08/08mayo.html. Accessed May 2005.

———. 2002. Leaks, Double Standards, and the New Deputy Chief Constable. *An Phoblacht,* 21 January. http://republican-news.org/archive/2002/November21/21mcqu.html. Accessed June 2005.

Gallaher, Carolyn, and Oliver Froehling. 2002. New World Warriors: "Nation" and "State" in the Politics of the Zapatista and U.S. Patriot Movements. *Social and Cultural Geography* 3 (1): 81–102.

Gallaher, Carolyn, and Peter Shirlow. 2006. The Geography of Loyalist Paramilitary Feuding in Belfast. *Space and Polity* 10 (2): 149–69.

Gamba, Virginia. 2006. Post-Agreement Demobilization, Disarmament, and Reintegration: Toward a New Approach. In *Violence and Reconstruction*, ed. J. Darby, 53–76. South Bend, IN: University of Notre Dame Press.

Garland, Roy. 2001. *Gusty Spence*. Belfast: Blackstaff Press.

Gibson-Graham, J. K. 1996. *The End of Capitalism as We Knew It: A Feminist Critique of Political Economy*. London: Blackwell.

Gibson-Graham, J. K., Stephen Resnick, and Richard Wolff. 2000. Introduction: Class in a Poststructural Frame. In *Class and Its Others*, ed. J. K. Gibson-Graham, S. Resnick, and R. Wolff, 1–22. Minneapolis: University of Minnesota Press.

Gilligan, Chris, and Jonathan Tonge. 2003. Introduction: Instability and the Peace Process. *Global Review of Ethnopolitics* 3 (1): 3–7.

Glencree Centre for Reconciliation. 2005. Glencree History. http://www.glencree-cfr.ie. Accessed May 2005.

Gomes Porto, Joãao, and Imogen Parsons. 2003. Sustaining the Peace in Angola: An Overview of Current Demobilisation, Disarmament, and Reintegration. Paper 27. Bonn: Bonn International Centre for Conversion. http://www.bicc.de/publications/papers/paper27/paper27.pdf. Accessed June 2006.

Gordon, David. 2002. Police Face Grilling on McCord Case Probe: UVF Killed my Son, Says Father. *Belfast Telegraph*, 16 May.

——. 2003. Ervine Retracts Claim against UVF Victim. *Belfast Telegraph*, 17 November.

——. 2005a. Adair Taunts Ex-Comrades: Gray's Downfall Is "Long Overdue." *Belfast Telegraph*, 31 March.

——. 2005b. Councillor Who Took a Stand against the UDA Set to Quit. *Belfast Telegraph*, 17 March.

——. 2005c. UVF Blamed for McCord Death Threat. *Belfast Telegraph*, 30 March.

——. 2006a. Forced out of the Shadows. *Belfast Telegraph*, 31 May.

——. 2006b. Police "Let Loyalist Free to Kill and Kill Again." *Belfast Telegraph*, 28 April.

Gordon, David, and Jonathan McCambridge. 2005. Hain Urged to Act on UVF Ceasefire. *Belfast Telegraph*, 15 July.

Gordon, Victor. 2005. Parents Want to Meet Orde over Double Murder. *Portadown Times*, 18 March.

GoToBelfast. 2005. Sights and Sounds of Belfast. http://www.gotobelfast.com/index.cfm/level/page/category_key/199/Page_Key/381/Parent_Key/0/type/Page/PaGeName/Sights_&_Sounds_of_Belfast. Accessed March 2005.

Graham, Brian. 1998. Contested Images of Place among Protestants in Northern Ireland. *Political Geography* 17 (2): 129–44.

——. 2004. The Past in the Present: The Shaping of Identity in Loyalist Ulster. *Terrorism and Political Violence* 16 (3): 483–500.

Graham, Brian, and Peter Shirlow. 2002. The Battle of the Somme in Ulster Memory and Identity. *Political Geography* 21: 881–904.

Gray, Chris. 1997. *Post-Modern War: The New Politics of Conflicts*. London: Routledge.

Grimason, Stephen. 1999. Selling the Agreement. BBC News, 19 November. http://news.bbc.co.uk/1/hi/northern_ireland/527226.stm. Accessed April 2005.

Guevara, Che. 1998. *Guerilla Warfare*. Lincoln: University of Nebraska Press.

Hadden, Peter. 1995. Troubled Times: The National Question in Ireland. http://www.socialistworld.net/publications/tt/index.html.

Hansard Parliamentary Debates. 2004a. Written Answers to Questions to Her Majesty's Government by Lord Glentoran. 10 June. http://www.parliament.the-stationery-office.co.uk/pa/ld199900/ldhansrd/pdvn/lds04/text/40610wo1.htm#40610wo1_sbhdo. Accessed July 2006.

——. 2004b. Written Answers to Questions to Her Majesty's Government by Lord Laird. 10 June. http://www.parliament.the-stationery-office.co.uk/pa/ld199900/ldhansrd/pdvn/lds04/text/40610wo1.htm#40610wo1_sbhdo. Accessed July 2006.

——. 2005a. Oral Answers to Questions by Ian Paisley. 16 June. http://www.publications.parliament.uk/pa/cm200506/cmhansrd/cmo50616/debtext/50616-31.htm#50616-31_spnew2. Accessed July 2006.

——. 2005b. Oral Answers to Questions by Nigel Dodds. 16 June. http://www.publications.parliament.uk/pa/cm200506/cmhansrd/cmo50616/debtext/50616-31.htm#50616-31_spnew3. Accessed July 2006.

——. 2006. Orders of the Day, Northern Ireland (Miscellaneous Provisions) Bill. 17 May. http://www.publications.parliament.uk/pa/cm200506/cmhansrd/cmo60517/debtext/60517-0162.htm. Accessed July 2006.

Hall, Julia. 1997. *To Serve without Favor: Policing, Human Rights, and Accountability in Northern Ireland.* New York: Human Rights Watch.

Harding, Thomas. 2005a. Fury at IRA Offer to Shoot McCartney's Murderers. *Telegraph*, 9 March.

——. 2005b. McCartney Murder Campaign Goes to US. *Telegraph*, 1 March.

Harnden, Toby. 1999. *"Bandit Country": The IRA and South Armagh.* London: Hodder and Stoughton.

Harvey, David. 1998. The Humboldt Connection. *Annals of the Association of American Geographers* 88: 723–30.

Hayes, Bernadette, Ian McAllister, and Lizanne Dowds. 2005. The Erosion of Consent: Protestant Disillusionment with the 1998 Northern Ireland Agreement. *Journal of Elections, Public Opinion and Parties* 15 (2): 147–67.

Healing through Remembering Project. June 2002. *The Report of the Healing through Remembering Project.* Belfast.

Heatley, Colm. 2005. PUP Chief Says LVF Killed Lisa. *Irish Aires News*, 19 May. http://irishaires.blogspot.com/2005/05/pup-chief-says-lvf-killed-lisa.html. Accessed August 2006.

Henderson, Derek. 2000. Mandelson: Nothing More or Less Than Gang Warfare. *Irish Examiner*, 22 August.

Hennessey, Frank. 2004. New Collusion Allegations. *Forum Magazine* 14: 2.

Hennessey, Thomas. 2001. *The Northern Ireland Peace Process: Ending the Troubles?* New York: Palgrave.

Henry, Shaun. 2003. Peace II—Seeing the Wood Despite the Trees. *Scope*, February, 10–12.

Herbert, Wulf. 1996. Disarming and Demobilizing Ex-Combatants: Implementing Micro-Disarmament. *Disarmament* 19 (2): 51–58.

Higgins, Geraldine. 1999. The Quotable Yeats: Modified in the Guts of the Living. *South Carolina Review* 32: 184–92.

Hillyard, P. 1985. Popular Justice in Northern Ireland: Continuities and Change. *Research in Law, Deviance and Social Control* 7: 247–67.

Hoare, Anthony. 1981. Why They Go Where They Go: The Political Imagery of Industrial Location. *Transactions of the Institute of British Geographers* 6: 152–75.

Hofstadter, Richard. 1965. *The Paranoid Style in American Politics; and Other Essays.* Chicago: University of Chicago Press.

Home Truths. 2004. Radio interview with Martin Snodden. March 8. http://www
.bbc.co.uk/radio4/hometruths/20040308_martin_snodden.shtml. Accessed August 2005.

Hookham, Mark. 2006. Details of 2,195 People Stolen in "Stormontgate." *Belfast Telegraph*, 10 June.

Horowitz, Donald. 2002. Explaining the Northern Ireland Agreement: The Sources of an Unlikely Constitutional Consensus. *British Journal of Political Science* 32: 193–220.

Howe, Stephen. 2000. *Ireland and Empire: Colonial Legacies in Irish History and Culture*. Oxford: Oxford University Press.

Hulme, David, and Michael Edwards, eds. 1997. *NGOs, States and Donors: Too Close for Comfort*. New York: Palgrave Macmillan.

Hutchinson, Graeme, and Tony Simpson. 2000. Migration Flows between NI and GB: The Impact on the NI Labour Market. In *Labour Market Bulletin*, 14th ed. Belfast: Department of Higher and Further Education, Training and Employment. http://www.nics.gov.uk/el/markbull.htm. Accessed July 2005.

Hutton, Brian. 2005. Just What Is Going on at Garnerville? *Belfast Telegraph*, 26 July.

Hyland, Julie. 2000. Ulster Defence Association Leader Arrested after Intra-Loyalist Violence in Belfast. World Socialist Web site, 24 August. http://www.wsws.org/articles/2000/aug2000/ire-a24.shtml. Accessed July 2005.

———. 2002. Sectarian Tensions Lead to Riots and School Closures in Northern Ireland. World Socialist Web site, 14 July. http://www.wsws.org/articles/2002/jan2002/ire-j14.shtml. Accessed July 2005.

Ignatieff, Michael. 1998. *The Warrior's Honor: Ethnic War and the Modern Conscience*. New York: Henry Holt.

Ignatiev, Noel. 1996. *How the Irish Became White*. New York: Routledge.

Independent Commission on Policing in Northern Ireland. 1999. *A New Beginning: Policing in Northern Ireland*. London: Her Majesty's Stationery Office. Also available online at http://www.belfast.org.uk/report/fullreport.pdf.

Independent Monitoring Commission. 2004. *Third Report of the Independent Monitoring Commission*. London: Her Majesty's Stationery Office.

———. 2005. *Sixth Report of the Independent Monitoring Commission*. London: Her Majesty's Stationery Office.

———. 2006. *Tenth Report of the Independent Monitoring Commission*. London: Her Majesty's Stationery Office.

Irelandclick. 2004a. Kelly: End "Myth of Ethnic Cleansing." *North Belfast News*, 7 October. http://www.irelandclick.com. Accessed April 2005.

———. 2004b. Residents Call on UVF to Stand Down. *South Belfast News*, 13 August. http://www.irelandclick.com. Accessed April 2005.

Irish Examiner. 2005. Arrest Me Now, Challenges Politician. 20 July.

Irish Republican Socialist Party. 2004. UVF Leader Removed over Racism. *Plough*, no. 25, 6 February. http://www.morrigan.net/irsm/plough25.htm. Accessed July 2005.

Irwin, Tracy. 2003. Prison Education in Northern Ireland: Learning from our Paramilitary Past. *Howard Journal* 42 (5): 471–84.

Isles, K. S., and Norman Cuthbert. 1957. *An Economic Survey of Northern Ireland*. Belfast: Her Majesty's Stationery Office.

Jarman, Neil. 2002. *Managing Disorder: Responding to Interface Violence in North Belfast*. Belfast: Office of the First Minister and Deputy First Minister, Research Branch.

Jarman, Neil, Libby Keys, Jenny Pearce, and Derik Wilson. 2004. Changing Places Changing Minds—Community Cohesion: Learning Lessons from Northern Ireland. Belfast: Groundwork Northern Ireland. http://www.groundworkni.org.uk/publications.htm. Accessed May 2005.

Jarman, Neil, and C. O'Halloran. 2000. *Peacelines or Battlefield? Responding to Violence in Interface Areas*. Belfast: Community Development Centre.

Kaldor, Mary. 1999. *New and Old Wars: Organized Violence in a Global Era*. Stanford: Stanford University Press.

———. 2001. Wanted: Global Politics. *Nation*, 5 November.

Kalyvas, Stathis. 2001. "New" and "Old" Civil Wars: A Valid Distinction? *World Politics* 54: 99–118.

Kaplan, Robert. 1994. The Coming Anarchy: How Scarcity, Crime, Overpopulation, Tribalism, and Disease are Rapidly Destroying the Social Fabric of our Planet. *Atlantic Monthly*, February, 44–76.

———. 2001. *The Coming Anarchy: Shattering the Dreams of the Post Cold War*. New York: Vintage Books.

Kearney, Jarlath. 2005. Arson Suspected in Fire at Offices Previously Targeted by Loyalists. *Daily Ireland*, 31 October. http://www.irelandclick.com. Accessed September 2006.

Keenan, Dan. 2004. Loyalists behind Racists' Pamphlets. *Irish Times*, 12 March.

Kelly, Brian. 2001. *Race, Class and Power in the Alabama Coalfields, 1908–1921*. Champaign: University of Illinois Press.

———. 2002. Belfast's "Poor White Trash" and the Dead Dogmas of the Past. *Blanket*, 19 September. http://lark.phoblacht.net/belfastpoor.html. Accessed July 2005.

Kelly, Tom. 2005. Isn't It Time the North Did a Little Growing Up? *Irish News*, 13 June, opinions.

Kennedy, Liam. 2001. They Shoot Children Don't They? An Analysis of the Age and Gender of Victims of Paramilitary "Punishments" in Northern Ireland. A report compiled for the Northern Ireland Committee against Terror and the Northern Ireland Affairs Committee of the House of Commons.

Kerr, David. 1997. And You Think We Have Problems with Yankee Interference. *Ulster Nation*. http://www.ulsternation.org.uk/yankee%20interference.htm. Accessed August 2005.

Kirk, John. 2000. The New Written Scots Dialect in Present-day Northern Ireland. In *Linguistic Structure and Variation: A Festschrift for Gunnel Melchers*, ed. M. Ljung, 121–38. Stockholm: Almqvist and Wiksell International.

Kirk, Robin. 2003. *More Terrible Than Death: Massacres, Drugs, and America's War in Colombia*. New York: Public Affairs.

Kitson, Frank. 1991. *Low-Intensity Operations: Subversion, Insurgency and Peacekeeping*. Reprint. London: Faber and Faber.

Knox, Colin. 2002. "See No Evil, Hear No Evil": Insidious Paramilitary Violence in Northern Ireland. *British Journal of Criminology* 42: 164–85.

Kumar, Amitava. 2000. Forward to *Class and Its Others*, ed. J. K. Gibson-Graham, S. Resnick, and R. Wolff, vii–xii. Minneapolis: University of Minnesota Press.

LaClau, Ernesto. 1992. Universalism, Particularism, and the Question of Identity. *October* 61: 83–90.

Laganside Corporation. 2005. Bringing New Life to the River. http://www.laganside.com/home.asp. Accessed March 2005.

Lahav, Gallya. 2004. *Immigration and Politics in the New Europe: Reinventing Borders*. Cambridge: Cambridge University Press.

Lane, Fern. 2001. Media Decommissioning Bias Exposed. *An Phoblacht*, 22 February. http://republican-news.org/archive/2001/February22/22pfc.html. Accessed August 2005.

Langhammer, Mark. 2001. Mark Langhammer Battles Sectarianism: An Interview with *Fourthwrite*. *Fourthwrite*, no. 11. Also available online at http://www.fourthwrite.ie/issue11alt12.html.

———. 2003. Cutting with the Grain: Policy and the Protestant Community. What Is to Be Done. Paper submitted to the Secretary of State for Northern Ireland and the Northern Ireland Office Team.

———. 2004. State-Funded Sectarianism and Pandering to Paramilitarism. Speech given at the conference Interpreting Ongoing Crises in the Northern Ireland Peace Process: Civil Society Dimensions, Queens University School of Politics and International Studies, 30 September.

Lavery, Brian, and Alan Cowell. 2005. IRA Renounces Violence in Potentially Profound Shift. *New York Times*, 28 July.

Lee, Joseph. 1985. *Ireland: Politics and Society, 1912–1985*. Cambridge: Cambridge University Press.

Left, Sarah. 2004. Q&A: The Northern Ireland Peace Deal. *Guardian*, 8 December.

LINC Resource Centre. 2005. http://www.linc-ncm.org. Accessed July 2005.

Lipset, Seymour Martin. 1963. The Sources of the Radical Right. In *The Radical Right: The New American Right*, ed. D. D. Bell. New York: Anchor Books.

Lister, David, and Russell Jenkins. 2005. Neighbours Move Out as Neo-Nazis Rally to Adair's Side. *Times Online*, 12 January. http://www.timesonline.co.uk/tol/news/uk/article411261.ece. Accessed July 2006.

Lister, David, and Hugh Jordan. 2003. The Downfall of Mad Dog Adair. *Observer Magazine*, 5 October, 26–36.

———. 2005. *Mad Dog: The Rise and Fall of Johnny Adair and "C Company."* Edinburgh: Mainstream Publishing.

Loyalist Volunteer Force. 1998. Ceasefire statement. 15 May. http://cain.ulst.ack.uk/events/peace/docs/lvf15598.htm. Accessed July 2005.

Lustick, Ian. 1997. Lijphart, Lakatos, and Consociationalism. *World Politics* 50 (1): 88–117.

Macafee, C. I., ed. 1996. *A Concise Ulster Dictionary*. Oxford: Oxford University Press.

Mackay, Neil. 1999. Mo's Woes. *Sunday Herald*, 29 August.

Mac Poilin, Aodan. 1999. Language, Identity, and Politics in Northern Ireland. In *BBC's A State Apart: An Interactive Chronicle of the Northern Ireland*. http://www.bbc.co.uk/northernireland/learning/history/stateapart/agreement/culture/support/cul2_co14.shtml. Accessed April 2005.

Mallory, P. J., and T. E. McNeill. 1991. *The Archaeology of Ulster: From Colonization to Plantation*. Belfast: Dufour Editions.

Mao Tse-tung. 2000. *On Guerilla Warfare*. Trans. Samuel Griffith II. Champaign: University of Illinois Press.

Marksman, Jeremy. 2005. Nelson McCausland—What a Card! Letter to the Editor. *An Phoblacht*, 24 February.

McAdam, Noel. 2005. What Ulster Thinks Now. *Belfast Telegraph*, 11 March.

———. 2006. UUP Accused of a Cynical Ploy as Ervine Embraces Assembly Group. *Belfast Telegraph*, 15 May.

McAuley, James. 1991. Cuchullain and an RPG-7: The Ideology and Politics of the Ulster Defence Association. In *Culture and Politics in Northern Ireland, 1960–1990*, ed. Eamon Hughes, 45–68. London: Open University Press.

McCabe, Anton. 2001. The Bitter Legacy of Expulsions. *Sunday Business Post*, 7 January.

McCaffery, Steven. 2000a. UVF Bid Rejected by Victim's Father. *Irish News*, 16 May.

———. 2000b. UVF Blamed for Attack on Grave. *Irish News*, 5 May.

———. 2000c. Victim's Family Taunted by Card. *Irish News*, 6 May.

McCambridge, Jonathan. 2004. UVF Leader Removed after Attacks. *Belfast Telegraph*, 6 February.

———. 2005. Police Vow Tough Action over Feud. *Belfast Telegraph*, 5 August.

———. 2006. Haddock "Set Up" by His Former UVF Comrades. *Belfast Telegraph*, 1 June.

McCandless, Frances. 2003. Development and Division in Northern Ireland. Speech give at the Northern Ireland Council for Voluntary Action annual meeting, Divided Societies: Does Civil Society Bridge Them or Bear Them? http://www .nicva.org/uploads/docs/FrancesMcCandless_Speech.pdf. Accessed May 2005.

McCann, Eamonn. 2000. What's behind Loyalist Feuding? *Socialist Worker* 1712, 2 September, 10–11.

———. 2005. Ardoyne Fuelled by Politics of the Good Friday Agreement. *Socialist Worker* 245, 20 July, 8.

McDonald, Henry. 2003. PUP Campaigns to Drive Racists Out of Ballymena. *Observer*, 25 May.

———. 2005a. Looking for Lisa. *Observer*, 31 July.

———. 2005b. Loyalists Rule Out Surrender of Arms. *Observer*, 2 October.

McDowell, Jim. 2001. *Godfathers: Inside Northern Ireland's Drug Racket*. Glasgow: Gill and Macmillan.

McEvoy, Kieran. 2001. *Paramilitary Imprisonment in Northern Ireland: Resistance, Management, and Release*. Oxford: Oxford University Press.

McGarry, John, and Brendan O'Leary. 1995. *Explaining Northern Ireland: Broken Images*. Oxford: Blackwell.

———. 2006. Consociational Theory, Northern Ireland's Conflict, and Its Agreement. Part 1: What Consociationalists Can Learn from Northern Ireland. *Government and Opposition* 41 (1): 43–63.

McGirr, Lisa. 2001. *Suburban Warriors: The Origins of the New American Right*. Princeton: Princeton University Press.

McGovern, Mark, and Peter Shirlow. 1997. Counter-Insurgency, Deindustrialisation and the Political Economy of Ulster Loyalism. In *Who Are "the People"? Unionism, Protestantism and Loyalism in Northern Ireland*, ed. P. Shirlow and M. McGovern, 176–98. London: Pluto Press.

McGuigan, Ciaran. 2004. A***holes! Ervine's Bum Rap for Ulster Race Hate Scum. *Sunday Life*, 8 February.

McIntyre, Anthony. 2006. Billy Mitchell: A Tribute. http://www.theotherview.net/ billytribute.htm

McKay, S. 2000. *Northern Protestants—An Unsettled People*. Belfast: Blackstaff Press.

McKittrick, David. 2005. Latest Loyalist Paramilitary Feuding Costing Lives. *Irish Independent*, 26 July.

Mertus, Julie. 2000. *War's Offensive on Women: The Humanitarian Challenge in Bosnia, Kosovo, and Afghanistan.* Bloomfield, CT: Kumarian Press.

Millar, Frank. 2004. *David Trimble: The Price of Peace.* Dublin: Liffey Press.

Miller, David. 1978. *Queens Rebels: Ulster Loyalism in Historical Perspective.* Dublin: Gill and Macmillan.

Mitchell, Billy. 2000. Turf War: A Loyalist Perspective. *North Belfast News,* 1 September. http://www.irelandclick.com. Accessed June 2005.

———. 2002a. Addressing Organized Crime. *Blanket,* 3 November. http://lark.phoblacht.net/addressing.html. Accessed June 2005.

———. 2002b. Can the Course of Labour Afford to Wait? *Blanket,* 22 September. http://lark.phoblacht.net/courseoflabour.html. Accessed March 2005.

Mittelman, James. 2005. Globalization, Cosmopolitanism, and the Kantian Revival: Commentary on David Held's "At the Global Crossroads." *Globalizations* 2 (1): 114–16.

Monaghan, Rachel. 2005. Is There a Culture of Violence in Northern Ireland? Hate Crime and Paramilitarism. Democratic Dialogue working paper. http://www.democraticdialogue.org/documents/rachelmonaghan.pdf. Accessed June 2006.

Montgomery, Michael. 2002. What Is Ulster Scots? http://www.ulsterscotsagency.com/WhatisUlster-Scots.asp. Accessed April 2005.

Moore, Charlotte. 2006. Sinn Fein Spy Shot Dead. *Guardian,* 4 April.

Mouffe, Chantal. 1995. Post-Marxism: Democracy and Identity. *Environment and Planning D: Society and Space* 13: 259–65.

———. 2000. Deliberative Democracy or Agonistic Pluralism. Political Science series 72. Vienna: Department of Political Science, Institute for Advanced Studies.

Mueller, John. 2004. *The Remnants of War.* Ithaca: Cornell University Press.

Mulholland, Marc. 2002. *The Longest War: Northern Ireland's Troubled History.* Oxford: Oxford University Press.

Multi-party Negotiations. 1998. The Agreement. 10th April. Linked on Cain Web site: http://cain.ulst.ac.uk/events/peace/docs/agreement.htm.

Münkler, Herfried. 2004. *The New Wars.* Trans. from the German by Patrick Camiller. New York: Polity Press.

Murphy, Paul. 2004. Statement on the despecification of the Ulster Defence Association (UDA)/Ulster Freedom Fighters (UFF). Linked on CAIN Web site: http://cain.ulst.ac.uk/issues/politics/docs/nio/pm151104.htm. Accessed June 2005.

Murray, Alan. 2002. Revealed: The True Extent of Spy Ring. *Belfast Telegraph,* 22 December.

———. 2005a. Police Agent Set up Monaghan Bombing Claims McCord. *Sunday Life,* 1 May.

———. 2005b. Why Loyalists Decided "Doris" Has Had His Day. *Irish Independent,* 31 March.

Murtagh, Brendan. 2002. *The Politics of Territory: Policy and Segregation in Northern Ireland.* Basingstoke: Palgrave.

MyBelfast. 2005. Castle Court Shopping Centre. http://www.mybelfast.co.uk/belfast/shops-shorts.htm. Accessed March 2005.

Nairn, Tom. 1981. *The Breakup of Britain.* London: Verso.

National Council for Voluntary Organizations. 2005. Welcome to the NCVO Website. http://www.ncvo-vol.org.uk/asp/search/ncvo/main.aspx?siteID=1. Accessed June 2005.

Neuffer, Elizabeth. 2001. *The Key to My Neighbor's House: Seeking Justice in Bosnia and Rwanda.* New York: Picador.

Nic Craith, M. 2001. Politicised Linguistic Consciousness: The Case of Ulster-Scots. *Nations and Nationalism* 7 (1): 21–37.

Northern Ireland Affairs Committee, House of Commons. 2004. Social Housing Provision in Northern Ireland. Sixth Report of Session 2003–4, vol. 2. http://www.parliament.the-stationery-office.co.uk/pa/cm200304/cmselect/cmniaf/493/493ii.pdf. Accessed March 2005.

———. 2005. *The Challenge of Diversity: Hate Crime in Northern Ireland*. Ninth Report of Session 2004—5, vol. 2. http://www.publications.parliament.uk/pa/cm200405/cmselect/cmniaf/548/548ii.pdf. Accessed July 2005.

Northern Ireland Assembly. 2000. Written Answers. Northern Ireland Voluntary Trust. http://www.niassembly.gov.uk/qanda/writtenans/001201.htm. Accessed June 2005.

Northern Ireland Statistics and Research Agency (NISRA). 2001a. Data: Northern Ireland Ward Level Data and LGD Level Summaries—Spreadsheet. http://www.nisra.gov.uk/whatsnew/dep/index.html#Data. Accessed March 2005.

———. 2001b. Table KS06: Ethnic Groups. In *Northern Ireland Census 2001: Key Statistics*. http://www.nisra.gov.uk/Census/Census2001Output/KeyStatistics/keystats.html. Accessed July 2005.

———. 2001c. Table KS25: Migration. In *Northern Ireland Census 2001: Key Statistics*. http://www.nisra.gov.uk/Census/Census2001Output/KeyStatistics/keystats.html. Accessed March 2005.

O'Brien, Conor Cruise. 1974. *States of Ireland*. London: Panther Books.

Ó Cairealláin, Gearóid. 2002. Flagging up Equality. *Daily Ireland*, 7 September. http://www.irelandclick.com. Accessed June 2005.

O'Doherty, Cara. 2000. Police Are Protecting Killer Claim. *Irish News*, 20 March.

O'Grada, Cormac. 1995. *The Great Irish Famine*. Cambridge: Cambridge University Press.

Ó hAdhmaill, Féilim. 2005. *Equal Citizenship for a New Society? An Analysis of Training and Employment Opportunities for Republican Ex-Prisoners in Belfast*. Report issued by Coiste na n-larchimí. http://www.coiste.ie/articles/feilim/equal-menu.htm. Accessed March 2005.

O'Hearn, Denis. 1998. *Inside the Celtic Tiger: The Irish Economy and the Asian Model*. London: Pluto Press.

O'Leary, Brendan. 1999. The Nature of the British–Irish Agreement. *New Left Review* 233 (1): 66–96.

O'Loan, Nuala. 2007. Operation Ballast. Police Ombudsman of Northern Ireland Investigative Report. Archived at the Ombudsman's Web site http://www.policeombudsman.org. Accessed April 2007.

Oliver, Joe. 1999. Freed IRA Man Engaged in Violence to Be Named. *Irish Examiner*, 25 January.

———. 2000. Terror Stalks the Shankill in Loyalist Turf War. *Irish Examiner*, 6 September.

O'Malley, Padraig. 1984. *Ireland: The Uncivil Wars*. Belfast: Blackstaff Press.

O'Reilly, Camille. 1997. Nationalists and the Irish Language in Northern Ireland: Competing Perspectives. In *The Irish Language in Northern Ireland*, ed. A. Mac Poilin, 95–130. Belfast: ULTACH Trust.

Osborne, Robert. 1982. The Lockwood Report and the Location of a Second University in Northern Ireland. In *Integration and Division: Aspects of the Northern Ireland Problem*, ed. F. Boal and J. Douglas, 167–78. New York: Academic Press.

O'Toole, Fintan. 2000. When Bigotry Takes on a Life of Its Own. *Irish Times*, 29 August.

O'Toole, Slugger. 2005. IRA Statement in Full (8 March). Slugger O'Toole: Notes on Northern Ireland Politics and Culture. http://www.sluggerotoole.com/ archives/2005/03/ira_statement_i.php. Accessed July 2005.

Parliament, United Kingdom. 2002. *Proceeds of Crime Act*. London: Her Majesty's Stationery Office.

Pat Finucane Centre. 2005. Loyalist Feud: 31 July–2 September 2000. http://www .serve.com/pfc/sattacks/july005att.html.

Police Service of Northern Ireland (PSNI). 2005. *Statistical Report: 1st April 2004 – 31st March 2005*. Belfast: Northern Ireland Statistics and Research Agency.

Porter, Norman. 1996. *Rethinking Unionism: An Alternative Vision for Northern Ireland*. Belfast: Blackstaff Press.

Press Association. 2003. Father Claims Son Was Killed by RUC Informers. UTV Internet Newsroom. http://www.u.tv/newsroom/indepth.asp?id=40209&pt-. Accessed August 2005.

Proteus. 2001. *Employment: Lessons of Peace I*. Belfast: Proteus.

Redwatch. 2005. Ulster Reds: Any Further Info on the Freaks Below Will Be Gratefully Received. http://www.redwatch.org.uk/ulster1.html. Accessed June 2006.

Residentgroups. 2005. "Residents Groups." http://www.residentgroups.fsnet.co.uk/ shortstrand.htm. Accessed June 2006.

Reuters. 2000. British Troops Return to Belfast Streets. 21 August. http://archives .cnn.com/2000/WORLD/europe/08/21/ireland.shooting. Accessed July 2005.

Reynolds, Charlie. 2006. Ulster Scots Rhymes. http://www.ulsterscotsrhymes.home-stead.com/pageone.html. Accessed July 2006.

Richards, Paul. 1996. *Fighting for the Rain Forest: War, Youth, and Resources in Sierra Leone*. New York: Heinemann.

Robinson, Philip. 1997. *Ulster-Scots: A Grammar of the Traditional Written and Spoken Language*. Belfast: Ullans Press.

Rolston, Bill. 2004. Legacy of Intolerance: Racism and Unionism in South Belfast. Independent Race and Refugee News Network, 10 February. http://www.irr.org .uk/2004/february/ak000008.html. Accessed July 2006.

Rowan, Brian. 2006. UVF Leadership Sanctioned Haddock Murder Bid. *Belfast Telegraph*, 2 June.

Rowthorn, Bob, and Naomi Wayne. 1988. *Northern Ireland: The Political Economy of Conflict*. Cambridge: Polity Press.

RTE News. 2005. €144m More for NI in EU Initiative. 3 June. http://www.rte .ie/news/2005/0603/northfunds.html. Accessed July 2005.

Sassen, Saskia. 2000. *Guests and Aliens*. New York: New Press.

Sharrock, David. 2005. Few Tears as Loyalist Thugs Kill Their Own. *Times Online*, 6 October. http://www.timesonline.co.uk/tol/news/uk/article575102.ece. Accessed June 2006.

Shelby, Tommie. 2005. *We Who Are Dark: The Philosophical Foundations of Black Solidarity*. Cambridge: Cambridge University Press.

Shirlow, Peter. 2002. *Devolution, Identity and the Reproduction of Ethno-Sectarianism in Northern Ireland*. Paper presented at Royal Geographical Society–Institute of British Geographers annual meeting, Queens University, Belfast, 2–6 January.

——. 2003. "Who Fears to Speak": Fear, Mobility, and Ethno-Sectarianism in the Two "Ardoynes." *Global Review of Ethnopolitics* 3 (1): 76–91.

Shirlow, Peter, and Mark McGovern. 1997. Introduction to *Who Are "the People"? Unionism, Protestantism and Loyalism in Northern Ireland*, ed. P. Shirlow and M. McGovern, 1–15. London: Pluto Press.

Shirlow, Peter, and Brendan Murtagh. 2006. *Belfast: Segregation, Violence and the City*. London: Pluto Press.

Shirlow, Peter, and Ian Shuttleworth. 1999. "Who Is Going to Toss the Burgers?" Social Class and the Reconstruction of the Northern Irish Economy. *Capital and Class* 69: 27–46.

Silke, Andrew. 1998. The Lords of Discipline: The Methods and Motives of Paramilitary Vigilantism in Northern Ireland. *Low Intensity Conflict and Law Enforcement* 7 (2): 121–56.

Sinn Fein. 2005a. De Brún Makes Case for Peace III with EU Commissioner. Sinn Fein online newsroom. 18 April. http://sinnfein.ie/news/detail/9251. Accessed June 2005.

——. 2005b. Initial Considerations for the Development of a Peace III Programme. Sinn Fein European Union Election Headquarters. No date provided. http://sinnfein.ie/euteam/document/169. Accessed June 2006.

Slí Na mBan. 2002. Interview with Marian Jamison. December. http://www.tallgirlshorts.net/marymary/sli_arch_frameset.html. Accessed April 2005.

Sluka, Jeff. 1999. Review of *Symbols in Northern Ireland* by Anthony Buckley, ed. *American Ethnologist* 26 (1): 245–46.

Snodden, Martin. 1996. Culture behind the Wire. *Journal of Prisoners on Prisons* 7 (2): 25–29.

Special EU Programmes Body. 2005. Successful Applications. Details for reference no. 007982. http://www.seupbsuccessfulprojects.org. Accessed June 2005.

Springfield Intercommunity Development Project. 2005. http://www.peacewall.org. Accessed April 2005.

Stevenson, Jonathan. 1996. *"We Wrecked the Place": Contemplating an End to the Northern Ireland Troubles*. New York: Free Press.

Sunday Life. 2003. Murdered Man's Father Incensed by PUP Tag. 23 March.

——. 2004a. UVF "Restructured": Boss Linked to McCord Murder Stood Down. 28 November.

——. 2004b. Why No Convictions. 22 February.

——. 2005. Killing Will Go on Say Feuding Gangs. Unfinished Business Say the UVF. 7 August.

Sweeney, Paul. 2000. *The Celtic Tiger: Ireland's Continuing Economic Miracle*. Dublin: Oak Tree Press.

Taylor, Peter. 1999a. *Behind the Mask: The IRA and Sinn Fein*. New York: TV Books.

——. 1999b. *Loyalists: War and Peace in Northern Ireland*. New York: TV Books.

Times Online. 2005. "Arrest Me or Shut Up," Says Sinn Fein's Adams. 10 February. http://www.timesonline.co.uk/tol/news/uk/article512940.ece. Accessed August 2005.

Tonge, Jonathan. 2003. Victims of Their Own Success? Post-Agreement Dilemmas of Political Moderates in Northern Ireland. *Global Review of Ethnopolitics* 3 (1): 39–59.

Totten, Joan. 2002. North Belfast: A Resident's View. *Blanket*, 18 August. http://lark.phoblacht.net/northbelfast.html. Accessed June 2005.

Trimble, David. 1998. Nobel lecture. 10 December. Oslo, Norway. http://nobel prize.org/peace/laureates/1998/trimble-lecture.html. Accessed June 2006.

———. 2000. Violence Linked to Loyalist Feud: Statement by the First Minister, Rt. Hon. David Trimble MP MLA. 30 August. http://archive.nics.gov.uk/ofmdfm/000830c-ofmdfm.htm. Accessed June 2005.

———. 2003. Speech delivered to the Ulster Unionist Party annual conference. Linked on CAIN Web site. http://cain.ulst.ac.uk/issues/politics/docs/uup/dt181003.htm. Accessed June 2005.

Ulster-Scots Agency. 2005. Awareness: Overview. http://www.ulsterscotsagency.com/overviewawareness.asp. Accessed May 2005.

Ulster-Scots Language Society. 1994. The 23rd Psalm. *Ullans* 2:21–25.

Ulster Unionist Party. 2005. UUP MEP Says Extension of PEACE II Is Good News for NI. http://www.uup.org/media/media_03_06_05_nicholson.htm. Accessed June 2005.

Ulster Volunteer Force. 2002. Principles of Loyalism. Unpublished internal discussion paper for use by the PUP in Loyalist constituencies.

———. 2007. Stand Down Order. 3 May. Full statement available through the Belfast Telegraph Archive.

Universities Ireland. 2005. About Us. http://www.universitiesireland.ie/home/about us.php. Accessed May 2005.

van Creveld, Martin. 1991. *The Transformation of War*. New York: Free Press.

Vargas, Zaragosa. 2004. *Labor Rights Are Civil Rights: Mexican American Workers in Twentieth-Century America*. Princeton: Princeton University Press.

Vieira, Constanza. 2006. US Supervision of Colombian Paramilitary Demobilization Becomes Evident. http://www.antiwar.com/ips/Vieira.php?articleid=9565. Accessed July 2006.

Walker, Brian. 2006. Hermon Tells of Link-up "Distress." *Belfast Telegraph*, 18 May.

Warner, Richard. 1999. Celtic Ireland and Other Fables: Politics and Pre-history. Essay based on a talk delivered at the Annual Conference of the Irish Association. http://www.irish-association.org/archives/Richard warner11_99.html. Accessed May 2005.

Watt, Nicholas, and Jamie Wilson. 2000. Loyalist Adair Back in Prison. *Guardian*, 23 August.

Weir, Peter. 2006. UUP's Indecent Haste in Signing up the PUP. *Belfast Telegraph*, 18 May.

Whelan, Ken. 2003. Protestants "Wiped from Culture." *Irish Independent*, 18 August.

Whyte, John. 1983. How Much Discrimination Was There under the Unionist Regime, 1921–1968? In *Contemporary Irish Studies*, ed. T. Gallagher and J. O'Connell, 1–35. Manchester: Manchester University Press.

———. 1990. *Interpreting Northern Ireland*. Oxford: Oxford University Press.

Wiener, R. 1980. *The Rape and Plunder of the Shankill*. Belfast: Farset Press.

Wikipedia. 2005a. Agonism. http://en.wikipedia.org/wiki/Agonism. Accessed May 2005.

———. 2005b. Celtic Tiger. http://en.wikipedia.org/wiki/Celtic_Tiger. Accessed May 2005.

———. 2005c. Irish Language. http://en.wikipedia.org/wiki/Irish_language#Northern_Ireland. Accessed May 2005.

———. 2005d. Ulster Scots Language. http://en.wikipedia.org/wiki/ullans. Accessed May 2005.

Wilson, Robin. 2005. Social Democracy and Inter-ethnic Accommodation. In *New Democratic Spaces in Northern Ireland Politics? Trends, Opinions and Expectations*. Report of a seminar held under the Chatham House rule at the Institute of Governance, Public Policy and Social Research, Queen's University Belfast in conjunction with Democratic Dialogue. 18 June.

Winston, Tom. 1997. Alternatives to Punishment Beatings and Shootings in a Loyalist Community in Belfast. Critical Criminology 8 (1): 122–28.

Formal Interviews

Named Interviews

Michael Atcheson, 1 July 2003
Beverly Davidson-Stitt, 27 July 2004
East Belfast Concerned Women's Group, 22 July 2004
David Ervine, 10 July 2003
Stephen Farry, 10 July 2006
Frankie Gallagher, 28 July 2004
Neil Jarman, 18 June 2003
David Kerr, 24 June 2003
Mark Langhammer, 23 March 2005
Wilson MacArthur, 9 July 2002
Nelson McCausland, 4 July 2003
Kenny McClinton, 7 July 2003
Wendy McClinton, 7 July 2003
Hugh McMillen, 29 July 2004
Billy Mitchell, 1 July 2003
Martin O'Brien, 2 July 2002
Bill Patterson, 29 July 2004
Tom Roberts, 1 July 2003
William "Plum" Smith, 2 July 2003
Martin Snodden, 4 July 2002
Debbie Watters, 9 July 2003
Del Williams, 28 July 2004
John Wilson (pseudonym), 25 June 2003

Anonymous Sources

Anonymous 1, 16 March 2005
Anonymous 2, 29 June 2006
Anonymous 3, 10 July 2006
Anonymous 4, 27 July 2006
Anonymous 5, 4 July 2006
Anonymous 6, 7 July 2006
Anonymous 7, 8 July 2006
Anonymous 8, 9 August 2006
Anonymous 9, 11 August 2006

Index